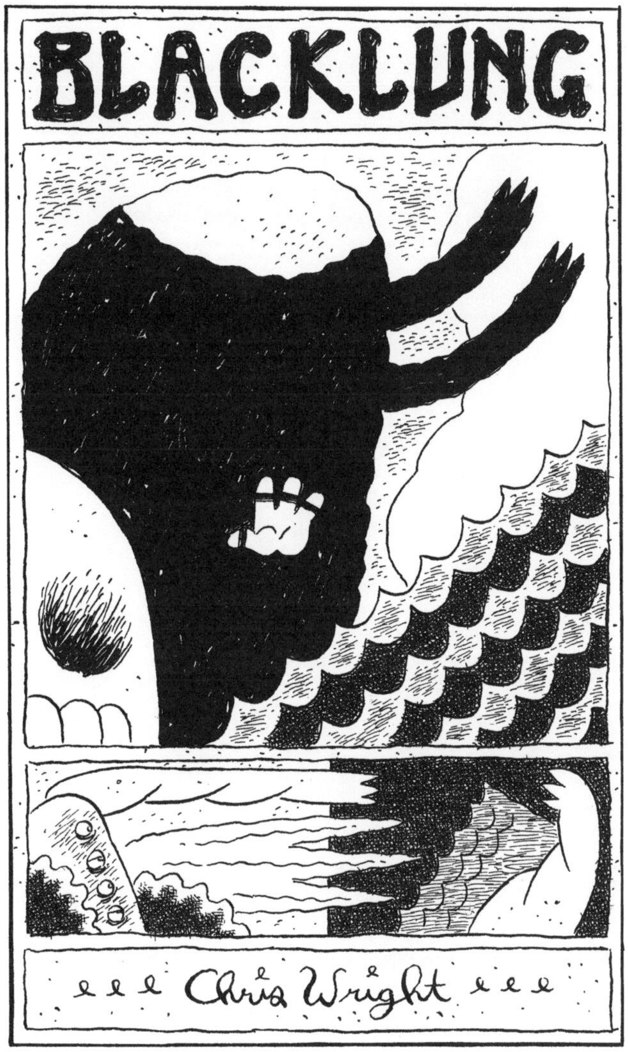
BLACKLUNG
Chris Wright

Fantagraphics Books
Seattle, Wash.

Special thanks to

Drew Weing, Eleanor Davis,
Max Clotfelter, David Yoder,
Chris Schweizer, Joey Weiser,
Michele Chidester, Brandon Elston,
Doug Frey, Tom Devlin, and
Dane Martin.

Extra special thanks to

James Sturm,
and
Matt Maloney.

Oh, the days, Matthew.

Blacklung
By Chris Wright

Editor and Associate Publisher Eric Reynolds
Designed by Chris Wright
Production by Chris Wright and Paul Baresh
Published by Gary Groth and Kim Thompson

Fantagraphics Books, Inc.
7563 Lake City Way NE
Seattle WA 98115 USA
fantagraphics.com

Distributed in the U.S. by W.W. Norton and Company, Inc. (800-233-4830)
Distributed in Canada by Canadian Manda Group (410-560-7100 x843)

Distributed in the UK by Turnaround distribution (44 020 8829-3002)

Distributed to comic book specialty stores by Diamond Comics Distributors (800-452-6642 x215)

ISBN 978-1-60699-587-7

First printing: September 2012

Printed in Singapore

Dedicated To Dylan Williams

Old Gods are terrible to look at when
they weep, all bloated like spoiled fish
One wonders if they ever understand
That they have caused their own grief.

Epic of Gilgamesh

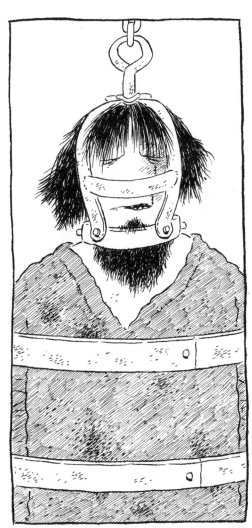

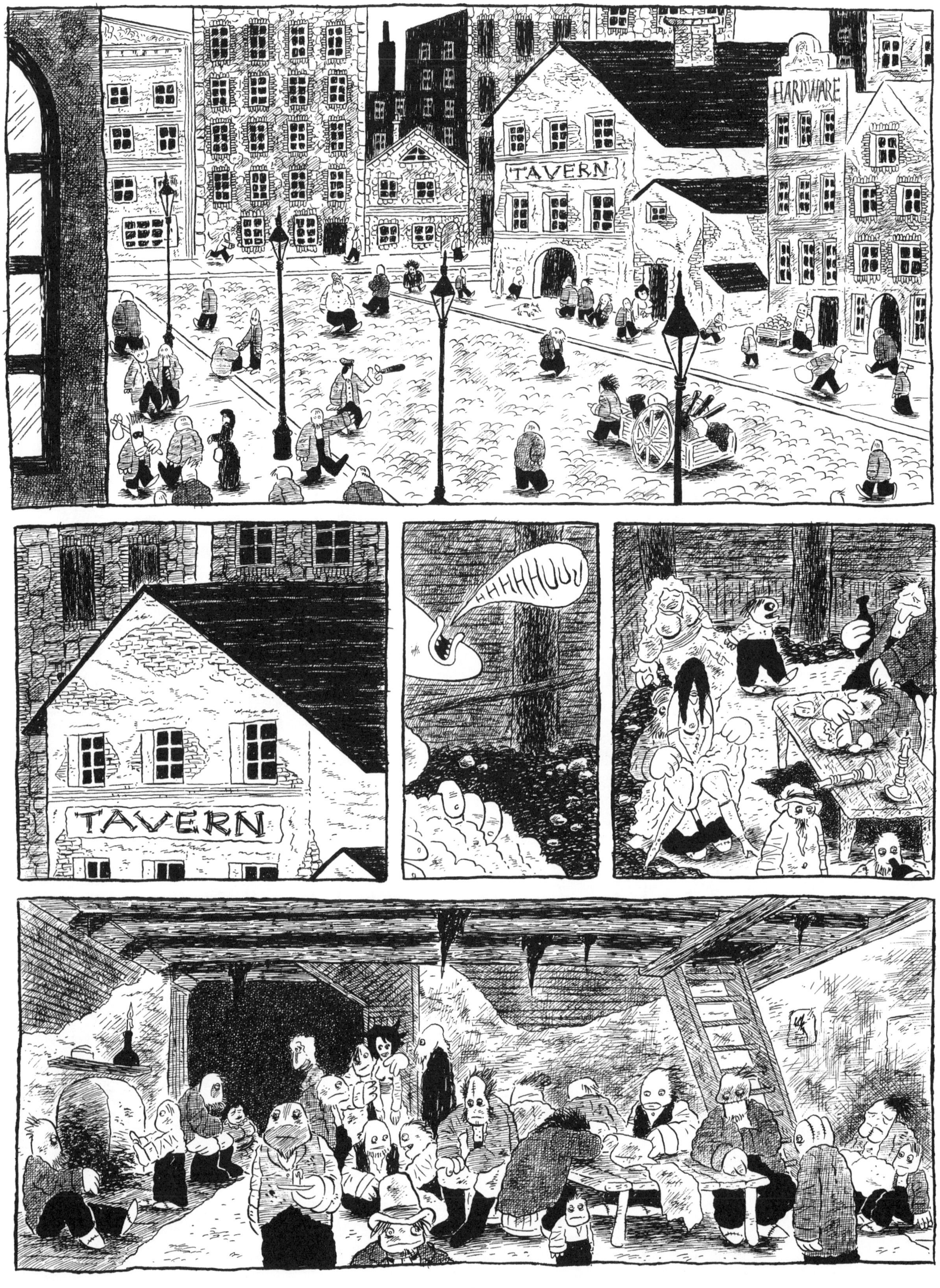
HARDWARE
TAVERN
TAVERN
HHHHHUUUU

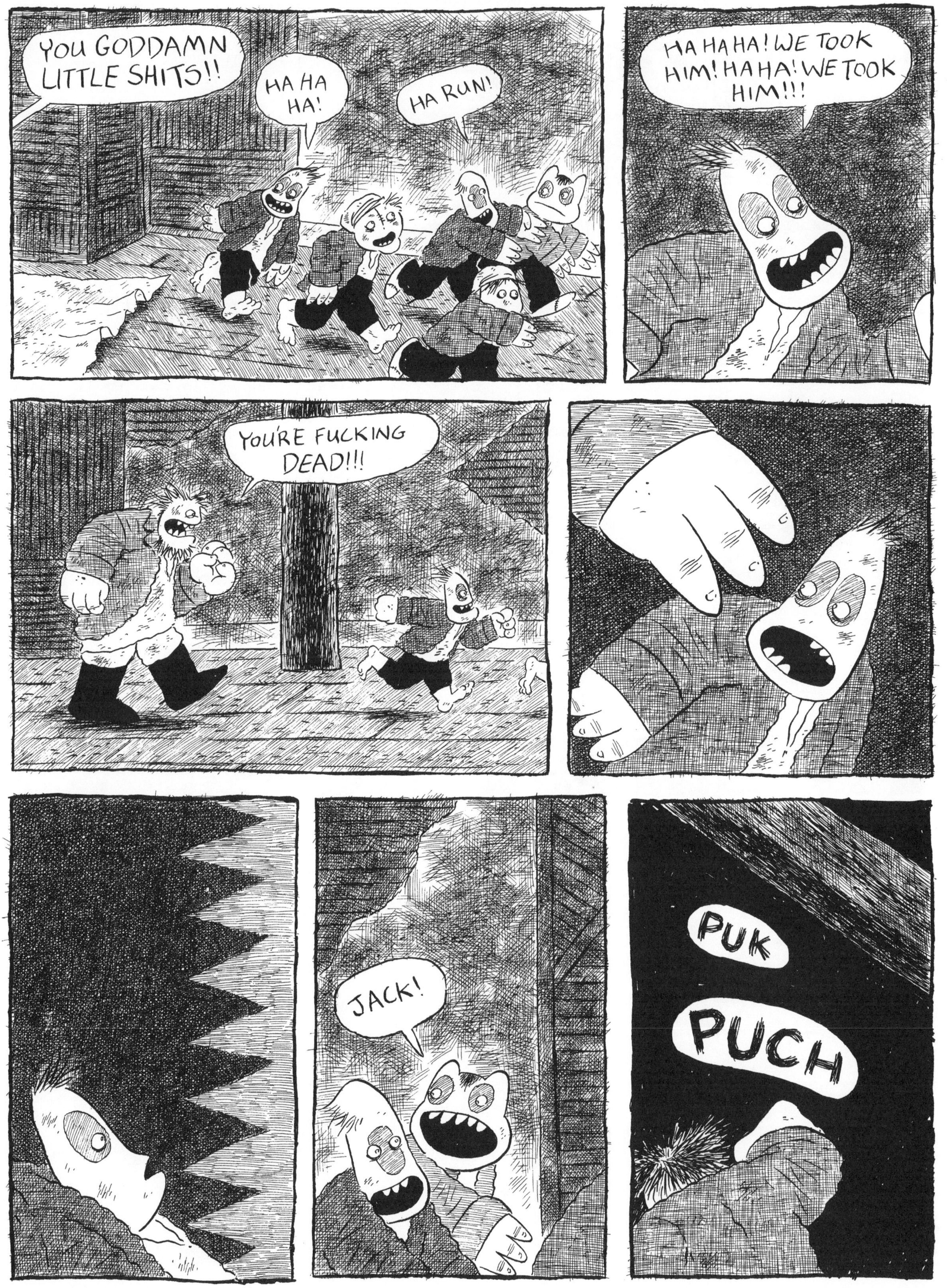
YOU GODDAMN LITTLE SHITS!!
HA HA HA!
HA RUN!
HA HA HA! WE TOOK HIM! HA HA! WE TOOK HIM!!!
YOU'RE FUCKING DEAD!!!
JACK!
PUK
PUCH

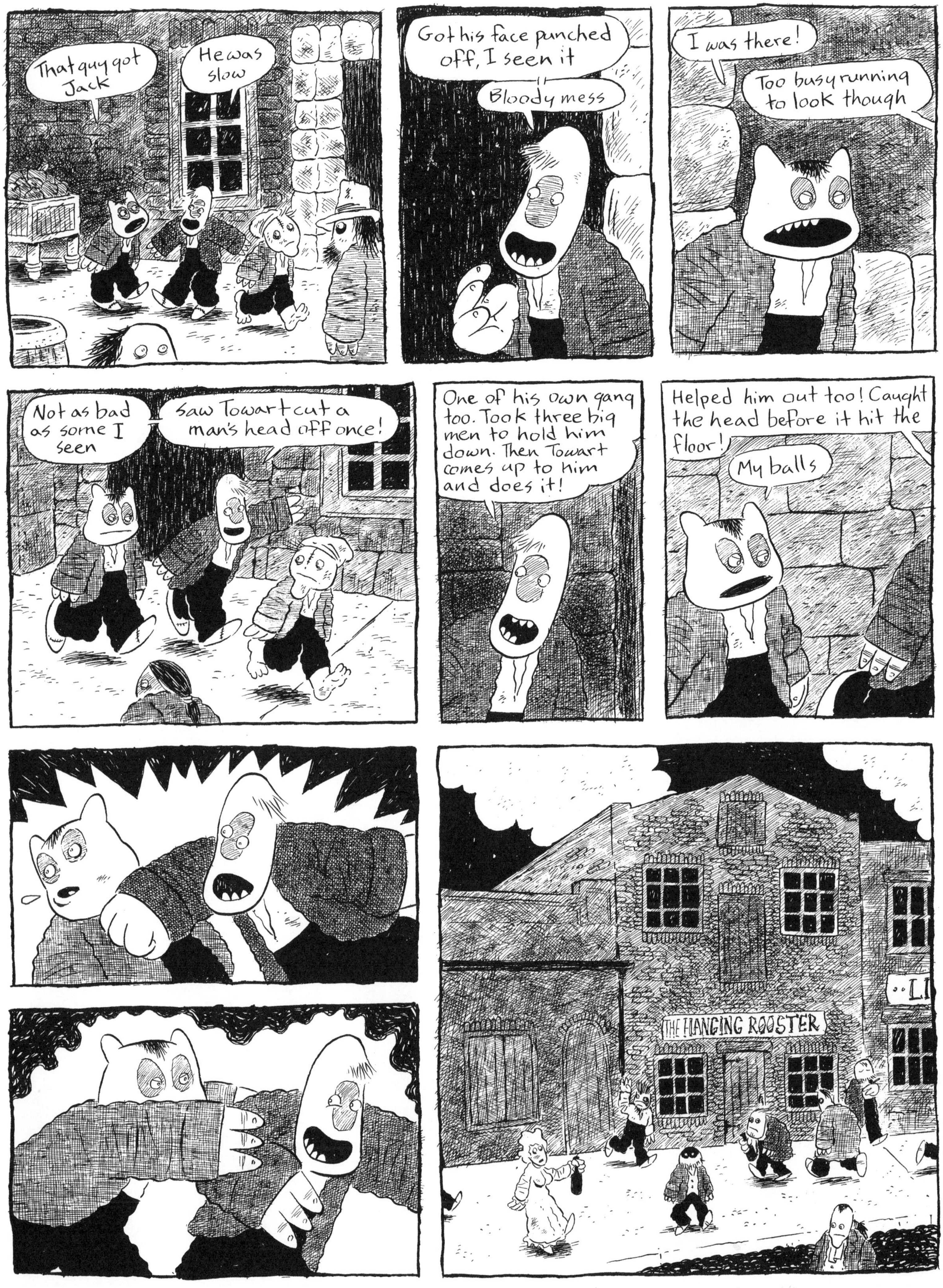

That guy got Jack
He was slow
Got his face punched off, I seen it
Bloody mess
I was there!
Too busy running to look though
Not as bad as some I seen
Saw Towart cut a man's head off once!
One of his own gang too. Took three big men to hold him down. Then Towart comes up to him and does it!
Helped him out too! Caught the head before it hit the floor!
My balls
THE HANGING ROOSTER

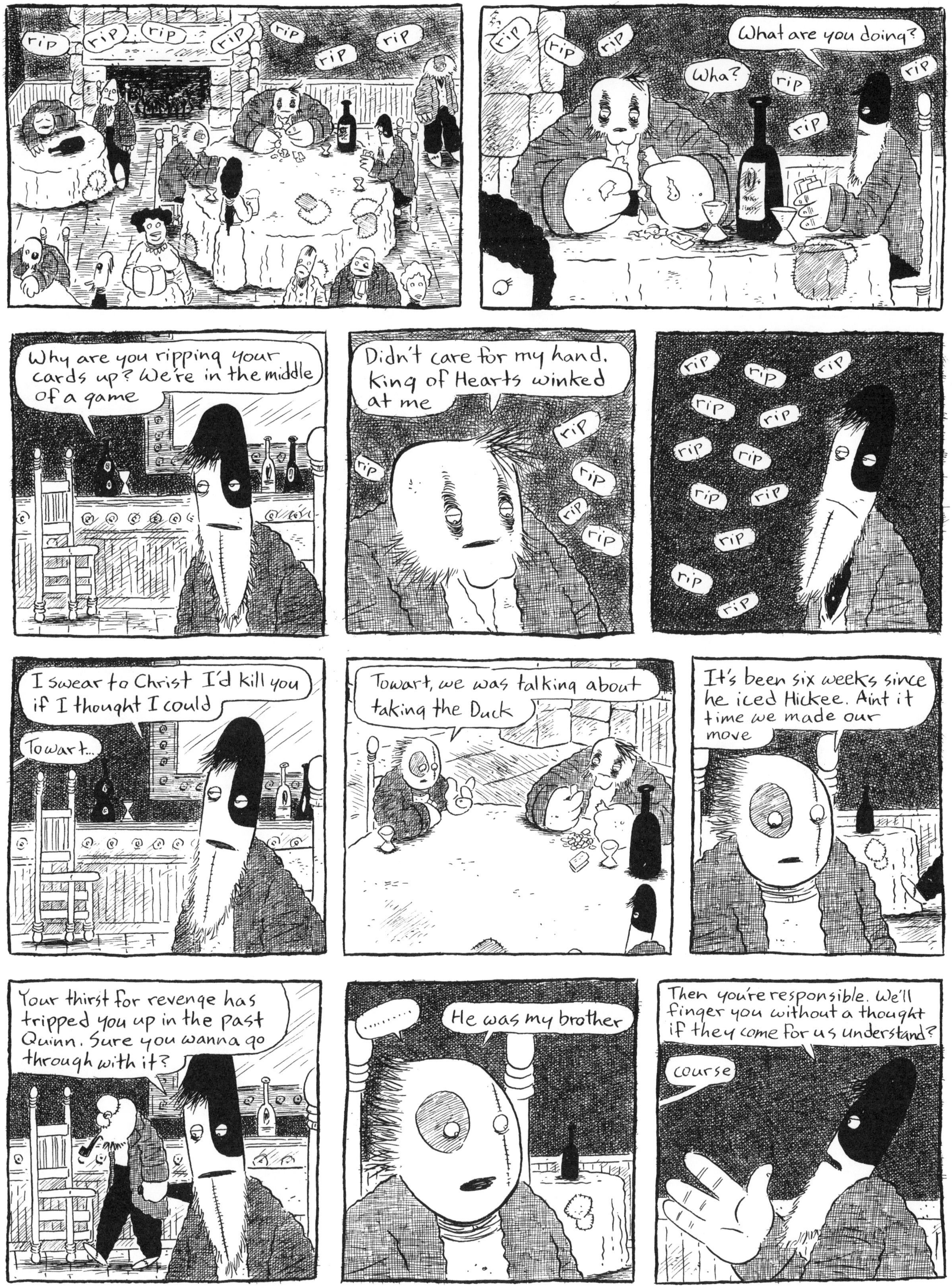
rip
rip
rip
rip
rip
rip
rip
rip
rip
rip
What are you doing?
Wha?
rip
rip
rip
Why are you ripping your cards up? We're in the middle of a game
Didn't care for my hand. King of Hearts winked at me
rip
rip
rip
rip
rip
I swear to Christ I'd kill you if I thought I could
Towart...
Towart, we was talking about taking the Duck
It's been six weeks since he iced Hickee. Aint it time we made our move
Your thirst for revenge has tripped you up in the past Quinn. Sure you wanna go through with it?
....
He was my brother
Then you're responsible. We'll finger you without a thought if they come for us understand?
course

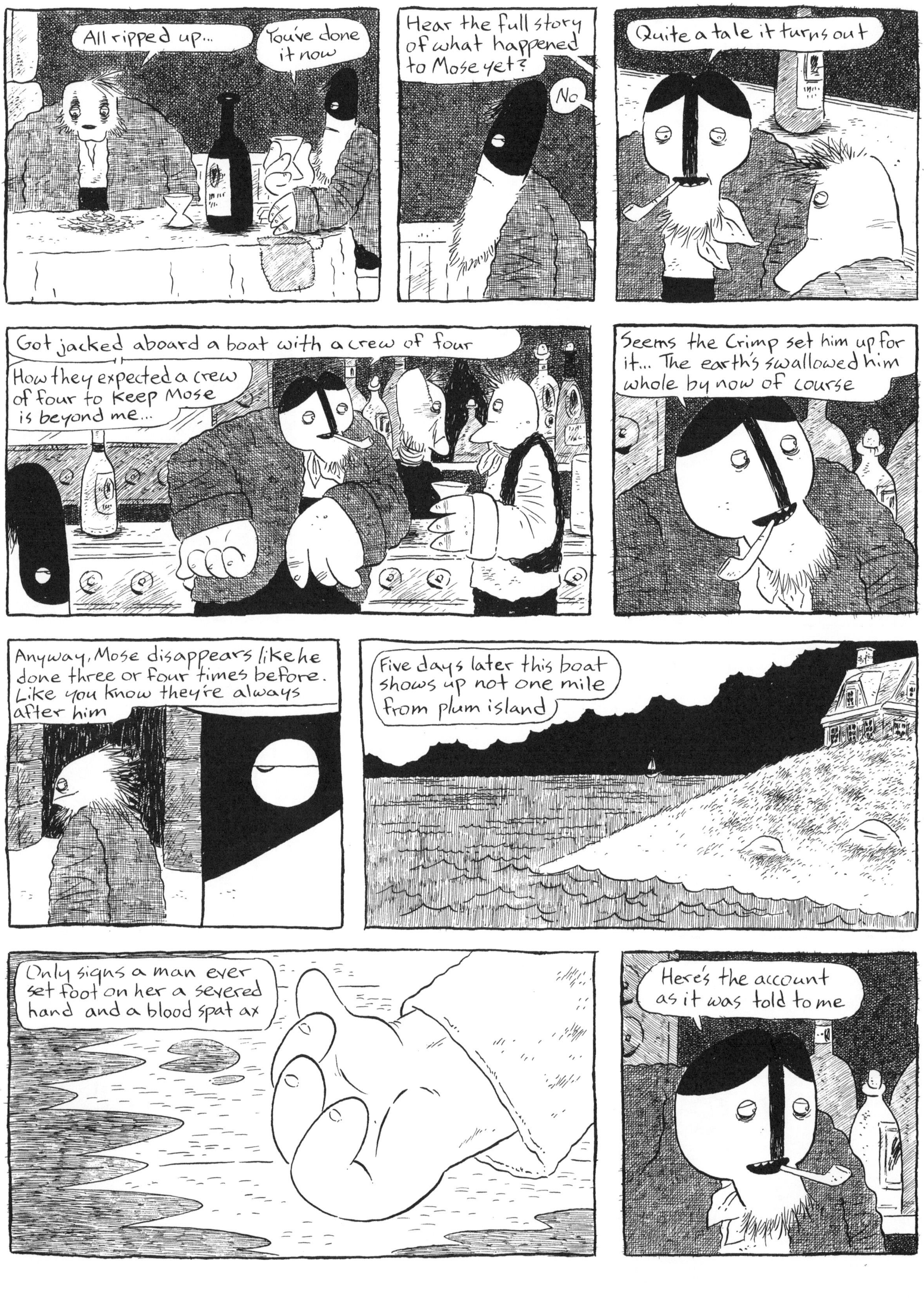
All ripped up...
You've done it now
Hear the full story of what happened to Mose yet?
No
Quite a tale it turns out
Got jacked aboard a boat with a crew of four
How they expected a crew of four to keep Mose is beyond me...
Seems the Crimp set him up for it... The earth's swallowed him whole by now of course
Anyway, Mose disappears like he done three or four times before. Like you know they're always after him
Five days later this boat shows up not one mile from plum island
Only signs a man ever set foot on her a severed hand and a blood spat ax
Here's the account as it was told to me

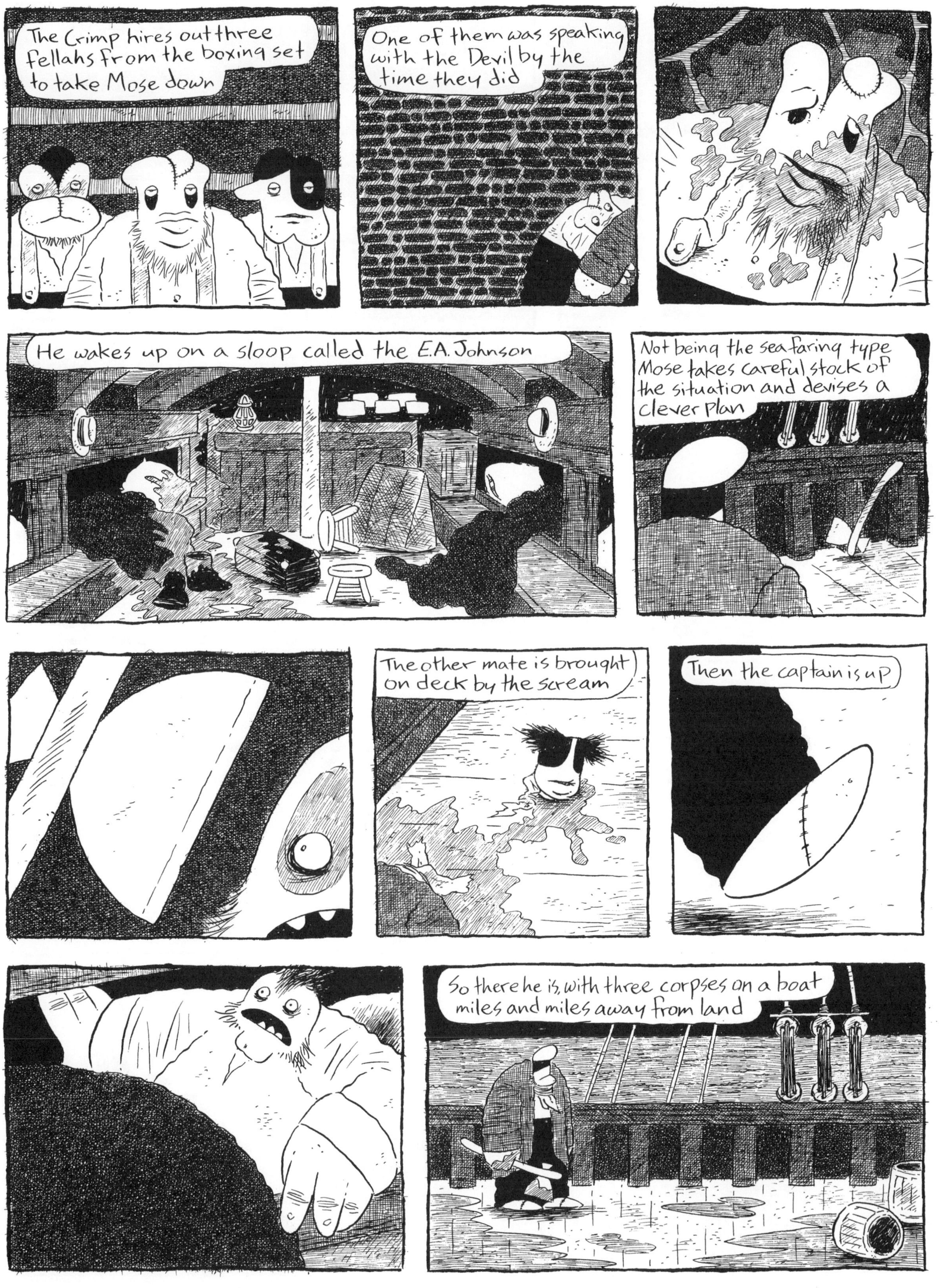
The Crimp hires out three fellahs from the boxing set to take Mose down
One of them was speaking with the Devil by the time they did
He wakes up on a sloop called the E.A. Johnson
Not being the seafaring type Mose takes careful stock of the situation and devises a clever plan
The other mate is brought on deck by the scream
Then the captain is up
So there he is, with three corpses on a boat miles and miles away from land

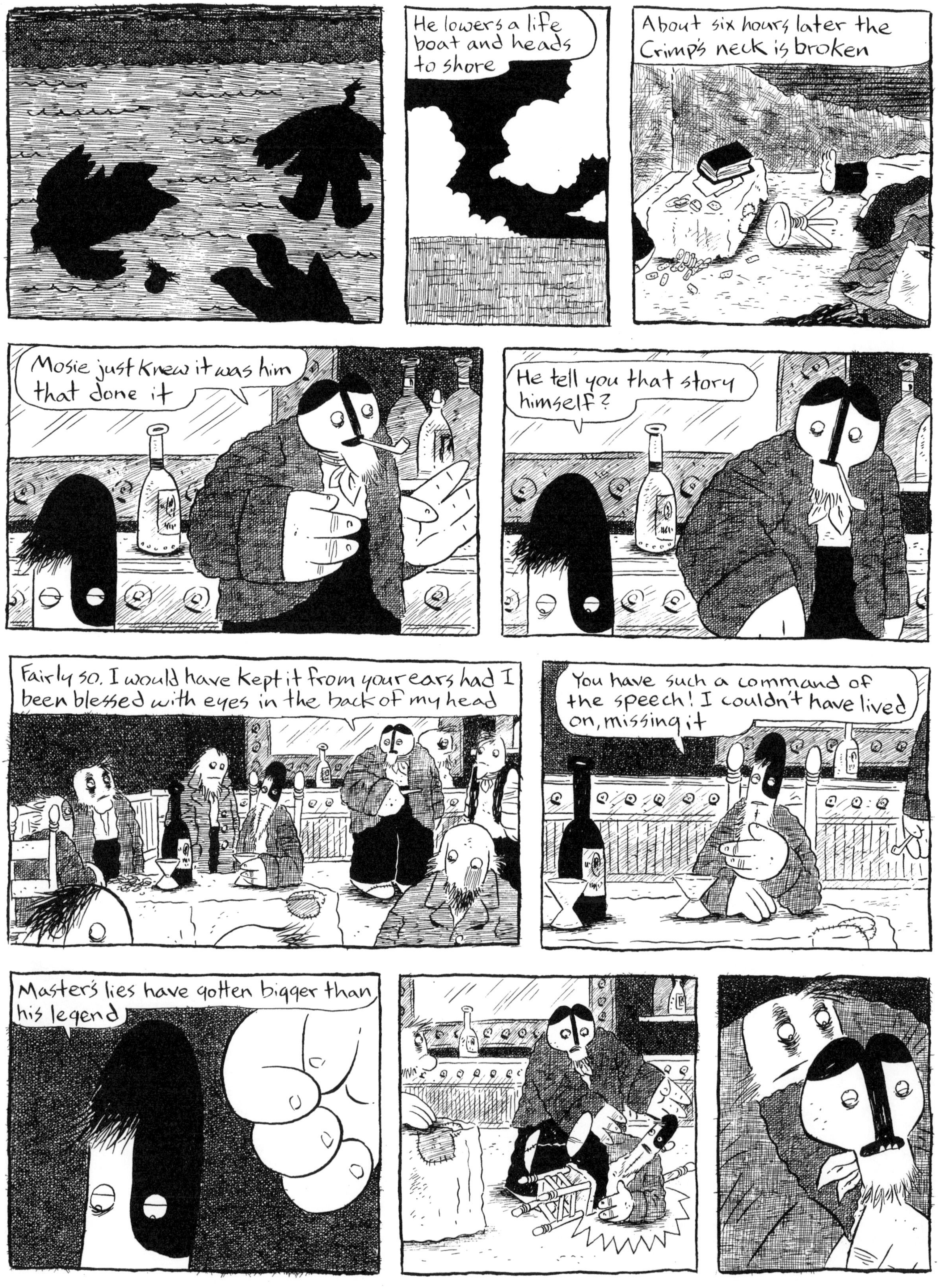

He lowers a life boat and heads to shore
About six hours later the Crimp's neck is broken
Mosie just knew it was him that done it
He tell you that story himself?
Fairly so. I would have kept it from your ears had I been blessed with eyes in the back of my head
You have such a command of the speech! I couldn't have lived on, missing it
Master's lies have gotten bigger than his legend

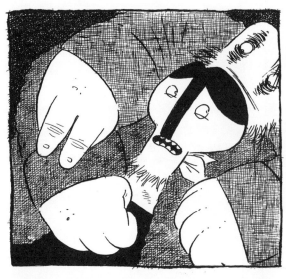

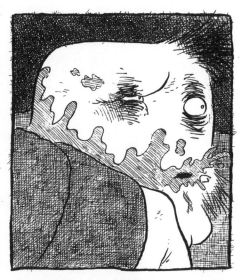

I need to go address this wound you've given me

I know you won't try to stop me, because your protection is asleep

Everyone watching should likewise hope they don't care enough for this man to stop me

Knock! knock!
SHAKESPEARE

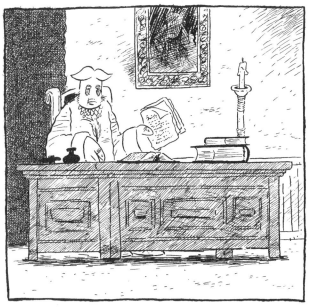

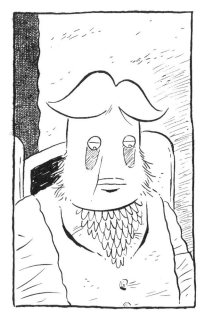

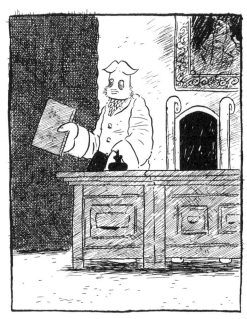

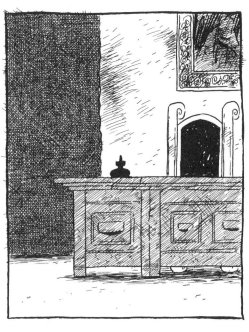

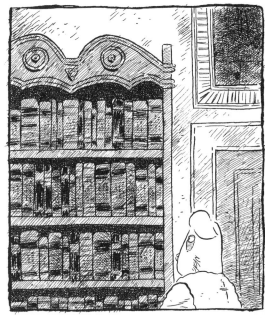

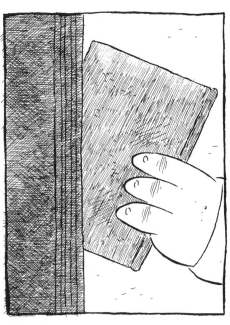

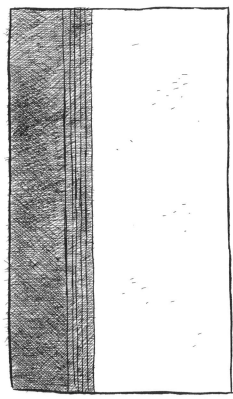

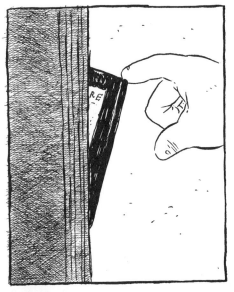

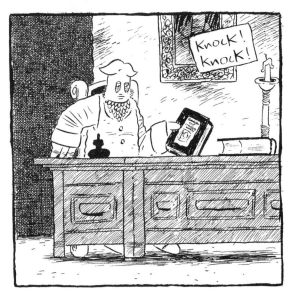

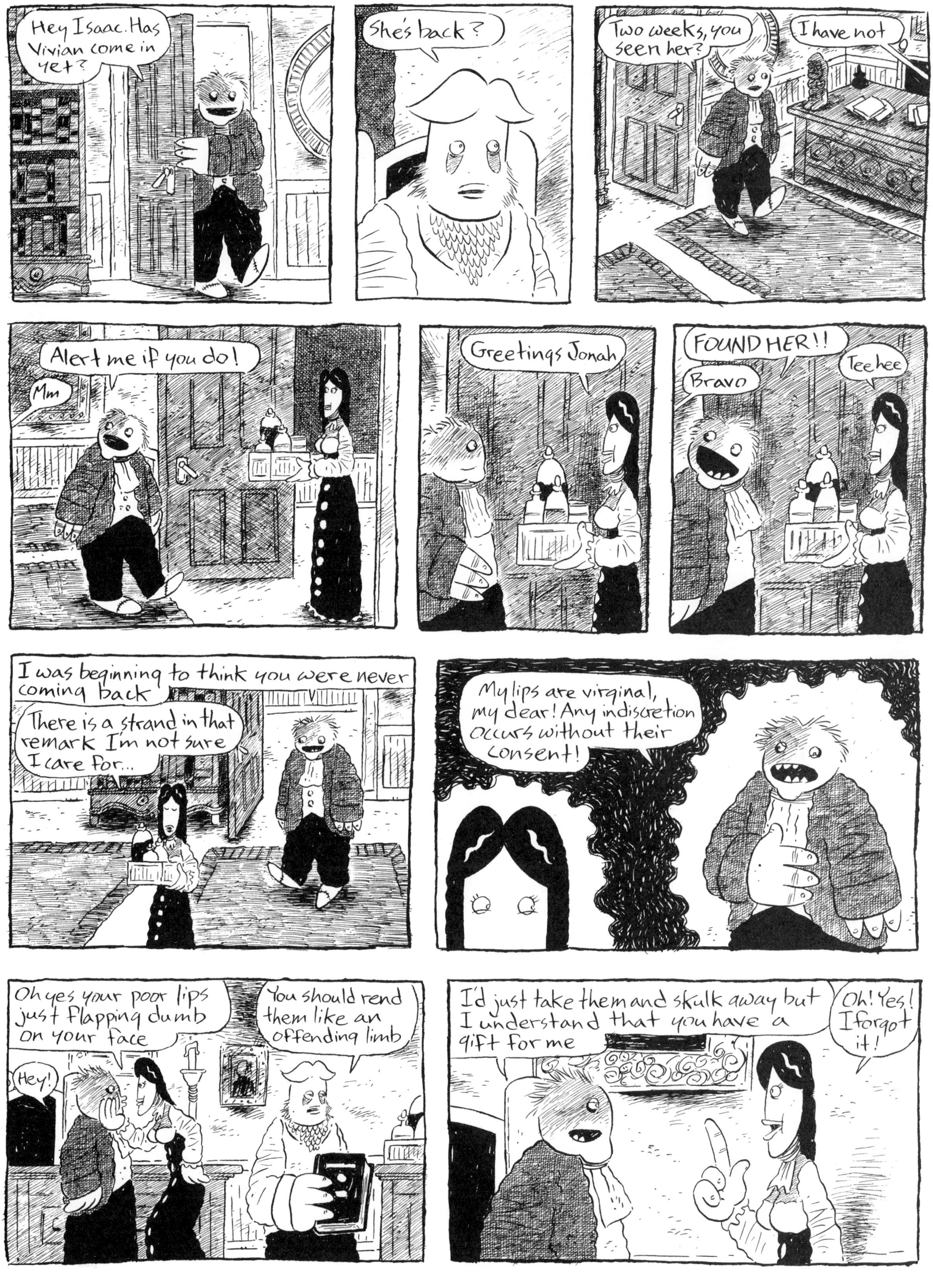
Hey Isaac. Has Vivian come in yet?
She's back?
Two weeks, you seen her?
I have not
Alert me if you do!
Mm
Greetings Jonah
FOUND HER!!
Bravo
Tee hee
I was beginning to think you were never coming back
There is a strand in that remark I'm not sure I care for...
My lips are virginal, my dear! Any indiscretion occurs without their consent!
Oh yes your poor lips just flapping dumb on your face
You should rend them like an offending limb
Hey!
I'd just take them and skulk away but I understand that you have a gift for me
Oh! Yes! I forgot it!

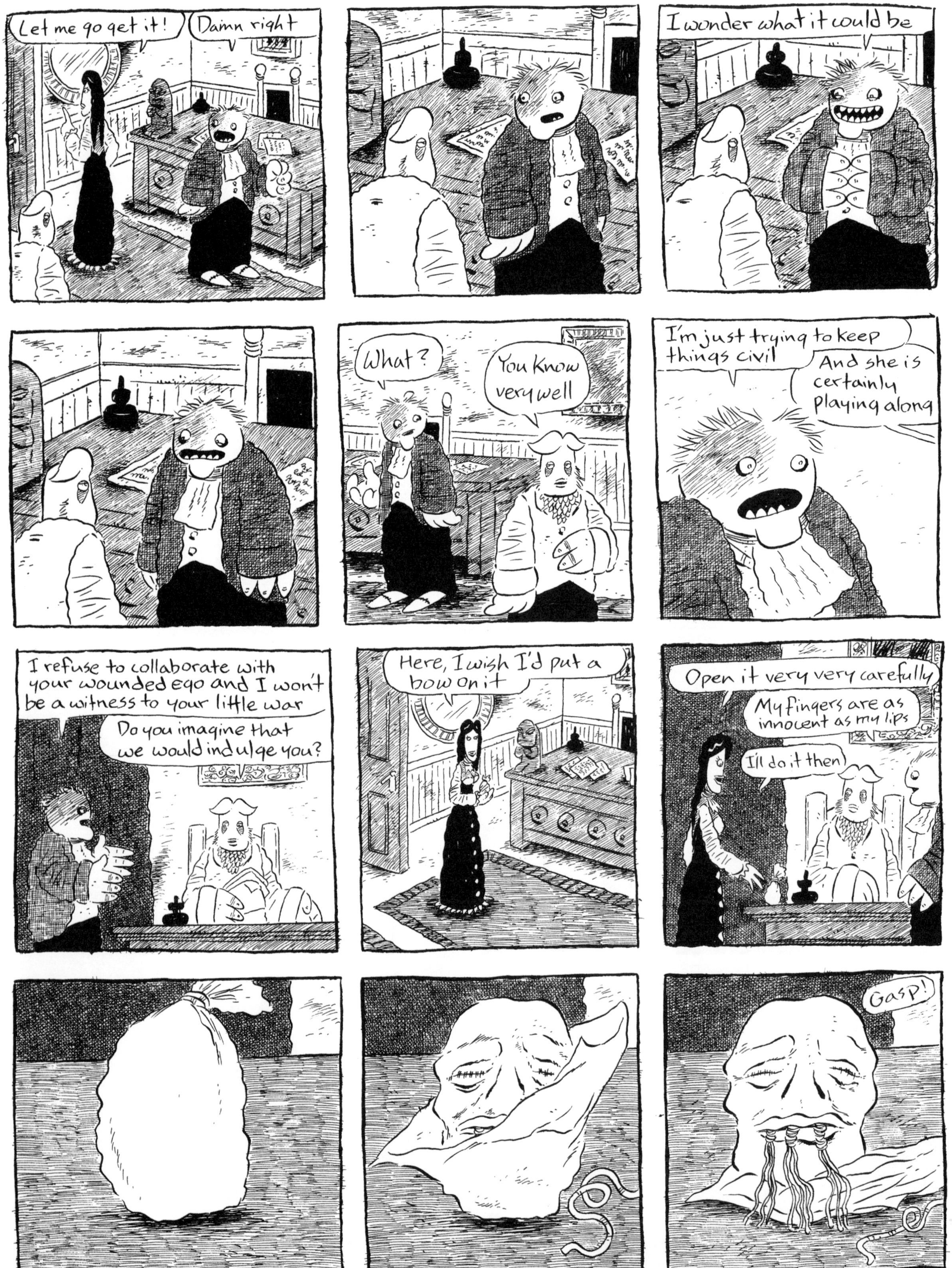
Let me go get it!
Damn right
I wonder what it could be
What?
You know very well
I'm just trying to keep things civil
And she is certainly playing along
I refuse to collaborate with your wounded ego and I won't be a witness to your little war
Do you imagine that we would indulge you?
Here, I wish I'd put a bow on it
Open it very very carefully
My fingers are as innocent as my lips
I'll do it then
Gasp!

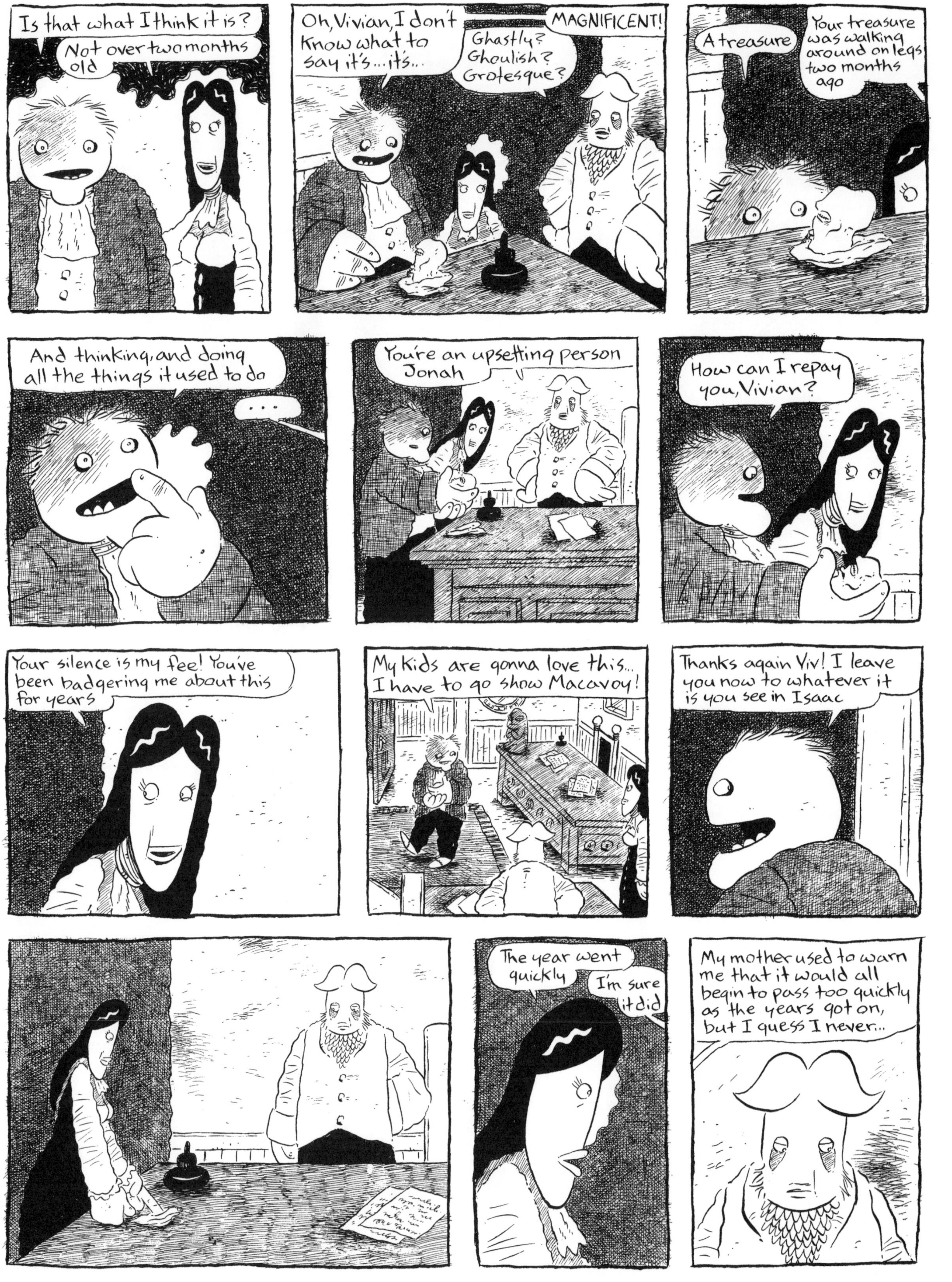

Is that what I think it is?
Not over two months old
Oh, Vivian, I don't know what to say it's... it's...
Ghastly? Ghoulish? Grotesque?
MAGNIFICENT!
A treasure
Your treasure was walking around on legs two months ago
And thinking, and doing all the things it used to do
...
You're an upsetting person Jonah
How can I repay you, Vivian?
Your silence is my fee! You've been badgering me about this for years
My kids are gonna love this... I have to go show Macavoy!
Thanks again Viv! I leave you now to whatever it is you see in Isaac
The year went quickly
I'm sure it did
My mother used to warn me that it would all begin to pass too quickly as the years got on, but I guess I never...

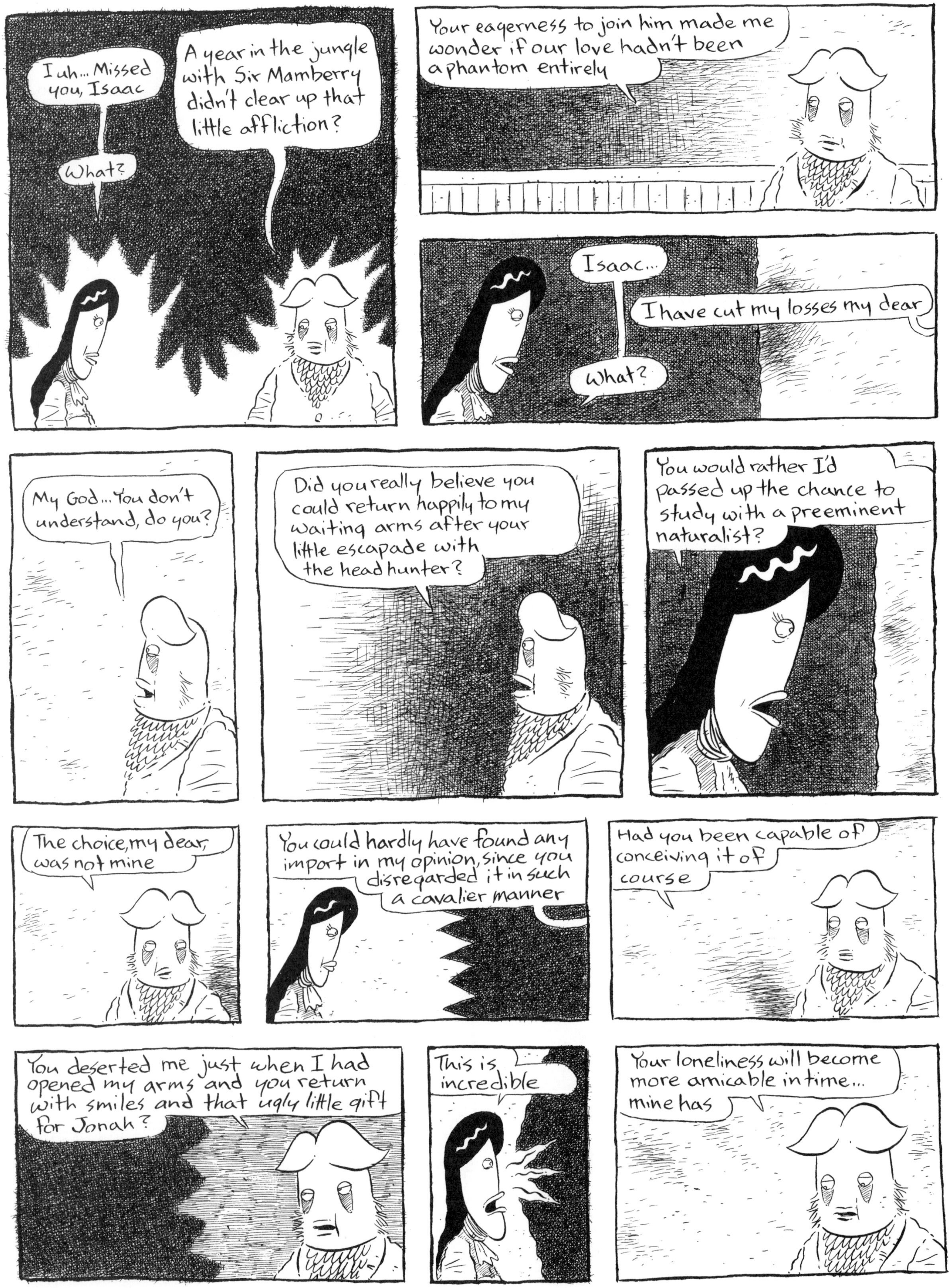
I uh... Missed you, Isaac
What?
A year in the jungle with Sir Mamberry didn't clear up that little affliction?
Your eagerness to join him made me wonder if our love hadn't been a phantom entirely
Isaac...
What?
I have cut my losses my dear
My God... You don't understand, do you?
Did you really believe you could return happily to my waiting arms after your little escapade with the head hunter?
You would rather I'd passed up the chance to study with a preeminent naturalist?
The choice, my dear, was not mine
You could hardly have found any import in my opinion, since you disregarded it in such a cavalier manner
Had you been capable of conceiving it of course
You deserted me just when I had opened my arms and you return with smiles and that ugly little gift for Jonah?
This is incredible
Your loneliness will become more amicable in time... mine has

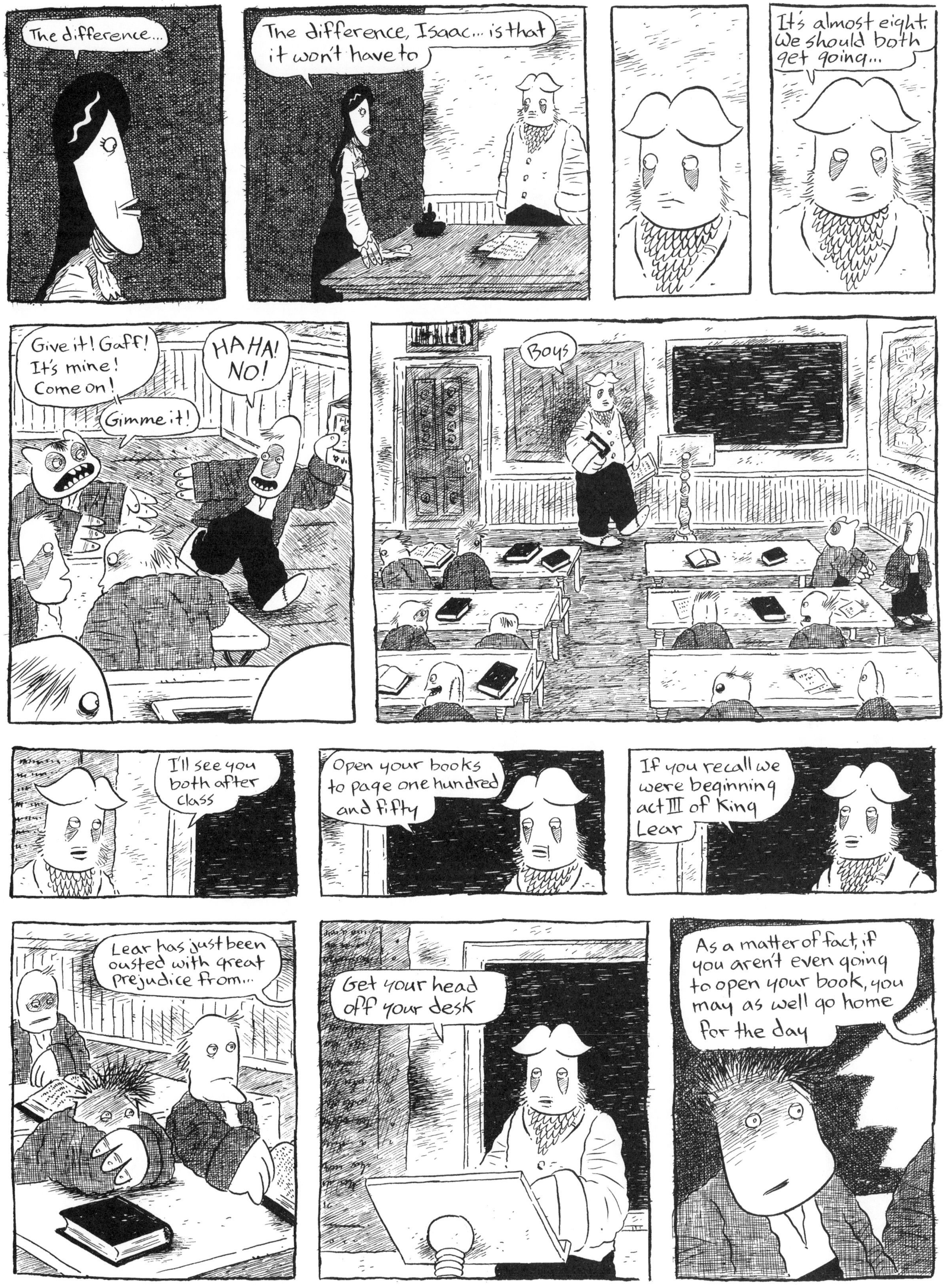
The difference...
The difference, Isaac... is that it won't have to
It's almost eight. We should both get going...
Give it! Gaff! It's mine! Come on!
HA HA! NO!
Gimme it!
Boys
I'll see you both after class
Open your books to page one hundred and fifty
If you recall we were beginning act III of King Lear
Lear has just been ousted with great prejudice from...
Get your head off your desk
As a matter of fact, if you aren't even going to open your book, you may as well go home for the day

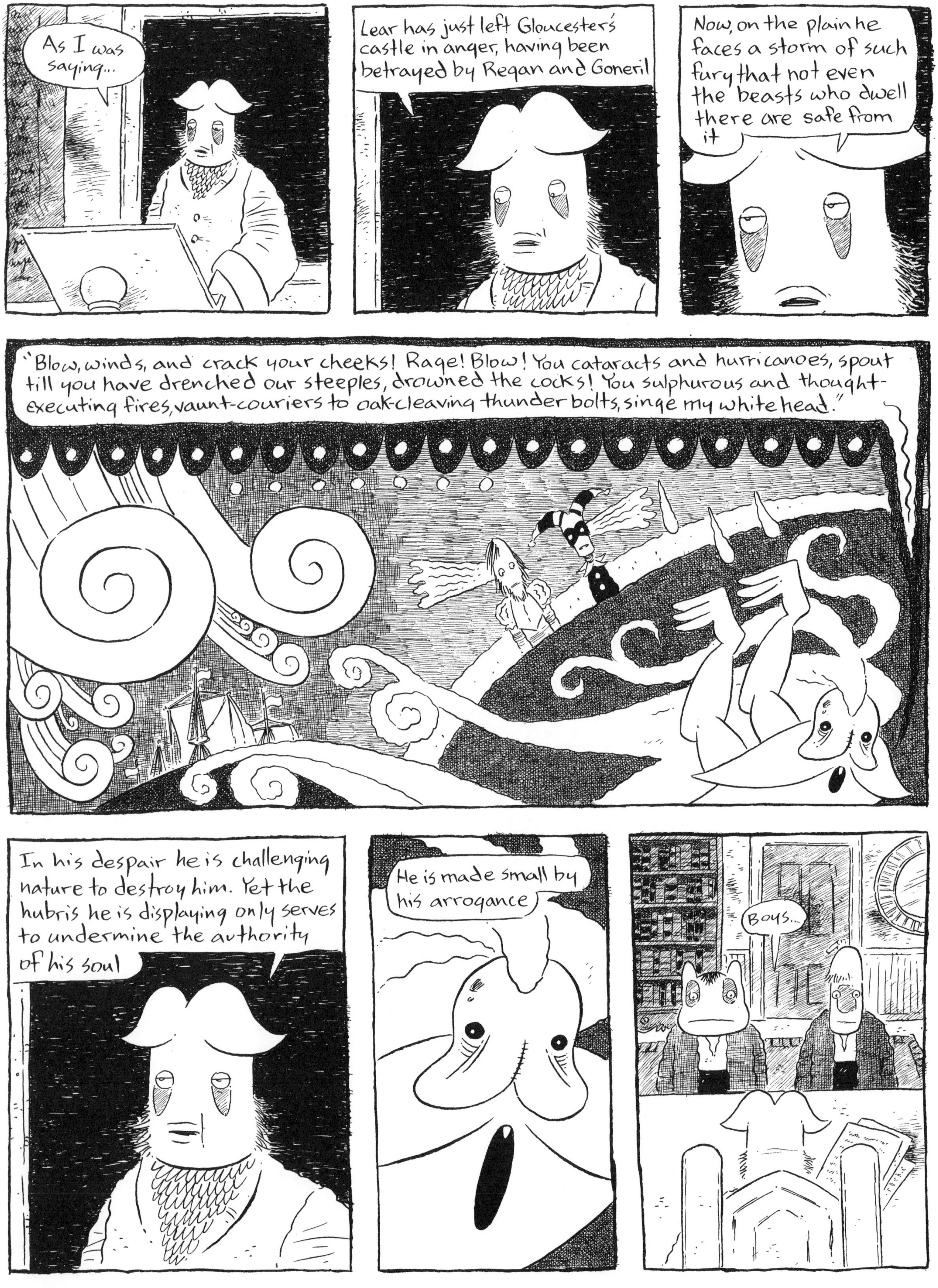

As I was saying...
Lear has just left Gloucester's castle in anger, having been betrayed by Regan and Goneril
Now, on the plain he faces a storm of such fury that not even the beasts who dwell there are safe from it
"Blow, winds, and crack your cheeks! Rage! Blow! You cataracts and hurricanoes, spout till you have drenched our steeples, drowned the cocks! You sulphurous and thought-executing fires, vaunt-couriers to oak-cleaving thunder bolts, singe my white head."
In his despair he is challenging nature to destroy him. Yet the hubris he is displaying only serves to undermine the authority of his soul
He is made small by his arrogance
Boys...

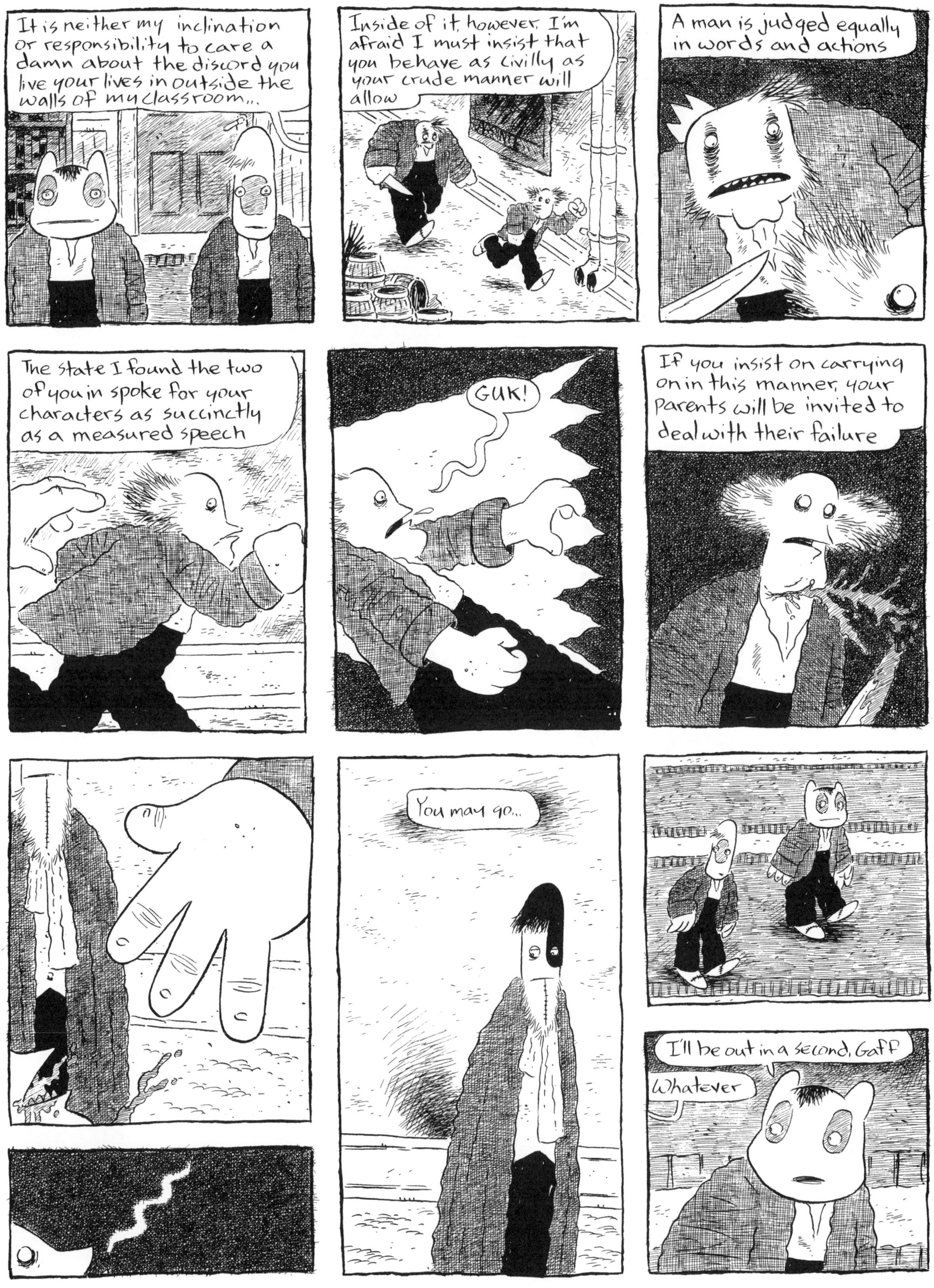

It is neither my inclination or responsibility to care a damn about the discord you live your lives in outside the walls of my classroom...
Inside of it, however, I'm afraid I must insist that you behave as civilly as your crude manner will allow
A man is judged equally in words and actions
The state I found the two of you in spoke for your characters as succinctly as a measured speech
GUK!
If you insist on carrying on in this manner, your parents will be invited to deal with their failure
You may go...
I'll be out in a second, Gaff
Whatever

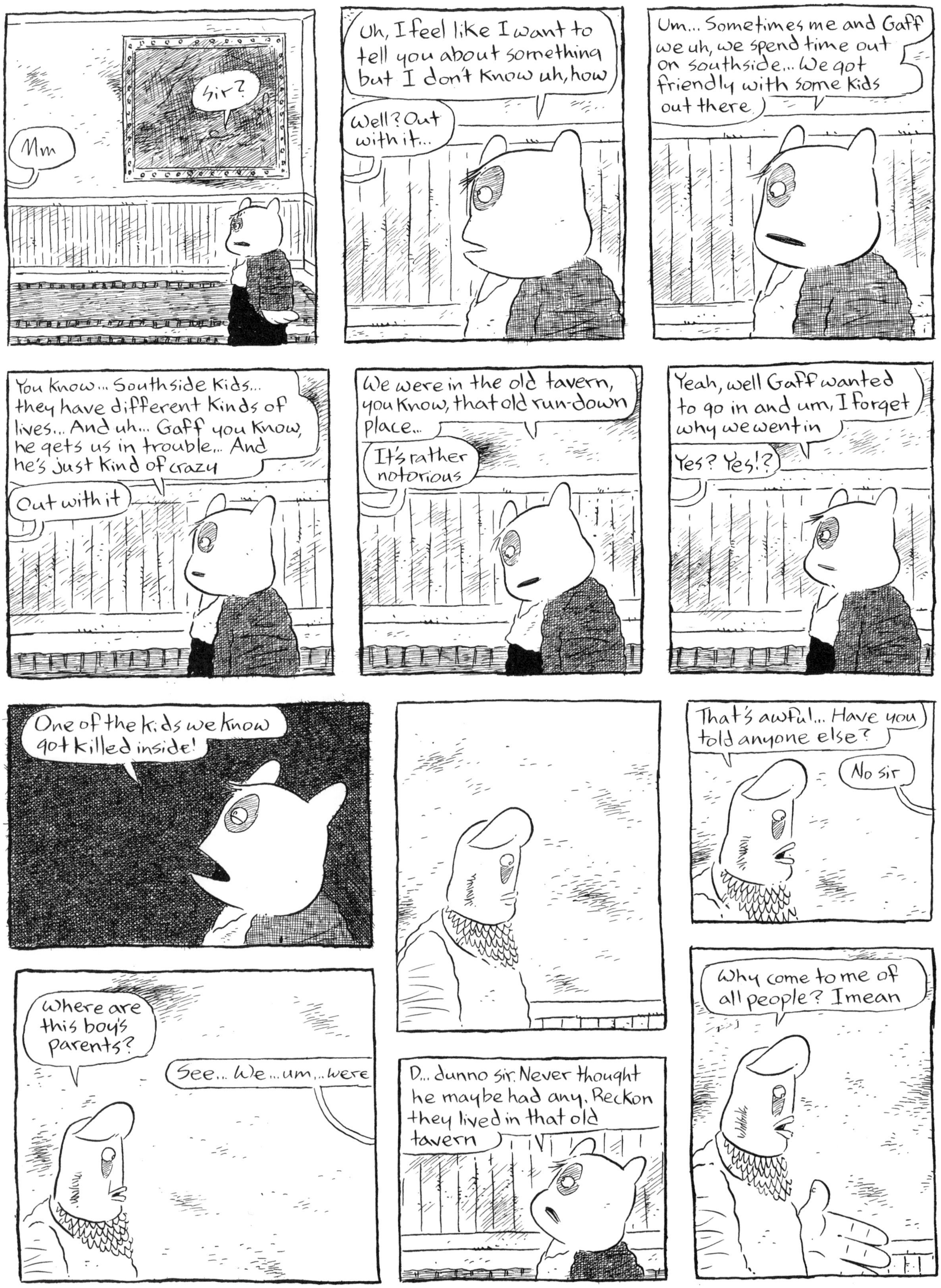
Sir?
Mm
Uh, I feel like I want to tell you about something but I don't know uh, how
Well? Out with it...
Um... Sometimes me and Gaff we uh, we spend time out on southside... We got friendly with some kids out there
You know... Southside kids... they have different kinds of lives... And uh... Gaff you know, he gets us in trouble... And he's just kind of crazy
Out with it
We were in the old tavern, you know, that old run-down place...
It's rather notorious
Yeah, well Gaff wanted to go in and um, I forget why we went in
Yes? Yes!?
One of the kids we know got killed inside!
That's awful... Have you told anyone else?
No sir
Where are this boy's parents?
See... We...um...were
D... dunno sir. Never thought he maybe had any. Reckon they lived in that old tavern
Why come to me of all people? I mean

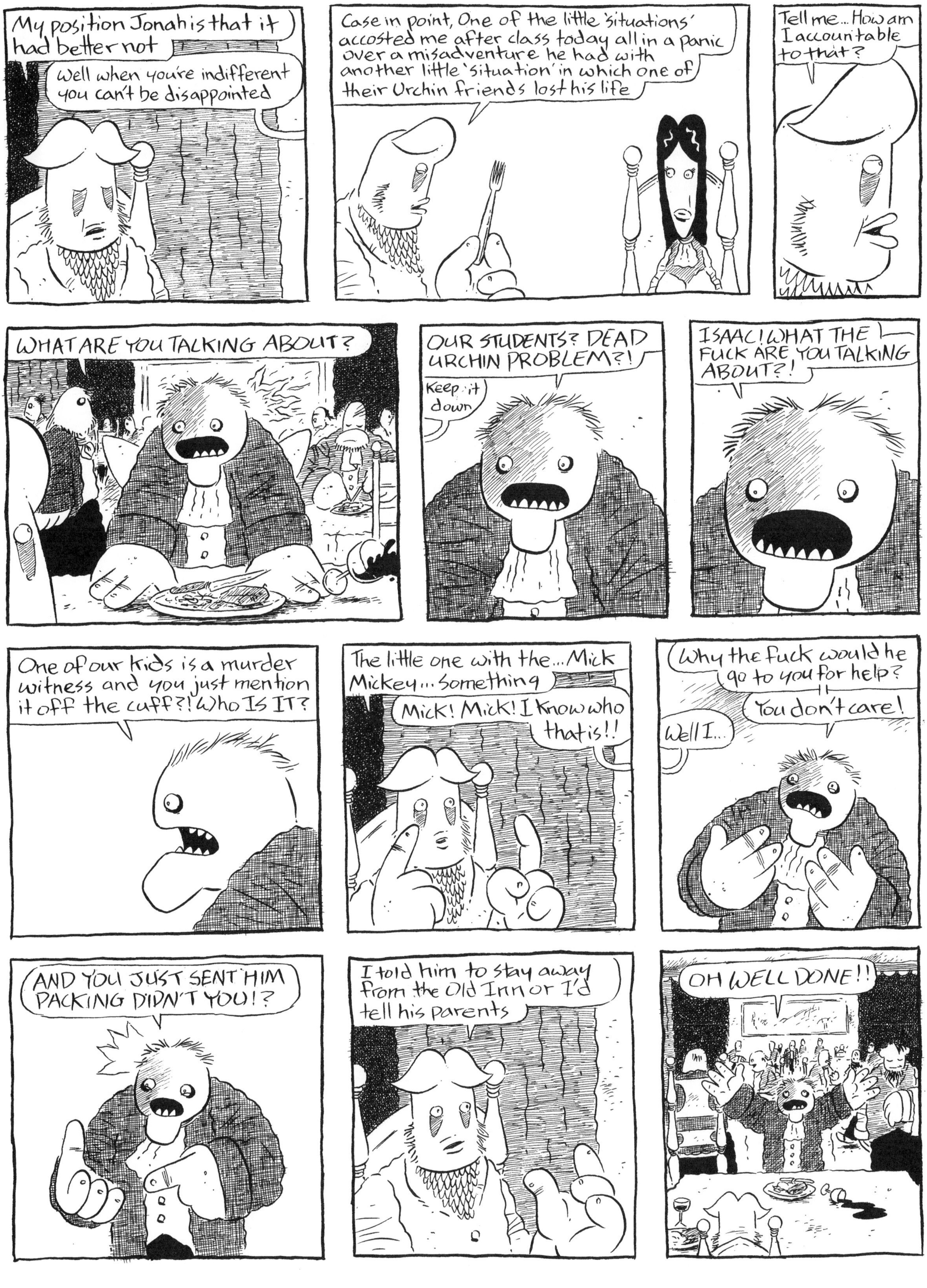
My position Jonah is that it had better not
Well when you're indifferent you can't be disappointed
Case in point, One of the little 'situations' accosted me after class today all in a panic over a misadventure he had with another little 'situation' in which one of their Urchin friends lost his life
Tell me... How am I accountable to that?
WHAT ARE YOU TALKING ABOUT?
OUR STUDENTS? DEAD URCHIN PROBLEM?!
Keep it down
ISAAC! WHAT THE FUCK ARE YOU TALKING ABOUT?!
One of our kids is a murder witness and you just mention it off the cuff?! Who IS IT?
The little one with the... Mick Mickey... Something
Mick! Mick! I know who that is!!
Why the fuck would he go to you for help?
You don't care!
Well I...
AND YOU JUST SENT HIM PACKING DIDN'T YOU!?
I told him to stay away from the Old Inn or I'd tell his parents
OH WELL DONE!!

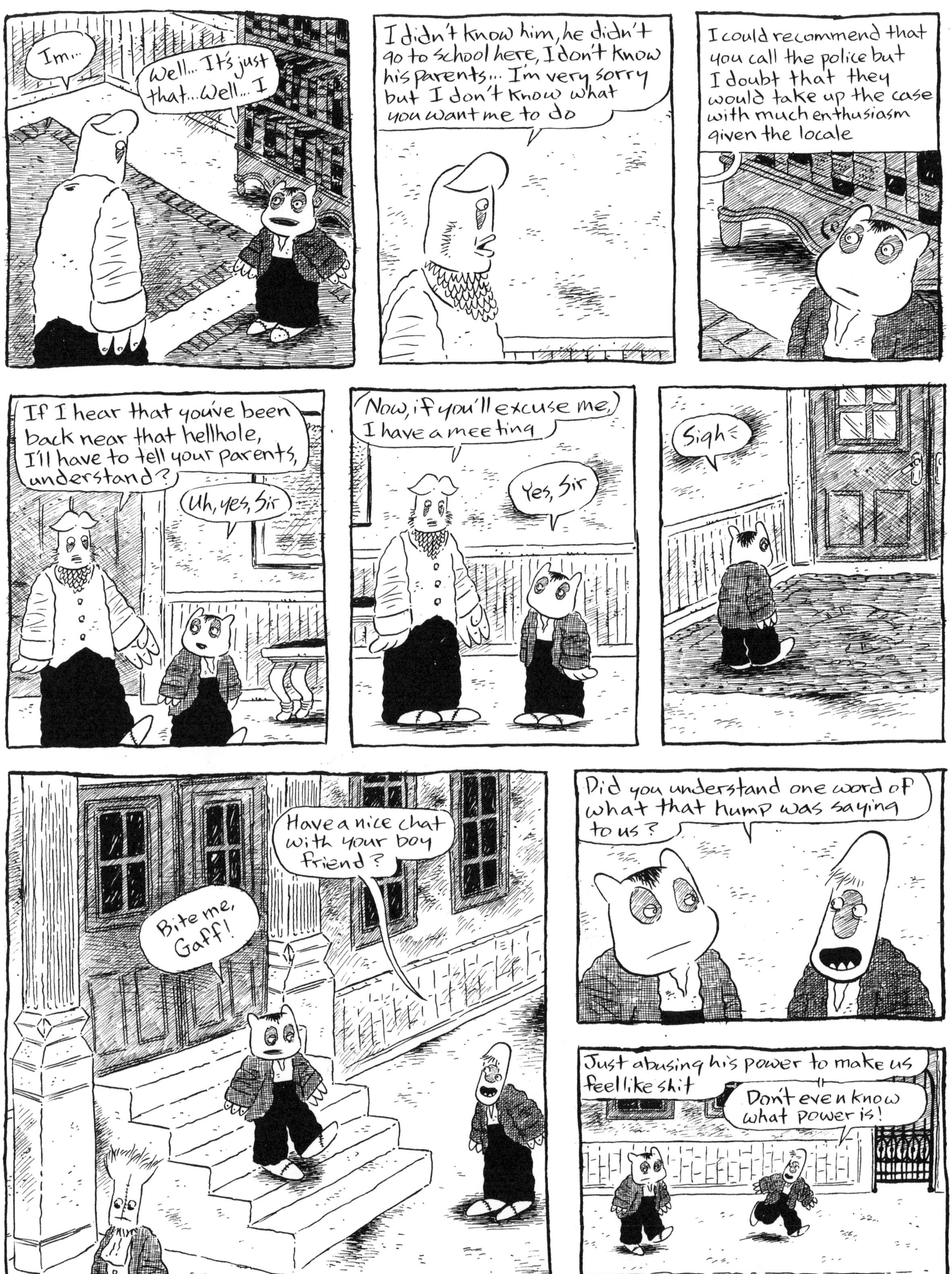
Im...
Well... It's just that... Well... I
I didn't know him, he didn't go to school here, I don't know his parents... I'm very sorry but I don't know what you want me to do
I could recommend that you call the police but I doubt that they would take up the case with much enthusiasm given the locale
If I hear that you've been back near that hellhole, I'll have to tell your parents, understand?
Uh, yes, Sir
Now, if you'll excuse me, I have a meeting
Yes, Sir
Sigh
Have a nice chat with your boy friend?
Bite me, Gaff!
Did you understand one word of what that hump was saying to us?
Just abusing his power to make us feel like shit
Don't even know what power is!

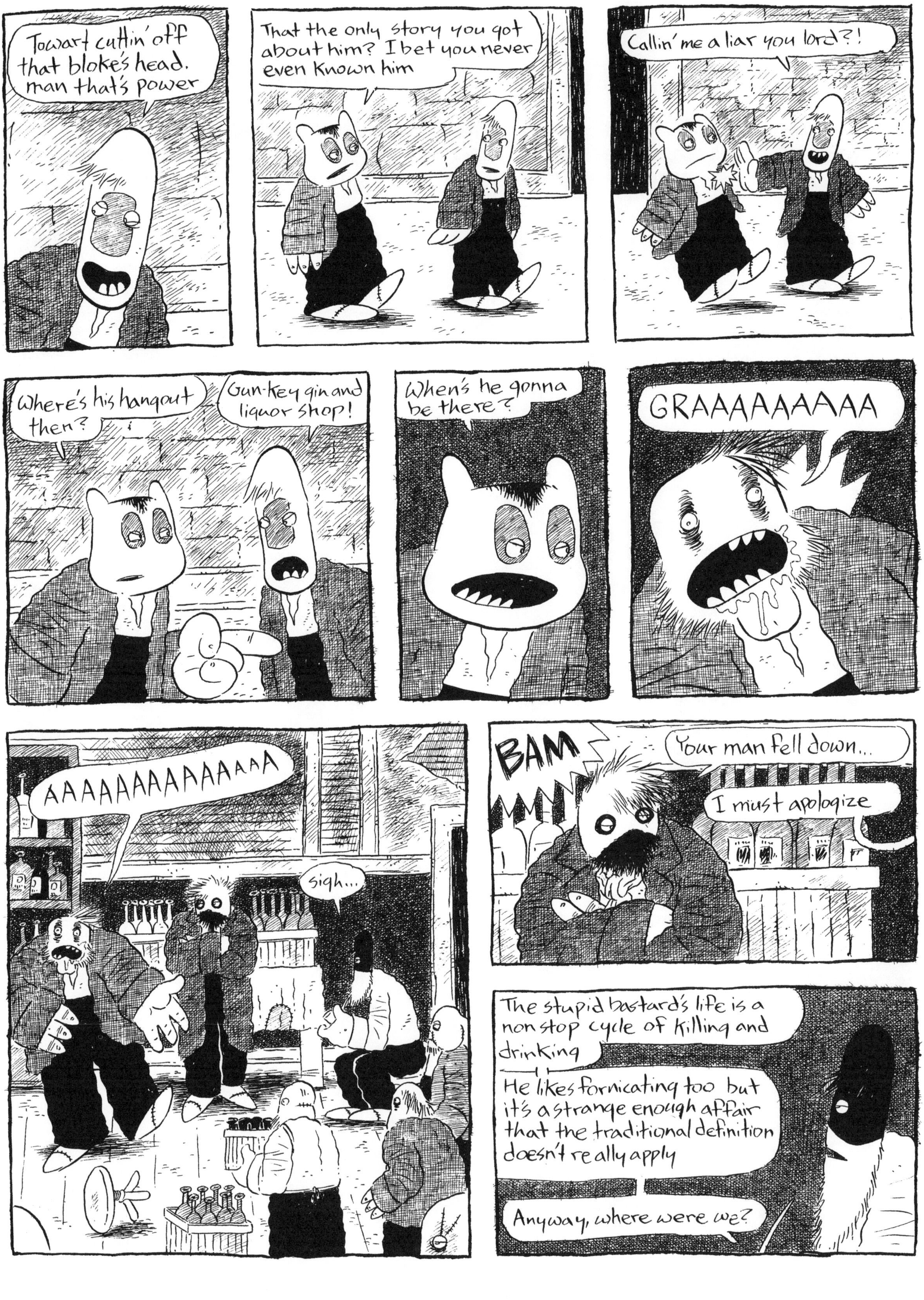
Towart cuttin' off that bloke's head. man that's power
That the only story you got about him? I bet you never even Known him
Callin' me a liar you lord?!
Where's his hangout then?
Gun-Key gin and liquor shop!
When's he gonna be there?
GRAAAAAAAAA
AAAAAAAAAAAAA
sigh...
BAM
Your man fell down...
I must apologize
The stupid bastard's life is a non stop cycle of Killing and drinking
He likes fornicating too but it's a strange enough affair that the traditional definition doesn't really apply
Anyway, where were we?

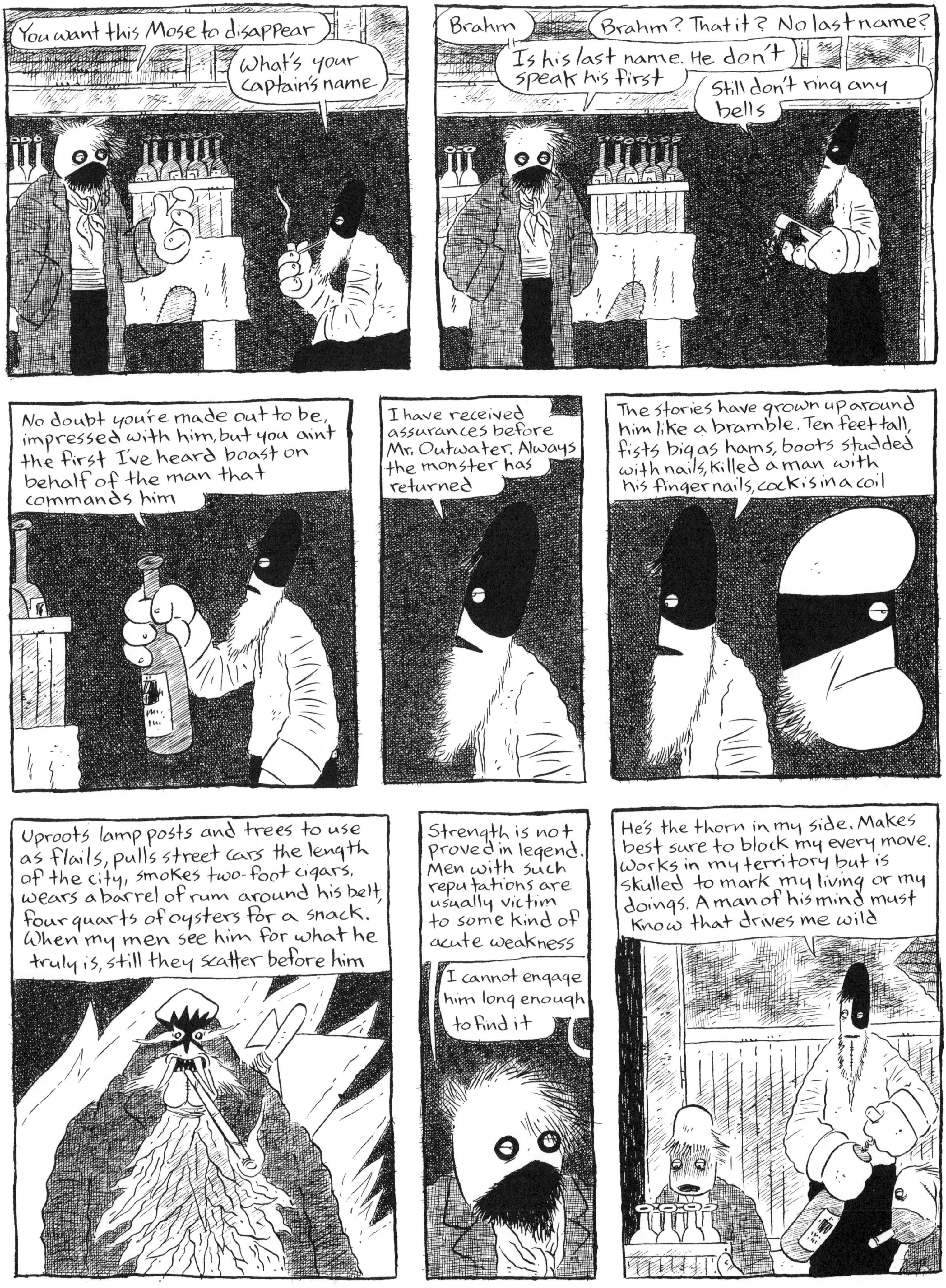
You want this Mose to disappear
What's your captain's name
Brahm
Brahm? That it? No last name?
Is his last name. He don't speak his first
Still don't ring any bells
No doubt you're made out to be, impressed with him, but you aint the first I've heard boast on behalf of the man that commands him
I have received assurances before Mr. Outwater. Always the monster has returned
The stories have grown up around him like a bramble. Ten feet tall, fists big as hams, boots studded with nails, killed a man with his fingernails, cock is in a coil
Uproots lamp posts and trees to use as flails, pulls street cars the length of the city, smokes two-foot cigars, wears a barrel of rum around his belt, four quarts of oysters for a snack. When my men see him for what he truly is, still they scatter before him
Strength is not proved in legend. Men with such reputations are usually victim to some kind of acute weakness
I cannot engage him long enough to find it
He's the thorn in my side. Makes best sure to block my every move. Works in my territory but is skulled to mark my living or my doings. A man of his mind must know that drives me wild

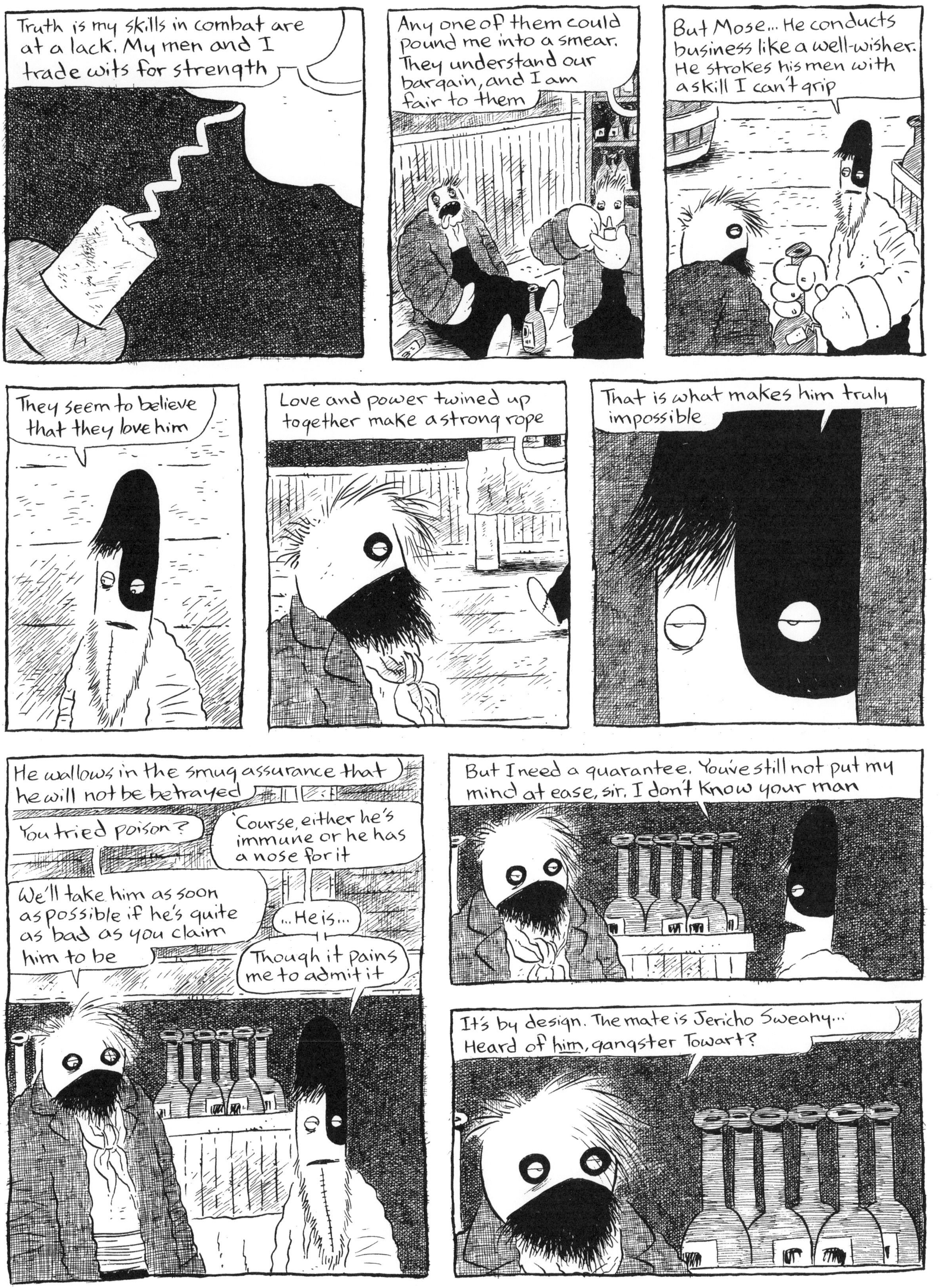

Truth is my skills in combat are at a lack. My men and I trade wits for strength
Any one of them could pound me into a smear. They understand our bargain, and I am fair to them
But Mose... He conducts business like a well-wisher. He strokes his men with a skill I can't grip
They seem to believe that they love him
Love and power twined up together make a strong rope
That is what makes him truly impossible
He wallows in the smug assurance that he will not be betrayed
You tried poison?
'Course, either he's immune or he has a nose for it
We'll take him as soon as possible if he's quite as bad as you claim him to be
...He is...
Though it pains me to admit it
But I need a guarantee. You've still not put my mind at ease, sir. I don't know your man
It's by design. The mate is Jericho Sweany... Heard of him, gangster Towart?

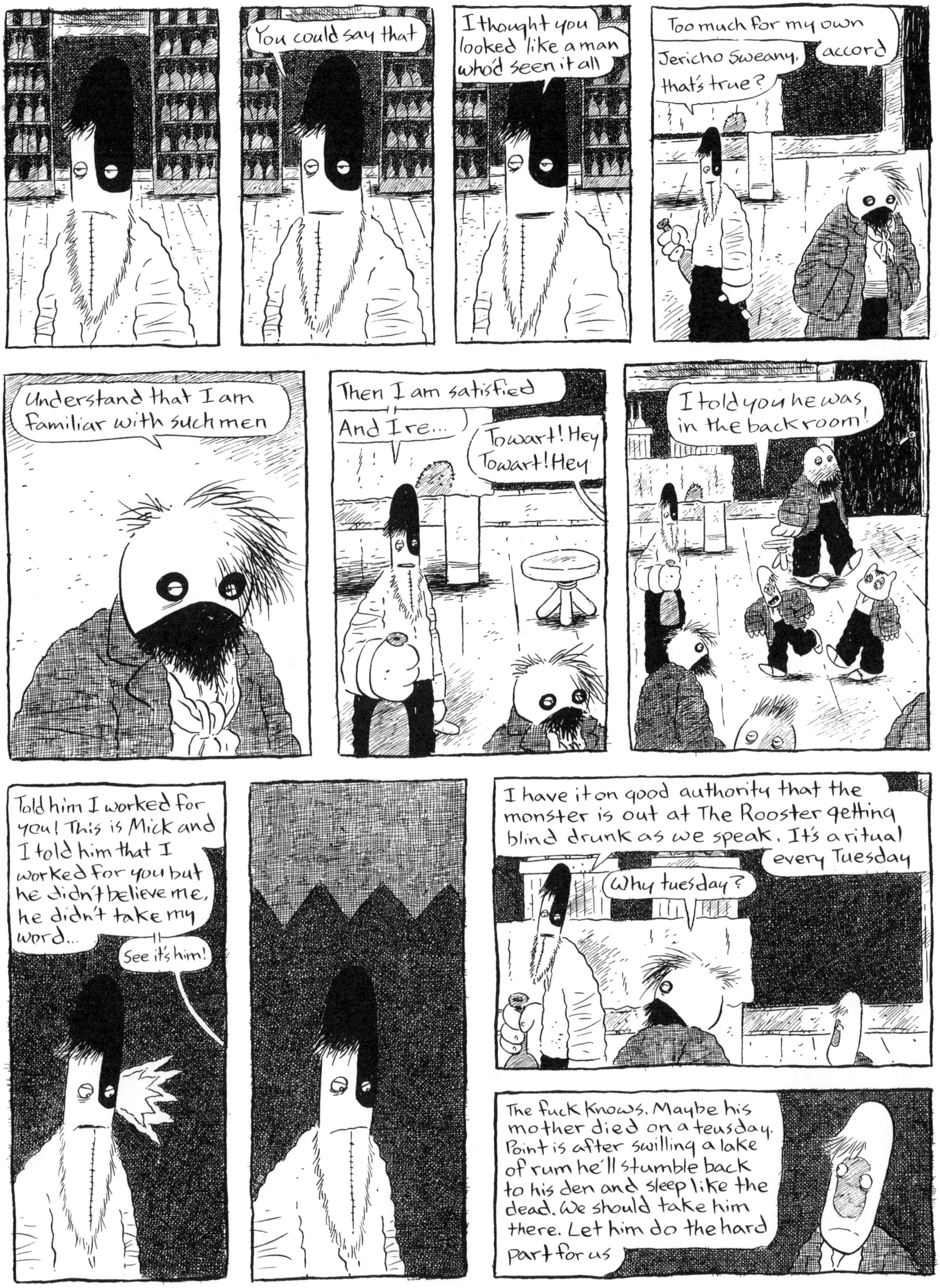
You could say that
I thought you looked like a man who'd seen it all
Too much for my own accord
Jericho Sweany, that's true?
Understand that I am familiar with such men
Then I am satisfied
And I re...
Towart! Hey Towart! Hey
I told you he was in the back room!
Told him I worked for you! This is Mick and I told him that I worked for you but he didn't believe me, he didn't take my word...
See it's him!
I have it on good authority that the monster is out at The Rooster getting blind drunk as we speak. It's a ritual every Tuesday
Why tuesday?
The fuck knows. Maybe his mother died on a teusday. Point is after swilling a lake of rum he'll stumble back to his den and sleep like the dead. We should take him there. Let him do the hard part for us

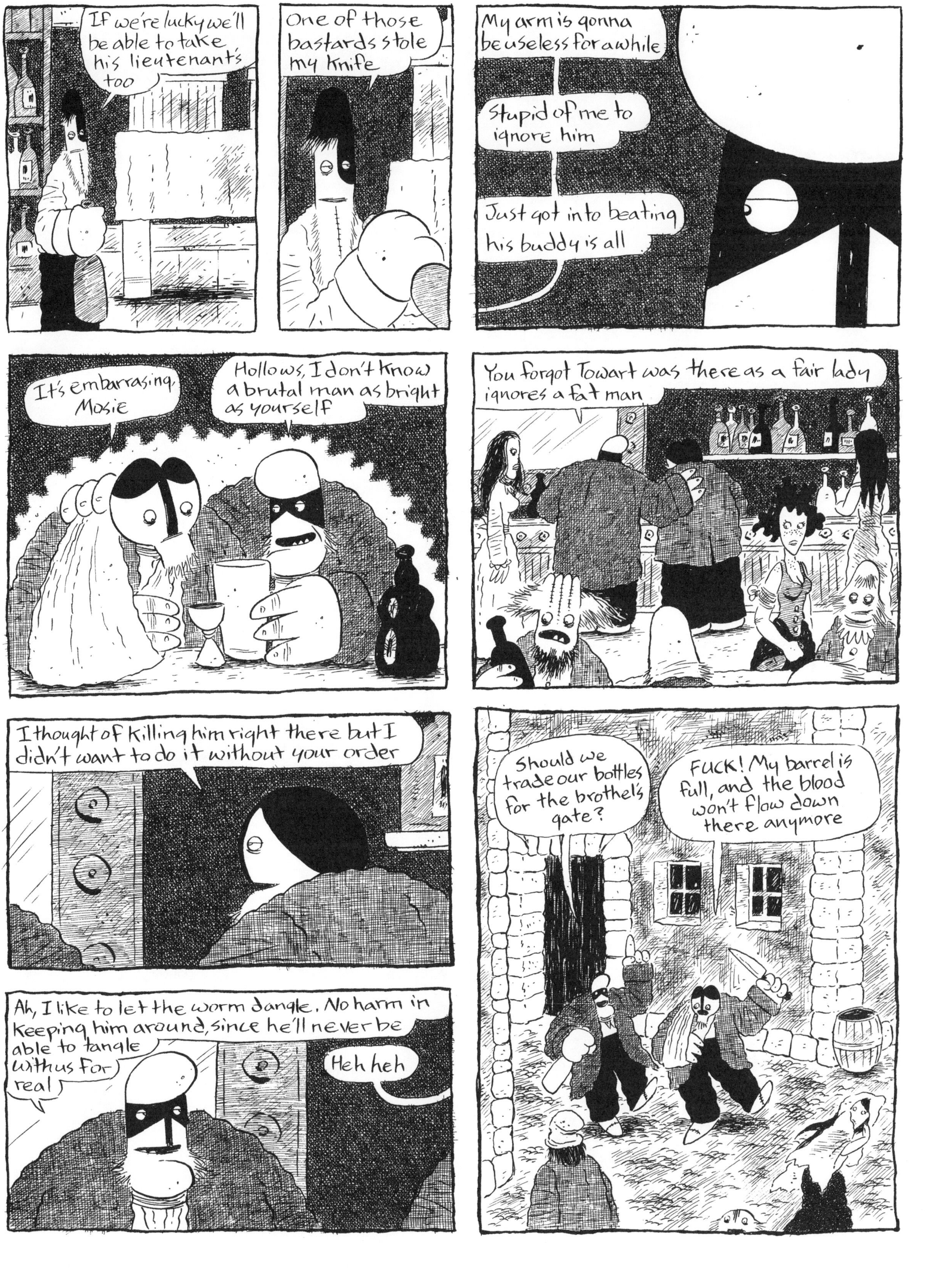
If we're lucky we'll be able to take his lieutenant's too
One of those bastards stole my knife
My arm is gonna be useless for a while
Stupid of me to ignore him
Just got into beating his buddy is all
It's embarrasing, Mosie
Hollows, I don't know a brutal man as bright as yourself
You forgot Towart was there as a fair lady ignores a fat man
I thought of killing him right there but I didn't want to do it without your order
Should we trade our bottles for the brothel's gate?
FUCK! My barrel is full, and the blood won't flow down there anymore
Ah, I like to let the worm dangle. No harm in keeping him around, since he'll never be able to tangle with us for real
Heh heh

HAW HAW HAW

SLAP

OW

What's wrong?

My arm got punched by a knife

I thought you were better

IT PUNCHED ME!

That knife is a shitface! RIGHT?

TOWART!

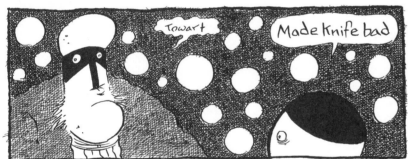

Towart

Made knife bad

IMA KILL THAT SHITFACE!!!

Okay

And I hear this awful gagging sound

I turn around, and everyone is looking at little Maxie Pinkser and there is vomit all over him

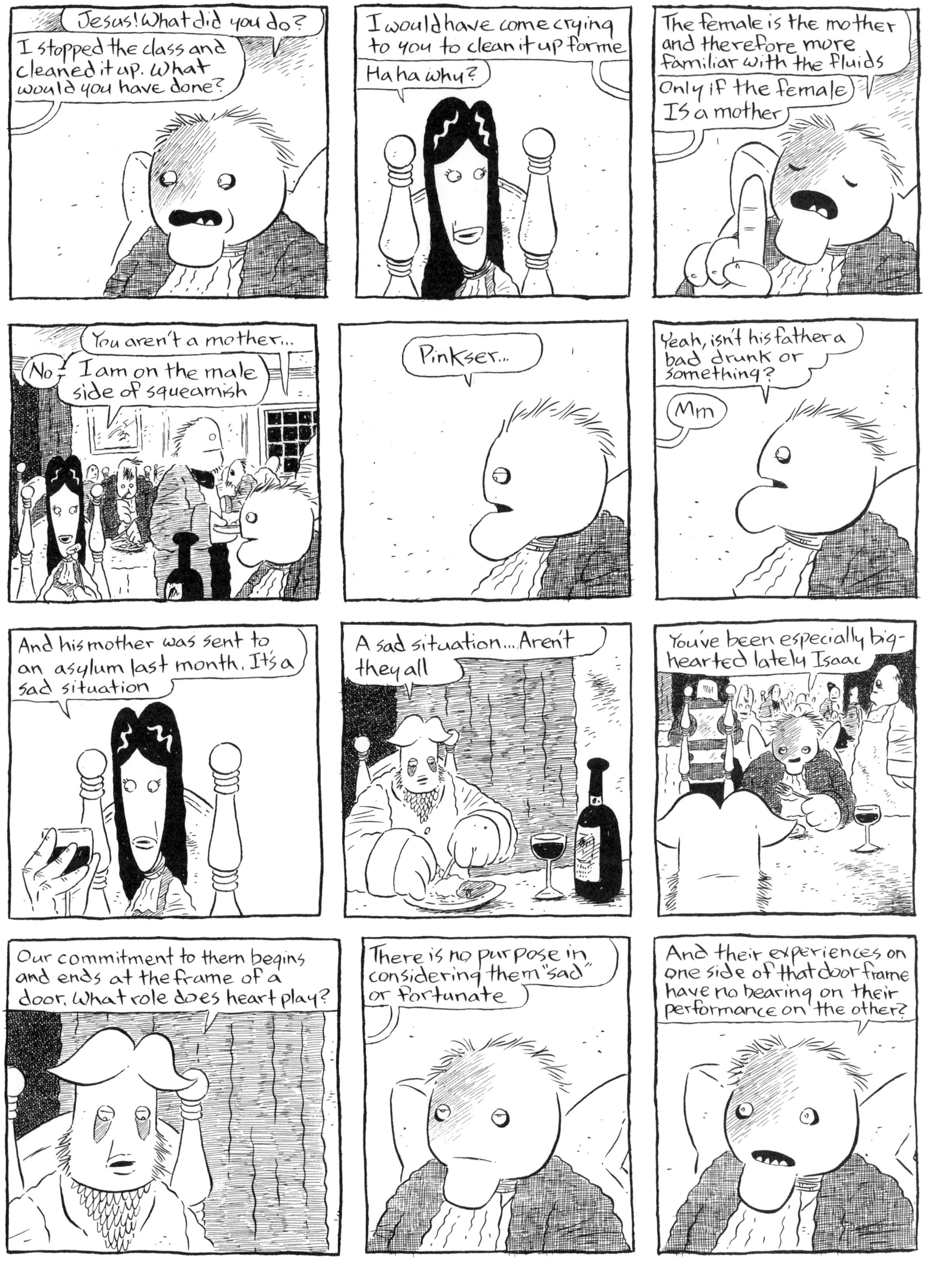
Jesus! What did you do?
I stopped the class and cleaned it up. What would you have done?
I would have come crying to you to clean it up for me
Ha ha why?
The female is the mother and therefore more familiar with the fluids
Only if the female IS a mother
You aren't a mother...
No
I am on the male side of squeamish
Pinkser...
Yeah, isn't his father a bad drunk or something?
Mm
And his mother was sent to an asylum last month. It's a sad situation
A sad situation.... Aren't they all
You've been especially big-hearted lately Isaac
Our commitment to them begins and ends at the frame of a door. What role does heart play?
There is no purpose in considering them "sad" or fortunate
And their experiences on one side of that door frame have no bearing on their performance on the other?

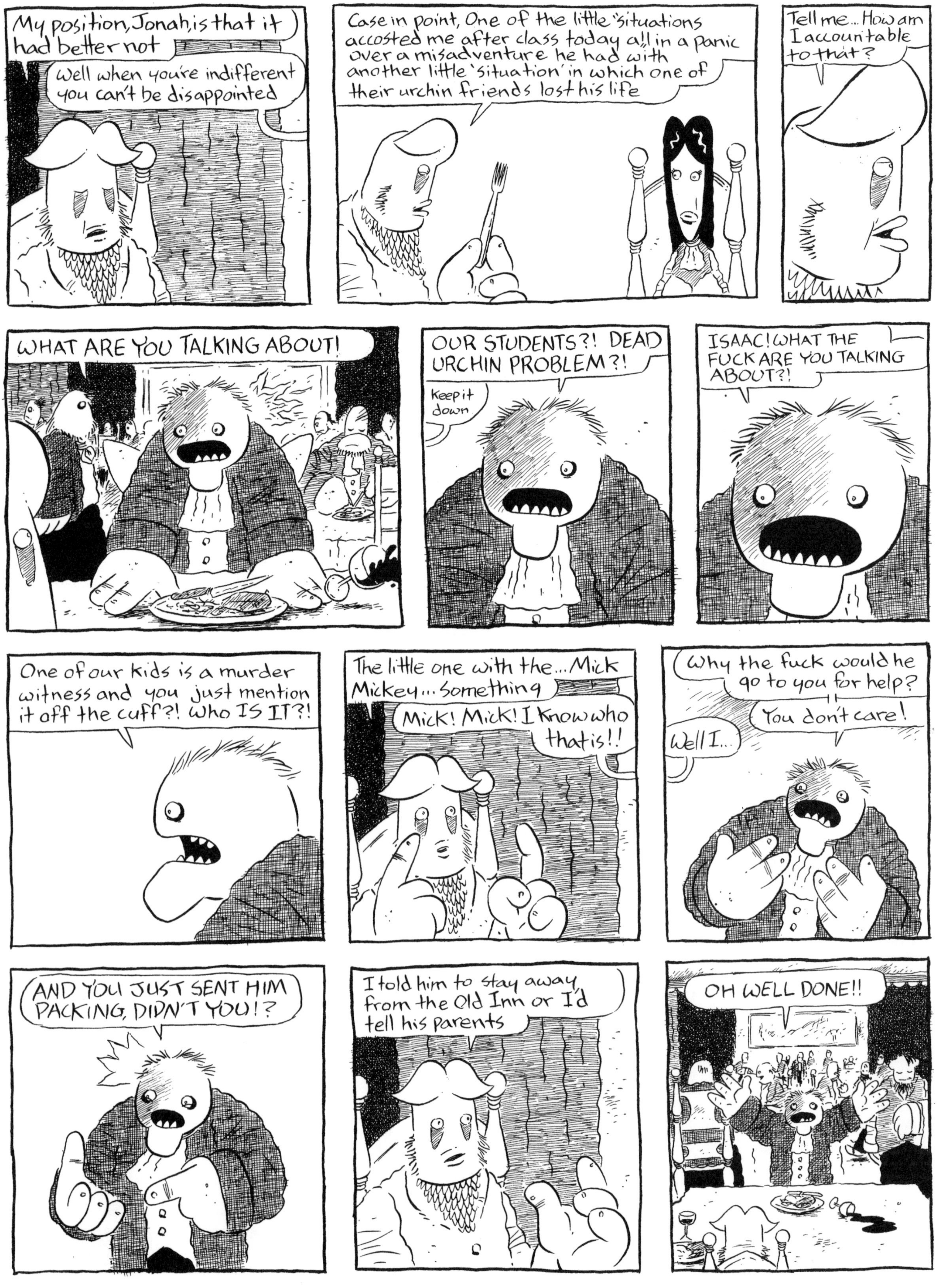
My position, Jonah, is that it had better not
Well when you're indifferent you can't be disappointed
Case in point, One of the little 'situations' accosted me after class today all in a panic over a misadventure he had with another little 'situation' in which one of their urchin friends lost his life
Tell me... How am I accountable to that?
WHAT ARE YOU TALKING ABOUT!
OUR STUDENTS?! DEAD URCHIN PROBLEM?!
Keep it down
ISAAC! WHAT THE FUCK ARE YOU TALKING ABOUT?!
One of our kids is a murder witness and you just mention it off the cuff?! Who IS IT?!
The little one with the... Mick Mickey... Something
Mick! Mick! I know who that is!!
Why the fuck would he go to you for help?
You don't care!
Well I...
AND YOU JUST SENT HIM PACKING, DIDN'T YOU!?
I told him to stay away from the Old Inn or I'd tell his parents
OH WELL DONE!!

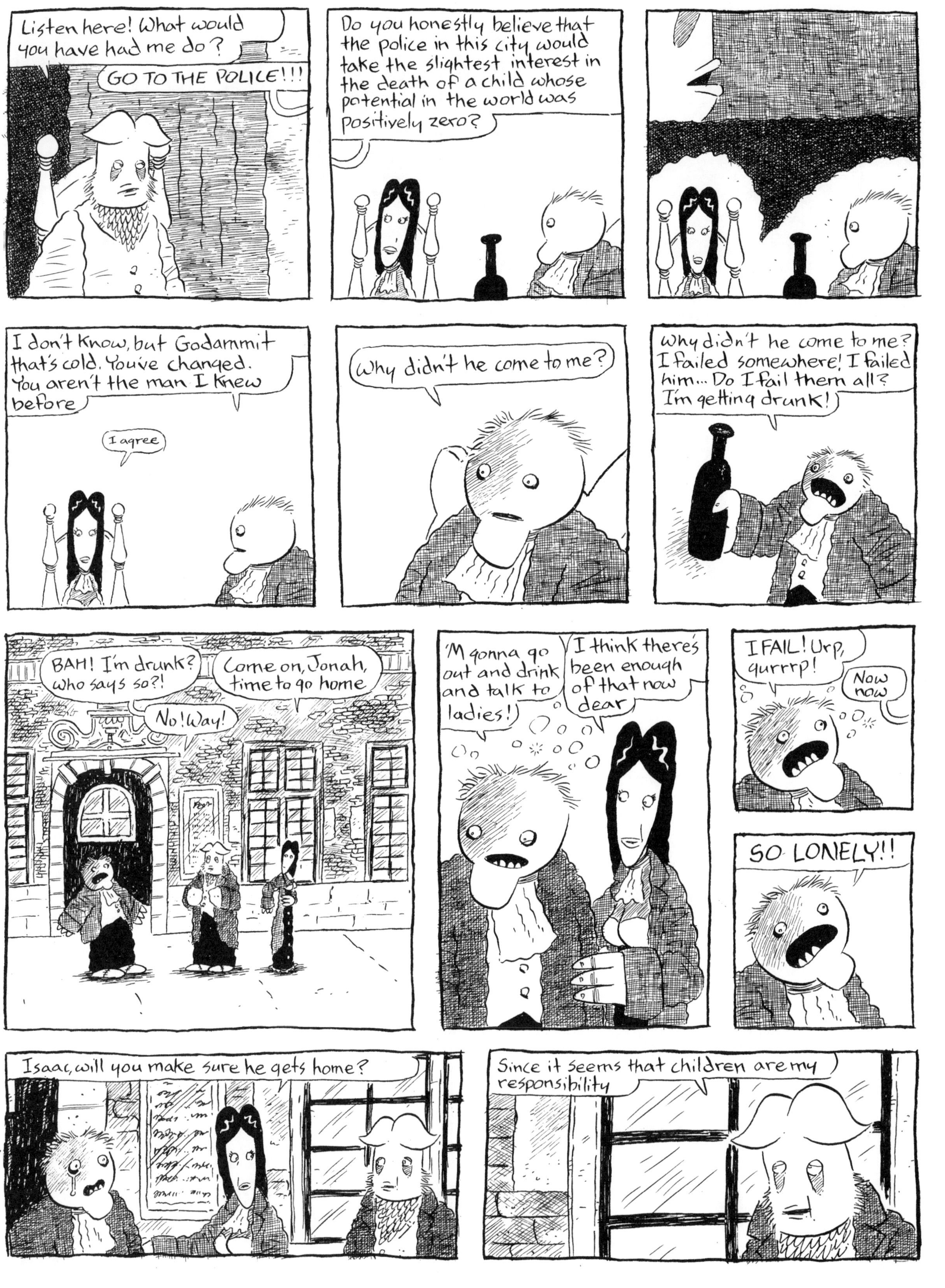
Listen here! What would you have had me do?
GO TO THE POLICE!!!
Do you honestly believe that the police in this city would take the slightest interest in the death of a child whose potential in the world was positively zero?
I don't Know, but Godammit that's cold. You've changed. You aren't the man I Knew before
I agree
Why didn't he come to me?
Why didn't he come to me? I failed somewhere! I failed him... Do I fail them all? I'm getting drunk!
BAH! I'm drunk? who says so?!
Come on, Jonah, time to go home
No! Way!
'M gonna go out and drink and talk to ladies!
I think there's been enough of that now dear
I FAIL! Urp, gurrrp!
Now now
SO LONELY!!
Isaac, will you make sure he gets home?
Since it seems that children are my responsibility

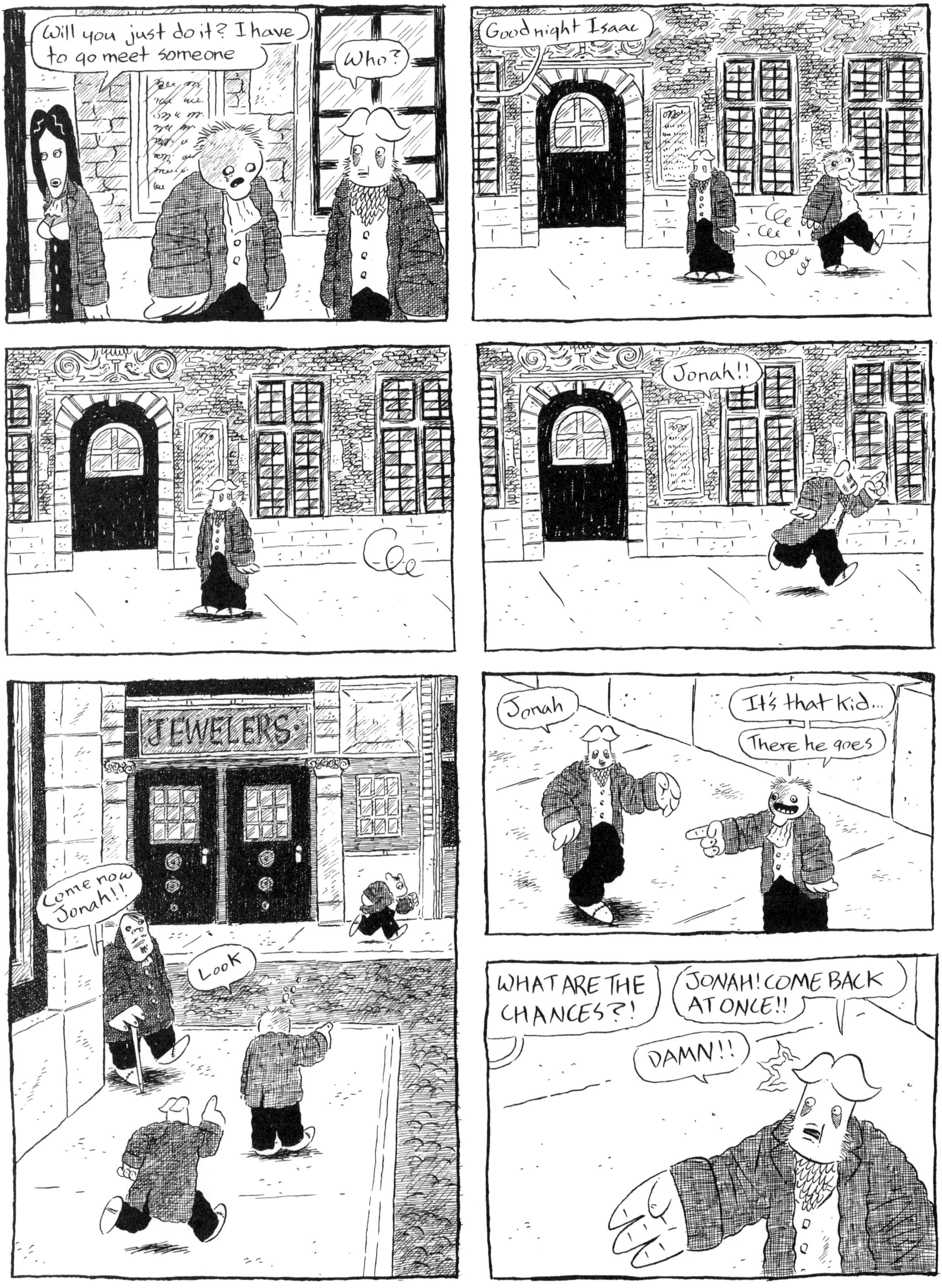
Will you just do it? I have to go meet someone
Who?
Good night Isaac
Jonah!!
JEWELERS
Come now Jonah!!
Look
Jonah
It's that kid...
There he goes
WHAT ARE THE CHANCES?!
JONAH! COME BACK AT ONCE!!
DAMN!!

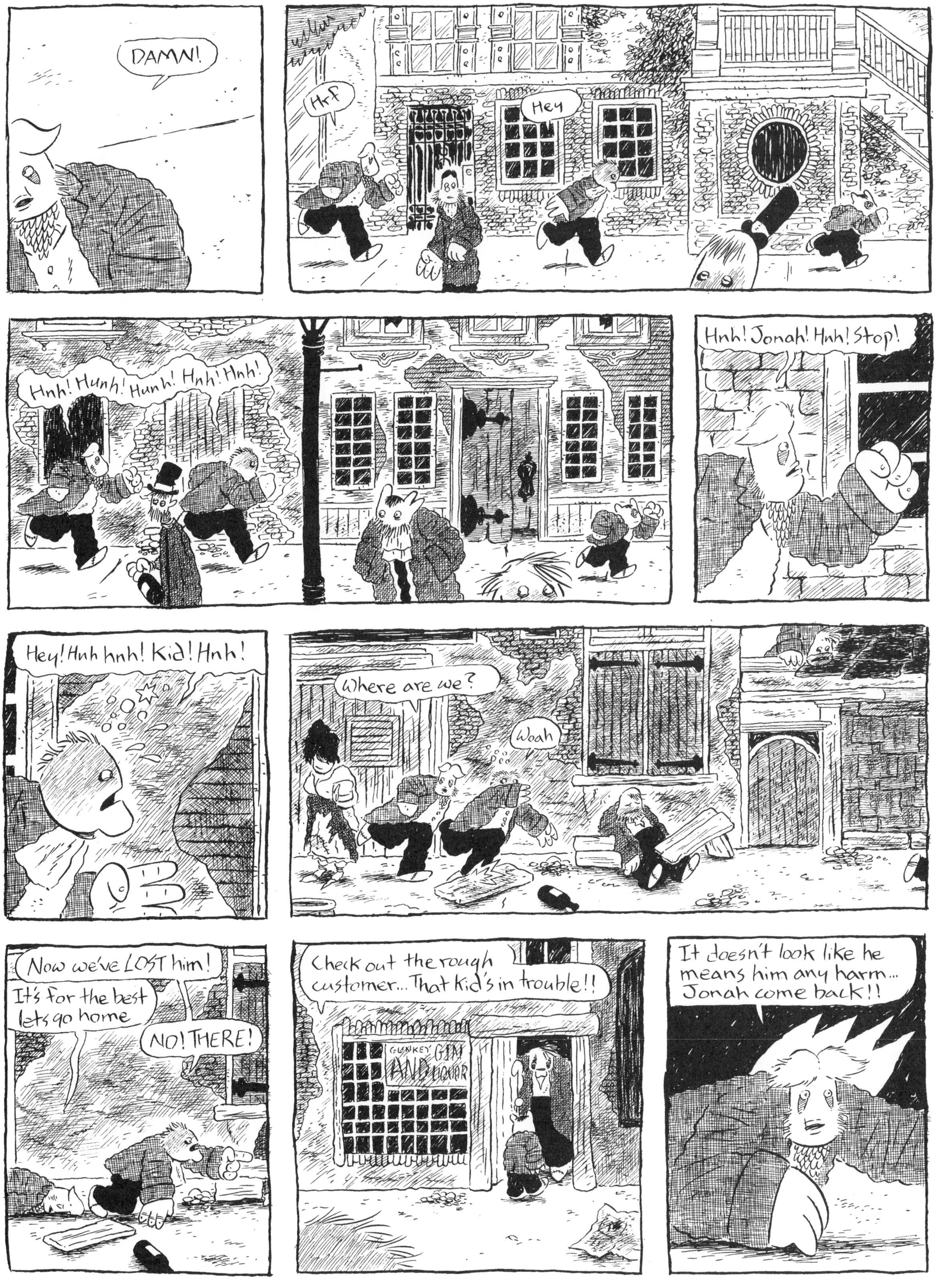
DAMN!
Hrf
Hey
Hnh! Hunh! Hunh! Hnh! Hnh!
Hnh! Jonah! Hnh! Stop!
Hey! Hnh hnh! Kid! Hnh!
Where are we?
Woah
Now we've LOST him!
It's for the best lets go home
NO! THERE!
Check out the rough customer... That kid's in trouble!!
GUNKEY GIN AND LIQUOR
It doesn't look like he means him any harm... Jonah come back!!

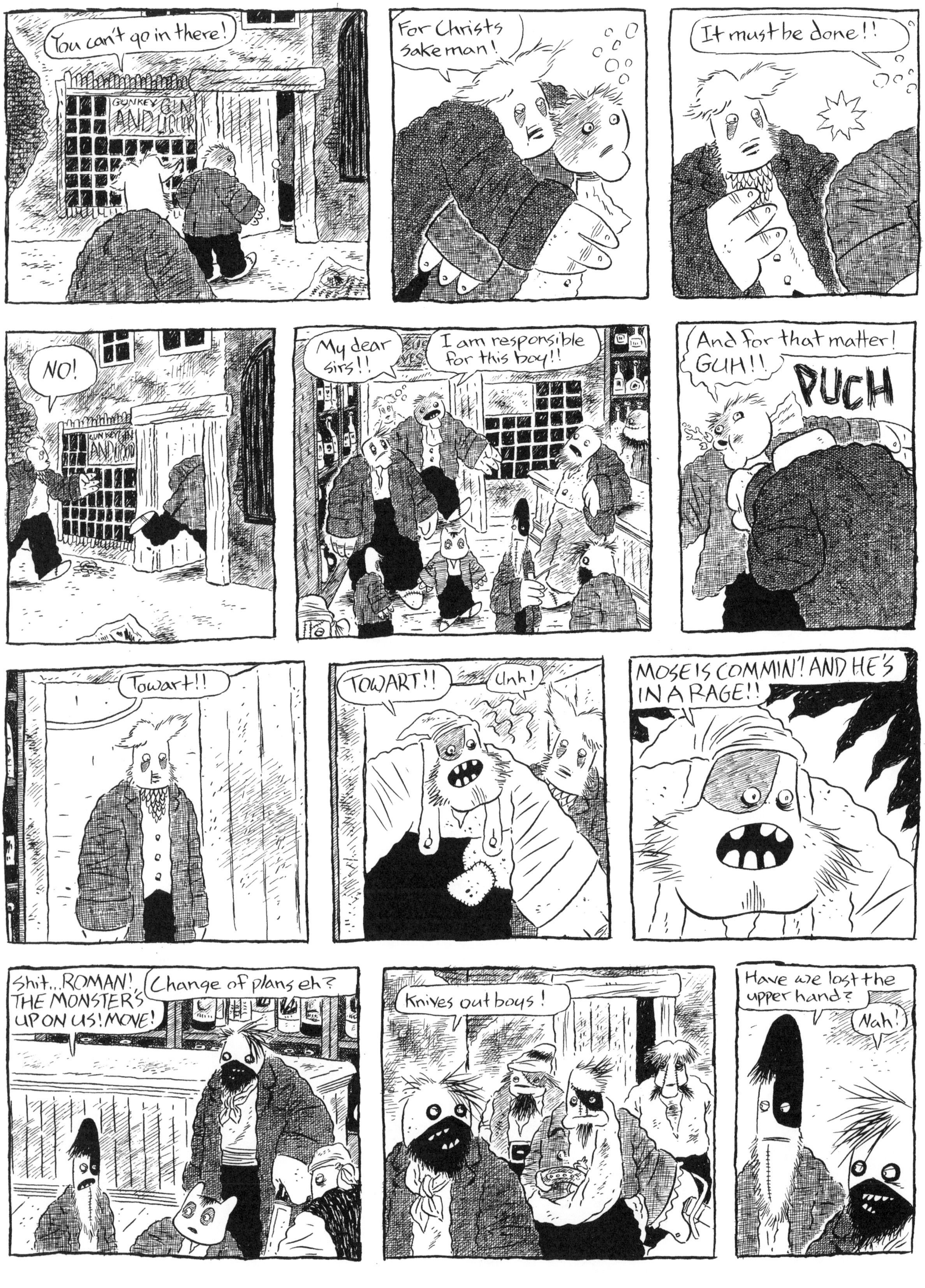
You can't go in there!
GUNKEY GIN AND LIQUOR
For Christs sake man!
It must be done!!
NO!
My dear sirs!!
I am responsible for this boy!!
And for that matter! GUH!!
PUCH
Towart!!
TOWART!!
Unh!
MOSE IS COMMIN'! AND HE'S IN A RAGE!!
Shit... ROMAN! THE MONSTER'S UP ON US! MOVE!
Change of plans eh?
Knives out boys!
Have we lost the upper hand?
Nah!

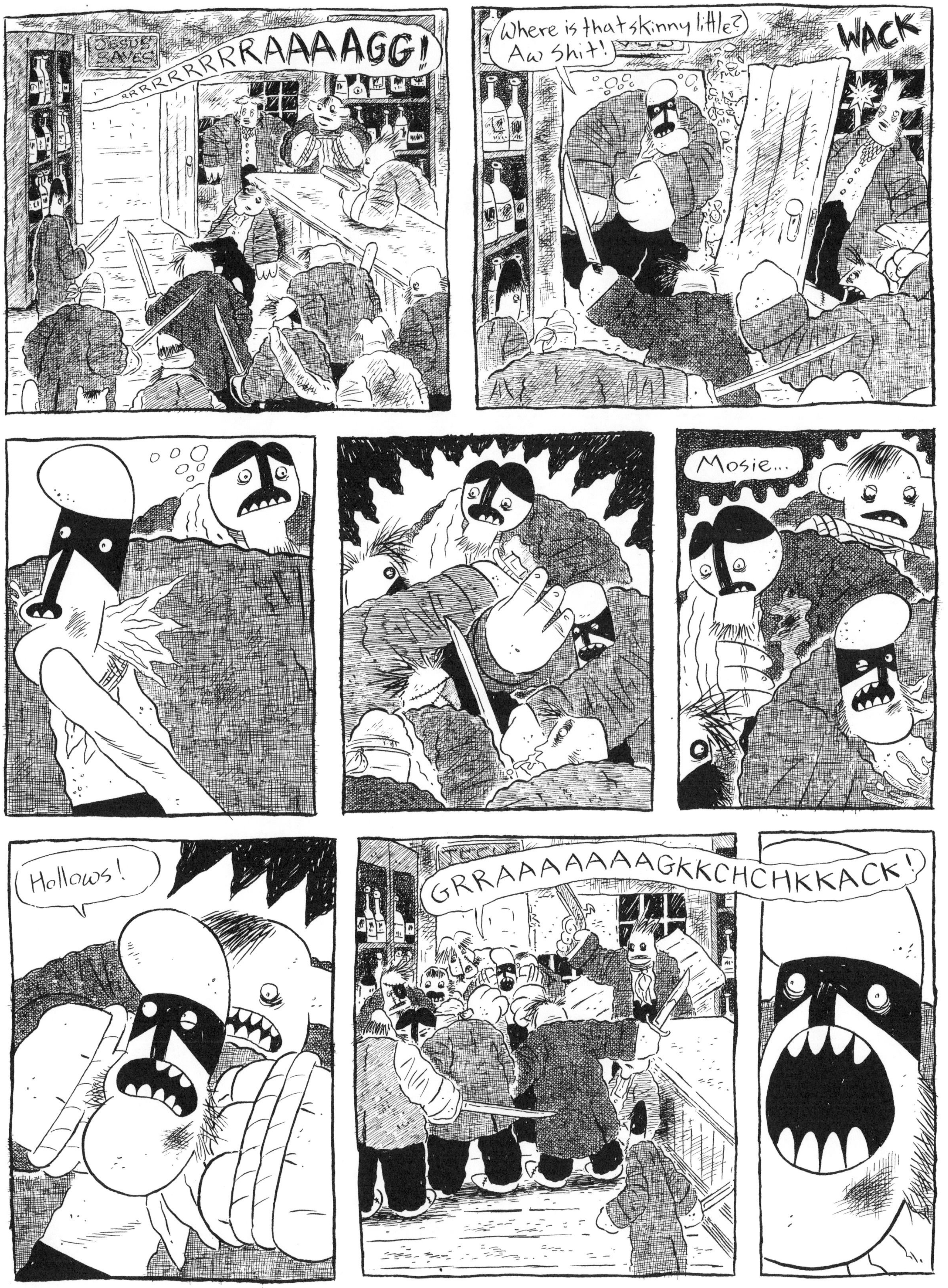

JESUS SAVES
RRRRRRRRRRRAAAAAGG!
Where is that skinny little? Aw Shit!
WACK
Mosie...
Hollows!
GRRAAAAAAAGKKCHCHKKACK!

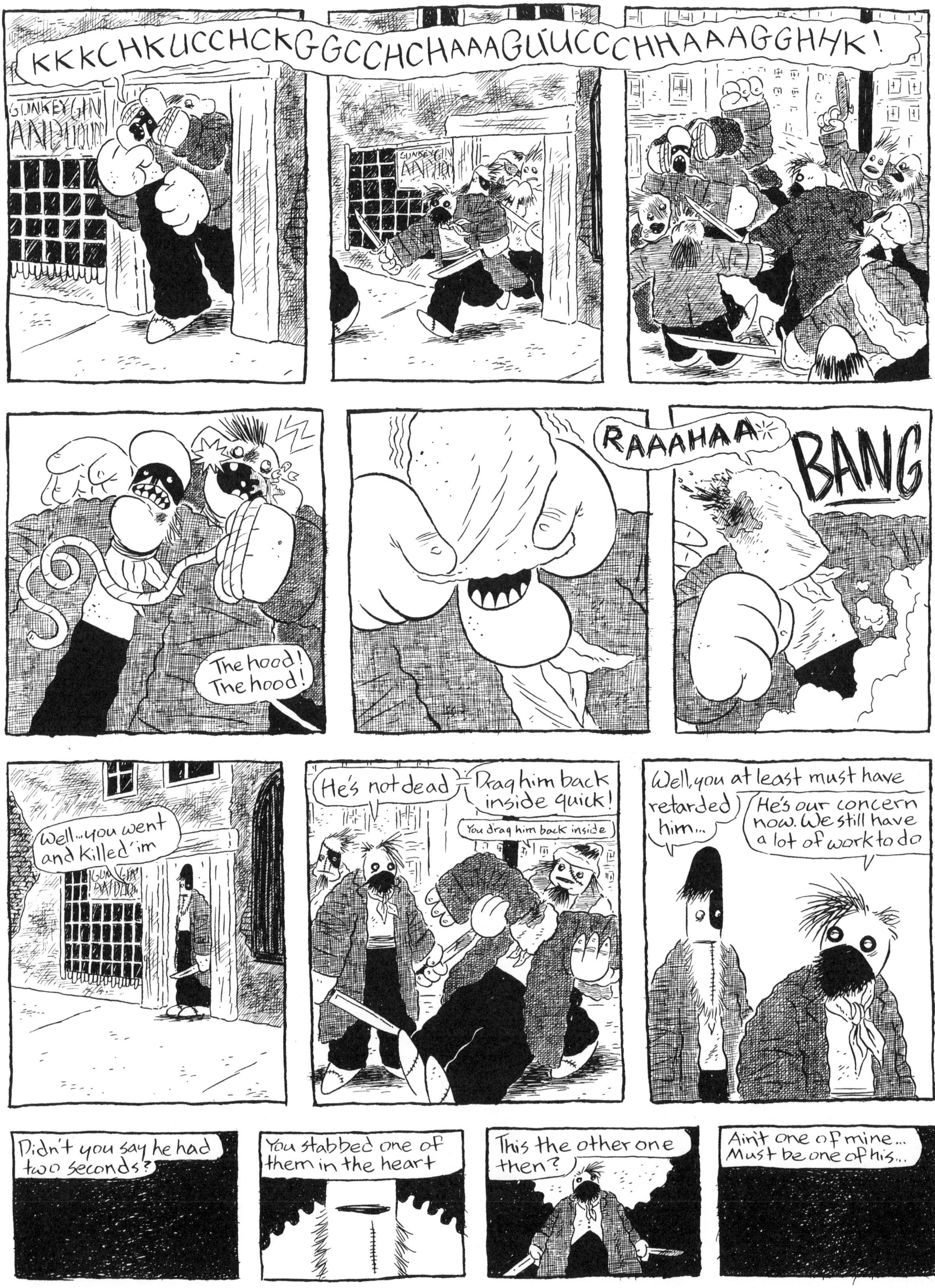
KKKCHKUCCHCKGGCCHCHAAAGUUCCCHHAAAGGHHK!
GUNKEY GIN AND LIQUOR
The hood! The hood!
RAAAHAA
BANG
Well...you went and killed 'im
He's not dead
Drag him back inside quick!
You drag him back inside
Well, you at least must have retarded him...
He's our concern now. We still have a lot of work to do
Didn't you say he had two seconds?
You stabbed one of them in the heart
This the other one then?
Ain't one of mine... Must be one of his...

Into the sacks with them!

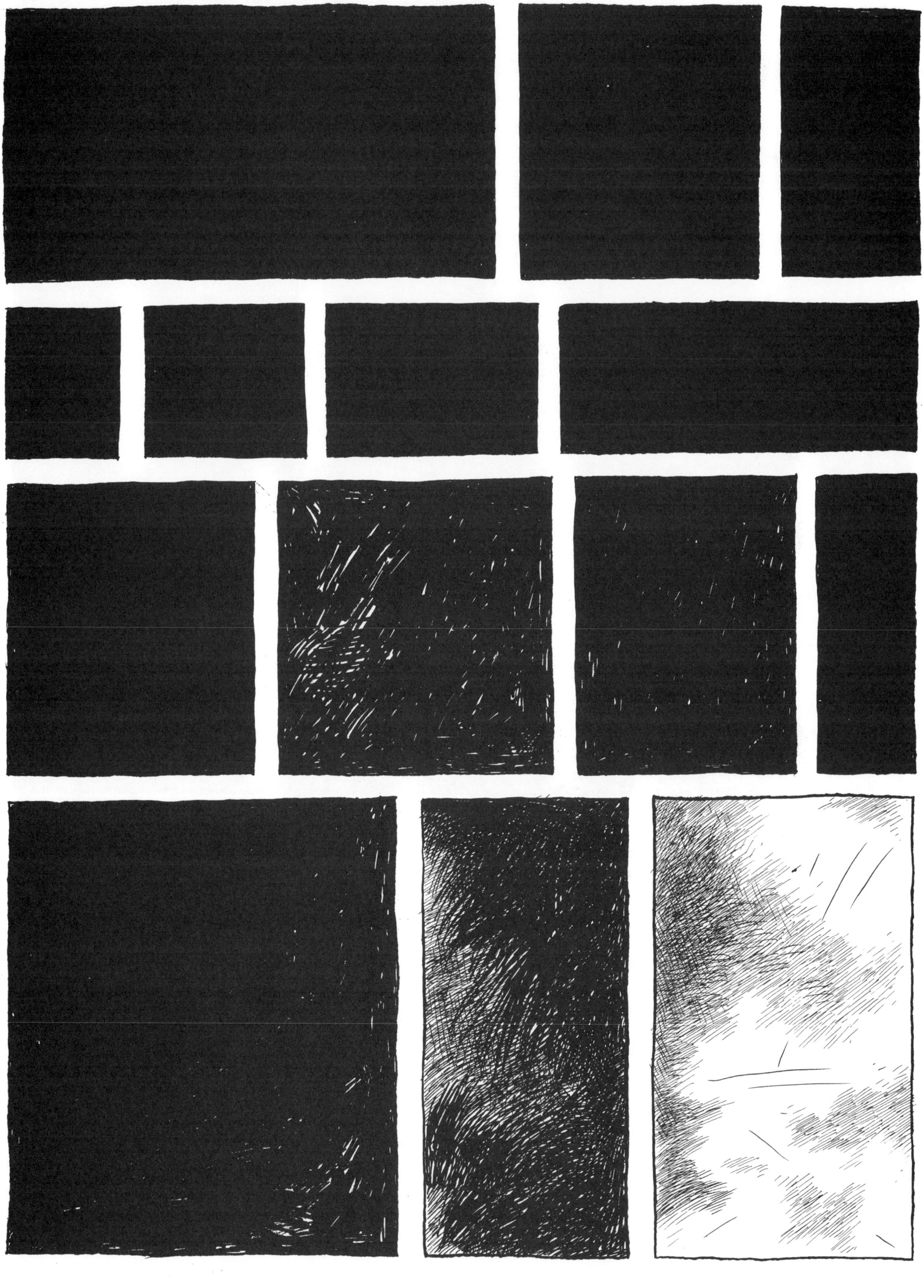

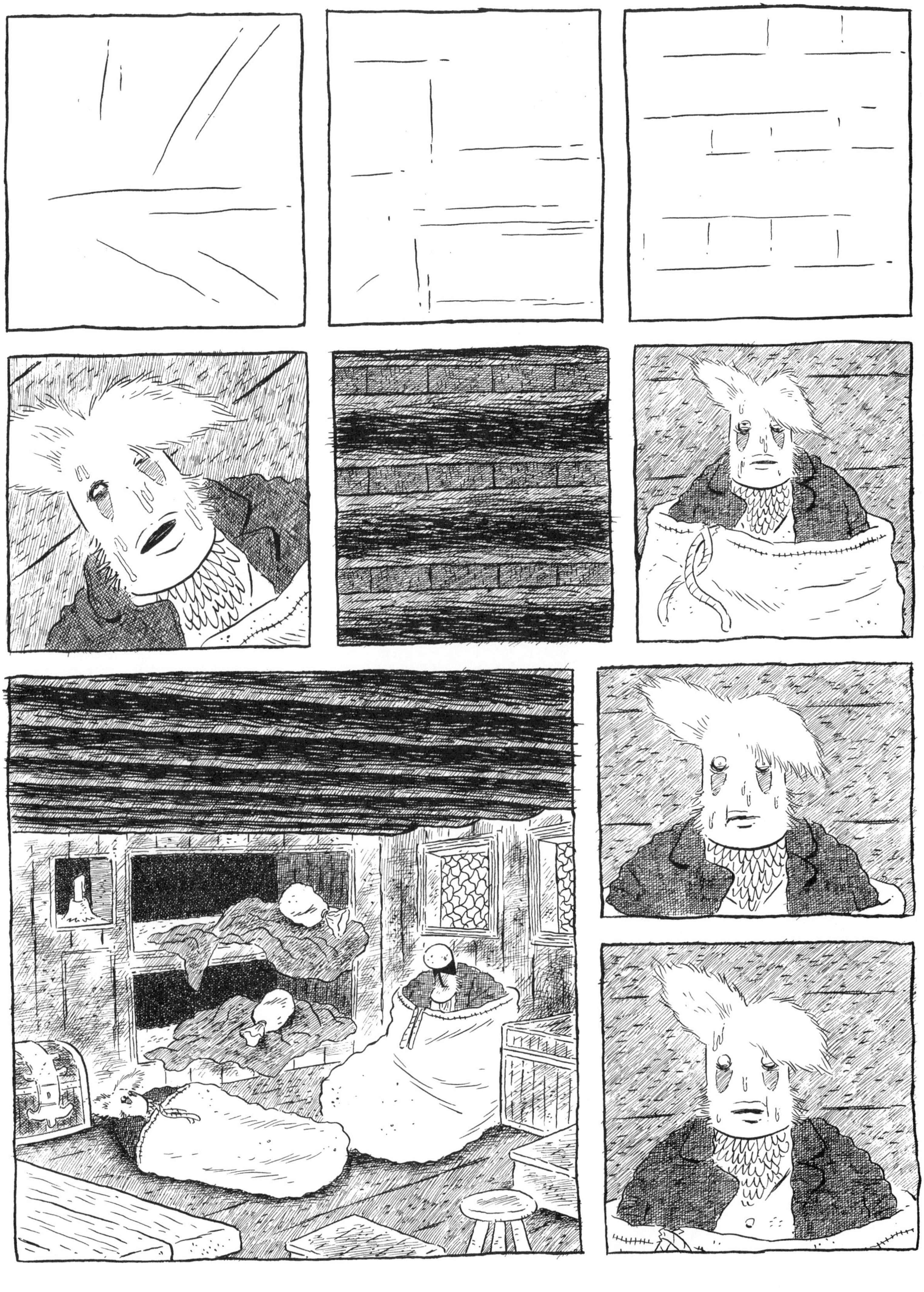

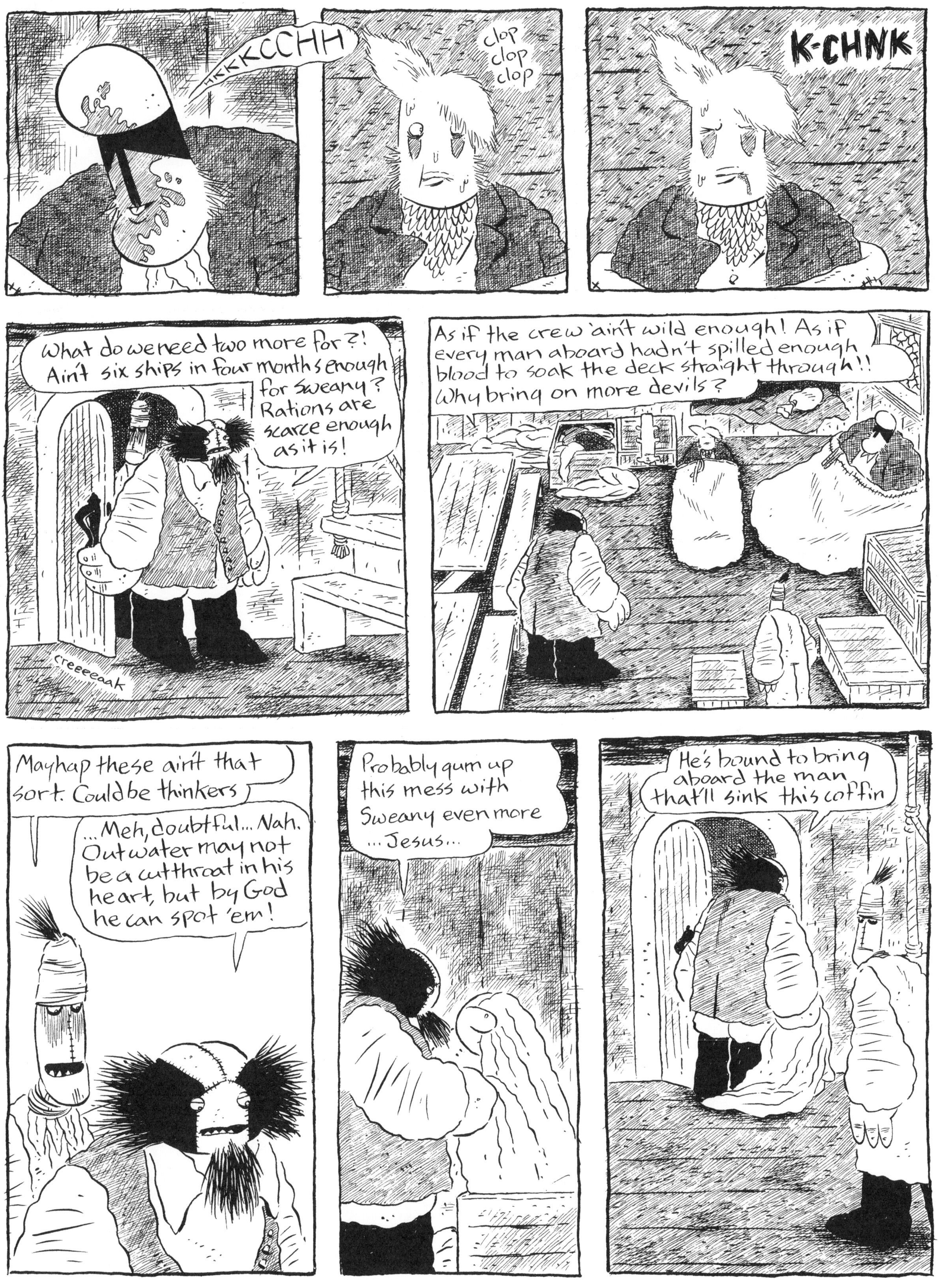
HKKKCCHH
clop
clop
clop
K-CHNK
What do we need two more for?! Ain't six ships in four months enough for Sweany? Rations are scarce enough as it is!
creeeeaak
As if the crew ain't wild enough! As if every man aboard hadn't spilled enough blood to soak the deck straight through!! Why bring on more devils?
Mayhap these ain't that sort. Could be thinkers
...Meh, doubtful... Nah. Outwater may not be a cutthroat in his heart, but by God he can spot 'em!
Probably gum up this mess with Sweany even more ...Jesus...
He's bound to bring aboard the man that'll sink this coffin

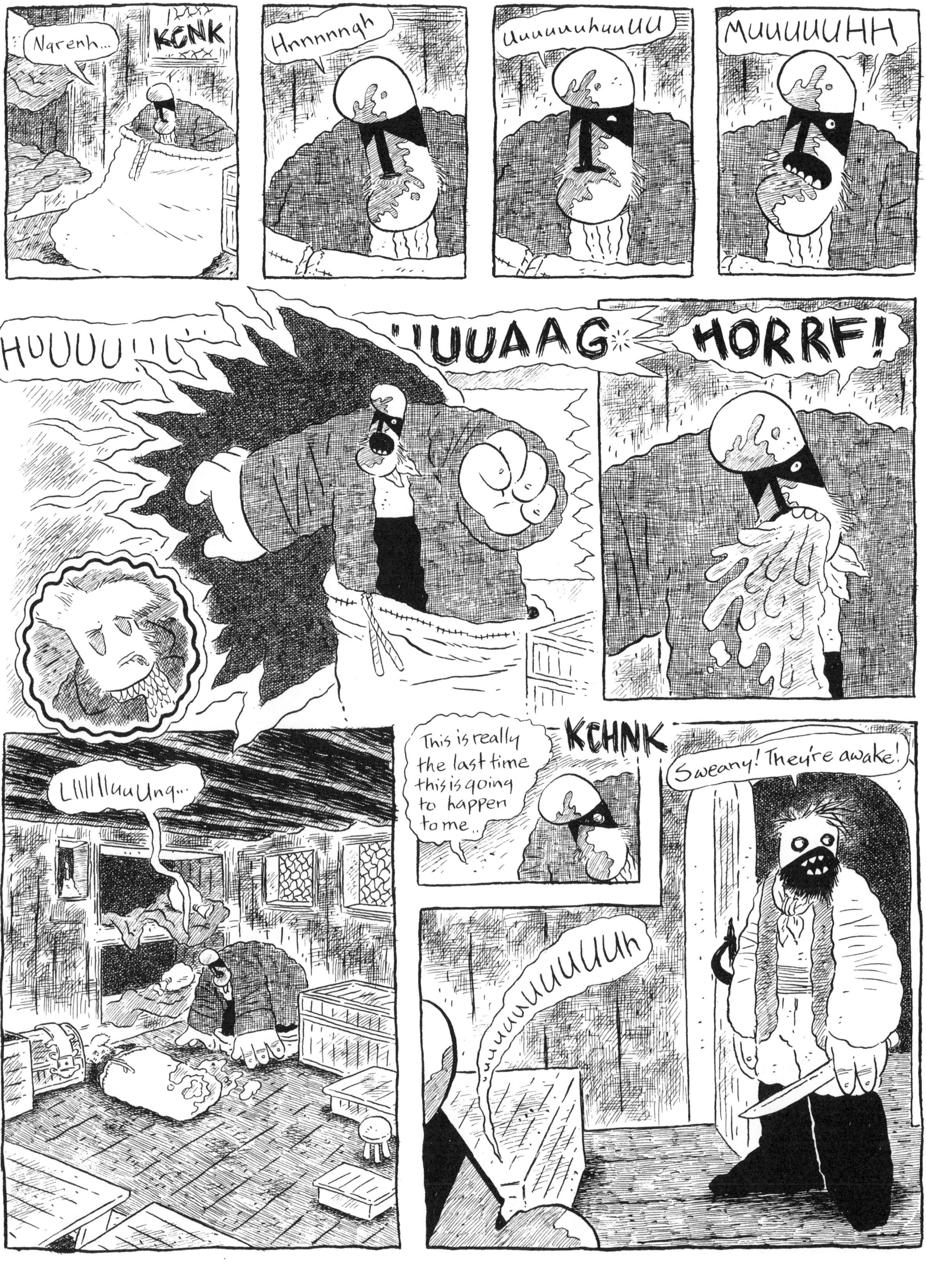
Nqrenh...
KCNK
Hnnnnngh
UuuuuuhuuUU
MUUUUUHH
HUUUUUU
UUUAAG
HORRF!
LlllllluuUng...
This is really the last time this is going to happen to me...
KCHNK
Sweany! They're awake!
UUUUUUUUUUUh

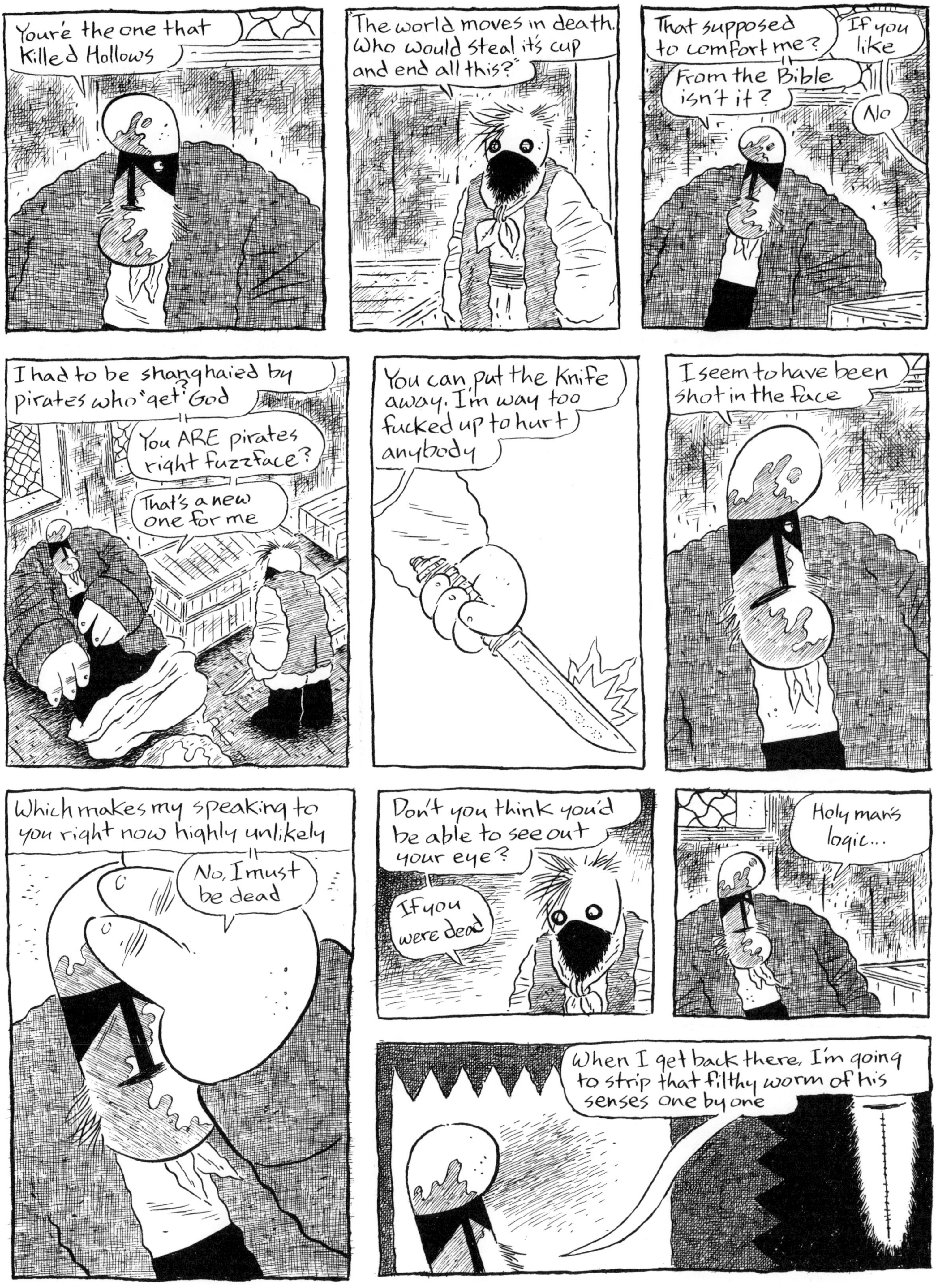
Youré the one that Killed Hollows
The world moves in death. Who would steal it's cup and end all this?
That supposed to comfort me?
If you like
From the Bible isn't it?
No
I had to be shanghaied by pirates who "get" God
You ARE pirates right fuzzface?
That's a new one for me
You can put the Knife away. I'm way too fucked up to hurt anybody
I seem to have been shot in the face
Which makes my speaking to you right now highly unlikely
No, I must be dead
Don't you think you'd be able to see out your eye?
If you were dead
Holy man's logic...
When I get back there, I'm going to strip that filthy worm of his senses one by one

You'd be blessed if you did, big man

His air somehow turned my stomach

Not ill enough that you would keep him from shooting me in the face

Not part of our plan I assure you

KCHNK

You say something, Outwater?...

Big one's awake, looks like the other one's still out

Great, who's this asshole

Other one?

We sent you out for one man. Why is there an "other" one?

It was bedlam. We grabbed him and ran

What exactly IS that, Outwater?

Looks like a fuckin' powder hair. You shanghaied us a fuckin' powder hair?

What are you doing to me, you little milksop?

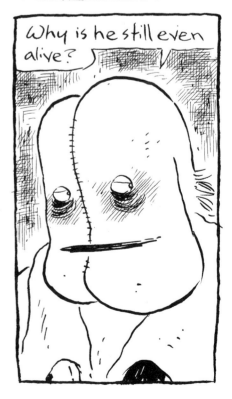

Why is he still even alive?

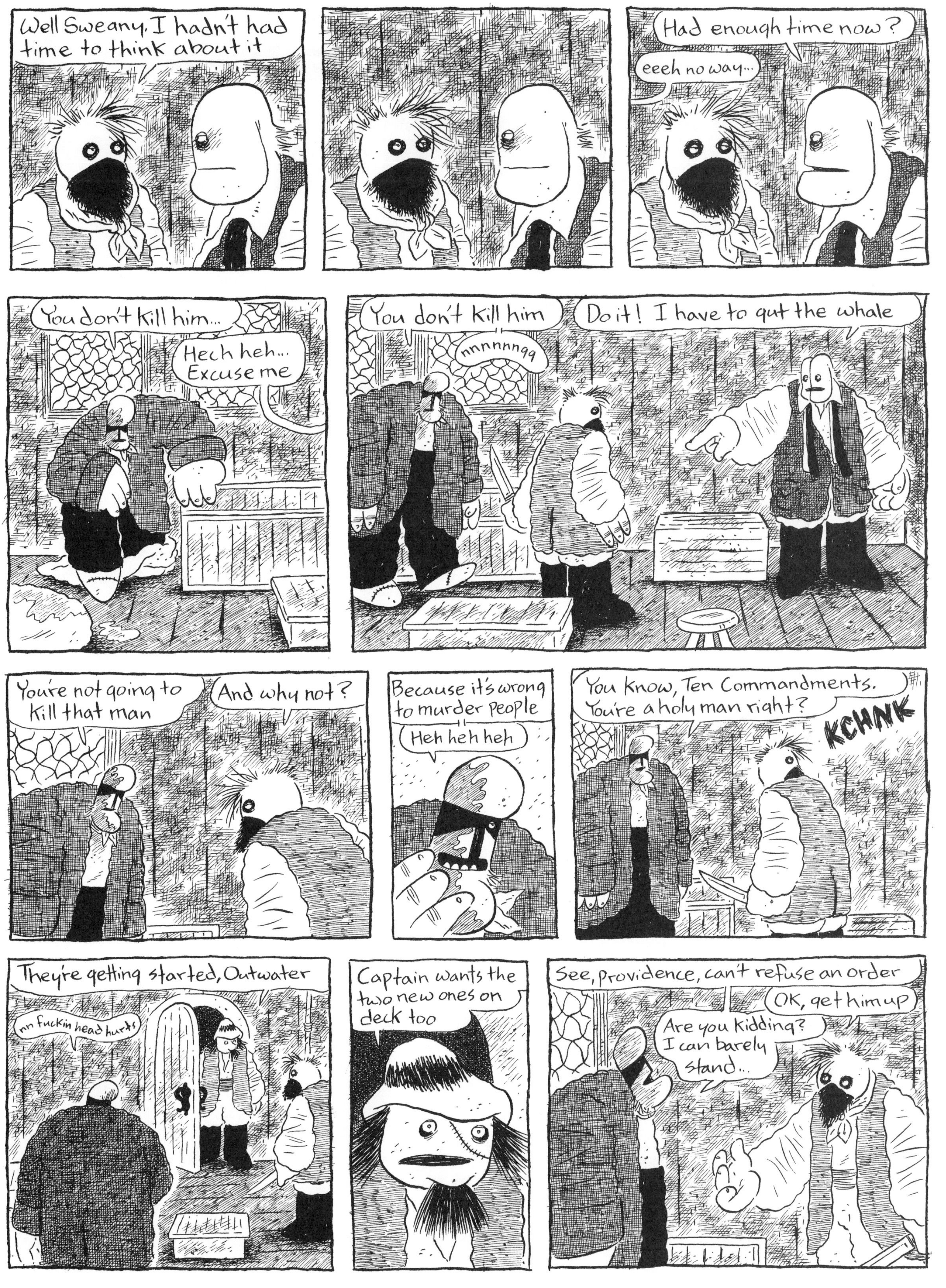

Well Sweany, I hadn't had time to think about it
Had enough time now?
eeeh no way...
You don't kill him...
Hech heh... Excuse me
You don't kill him
nnnnnnngg
Do it! I have to gut the whale
You're not going to kill that man
And why not?
Because it's wrong to murder people
Heh heh heh
You know, Ten Commandments. You're a holy man right?
KCHNK
They're getting started, Outwater
nn fuckin head hurts
Captain wants the two new ones on deck too
See, providence, can't refuse an order
OK, get him up
Are you kidding? I can barely stand...

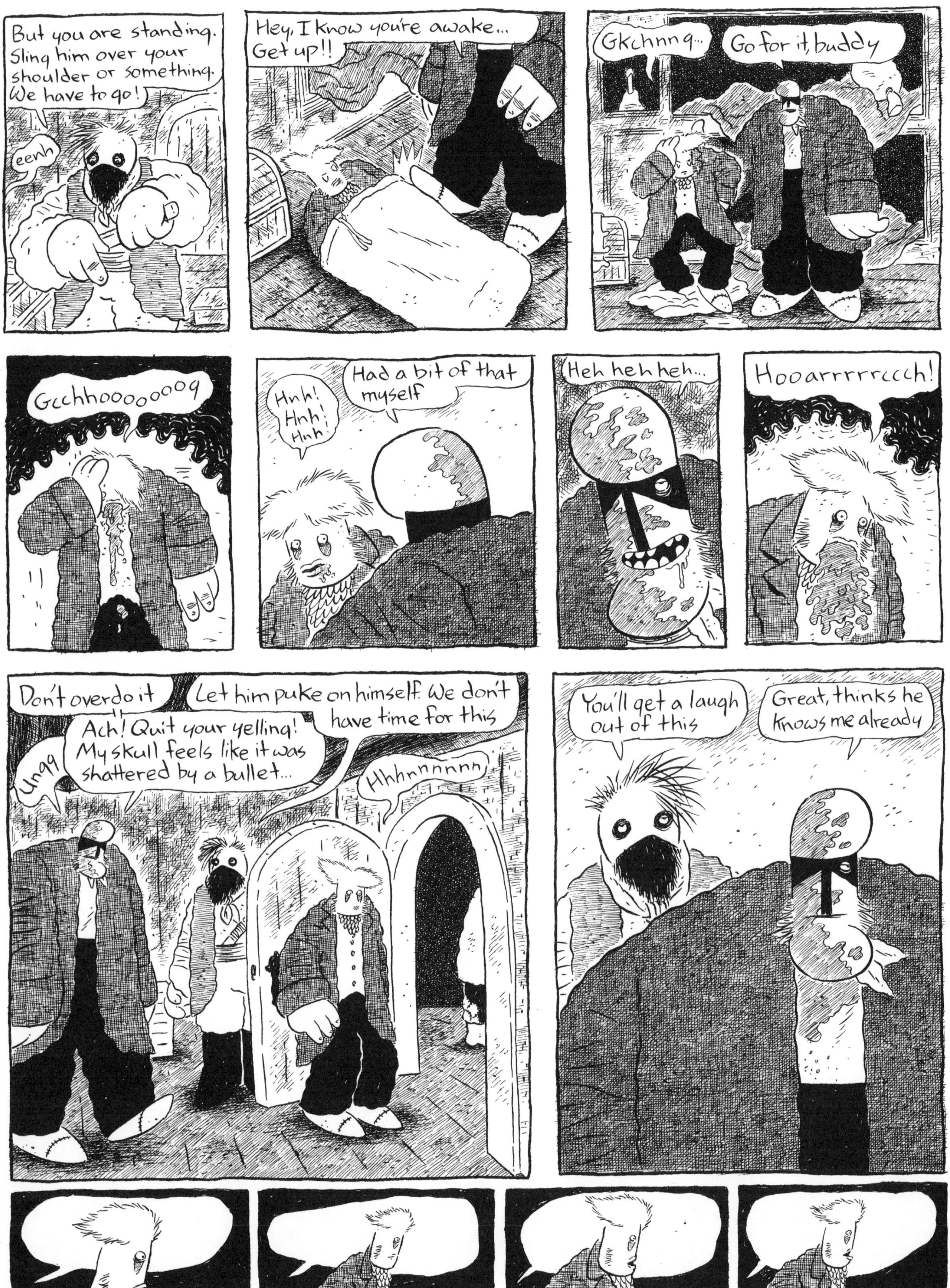
But you are standing. Sling him over your shoulder or something. We have to go!
eenh
Hey, I know you're awake... Get up!!
Gkchnnq...
Go for it, buddy
Gcchhoooooooog
Hnh! Hnh! Hnh!
Had a bit of that myself
Heh heh heh...
Hooarrrrrccch!
Don't overdo it
Let him puke on himself. We don't have time for this
Ach! Quit your yelling! My skull feels like it was shattered by a bullet...
Ungg
Hhhnnnnnn
You'll get a laugh out of this
Great, thinks he knows me already

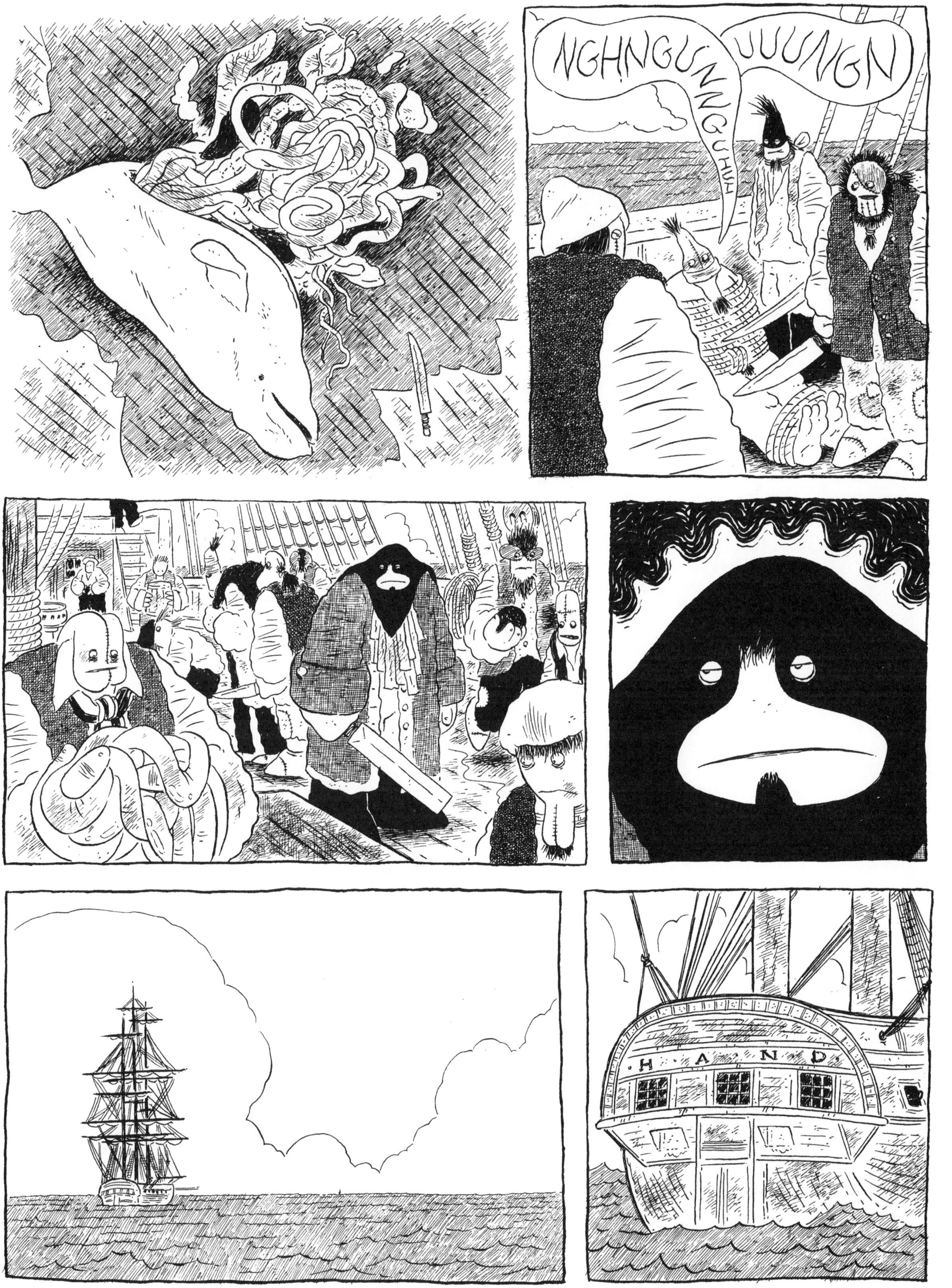
NGHNGUNNGUHH
UUUNGN
H A N D

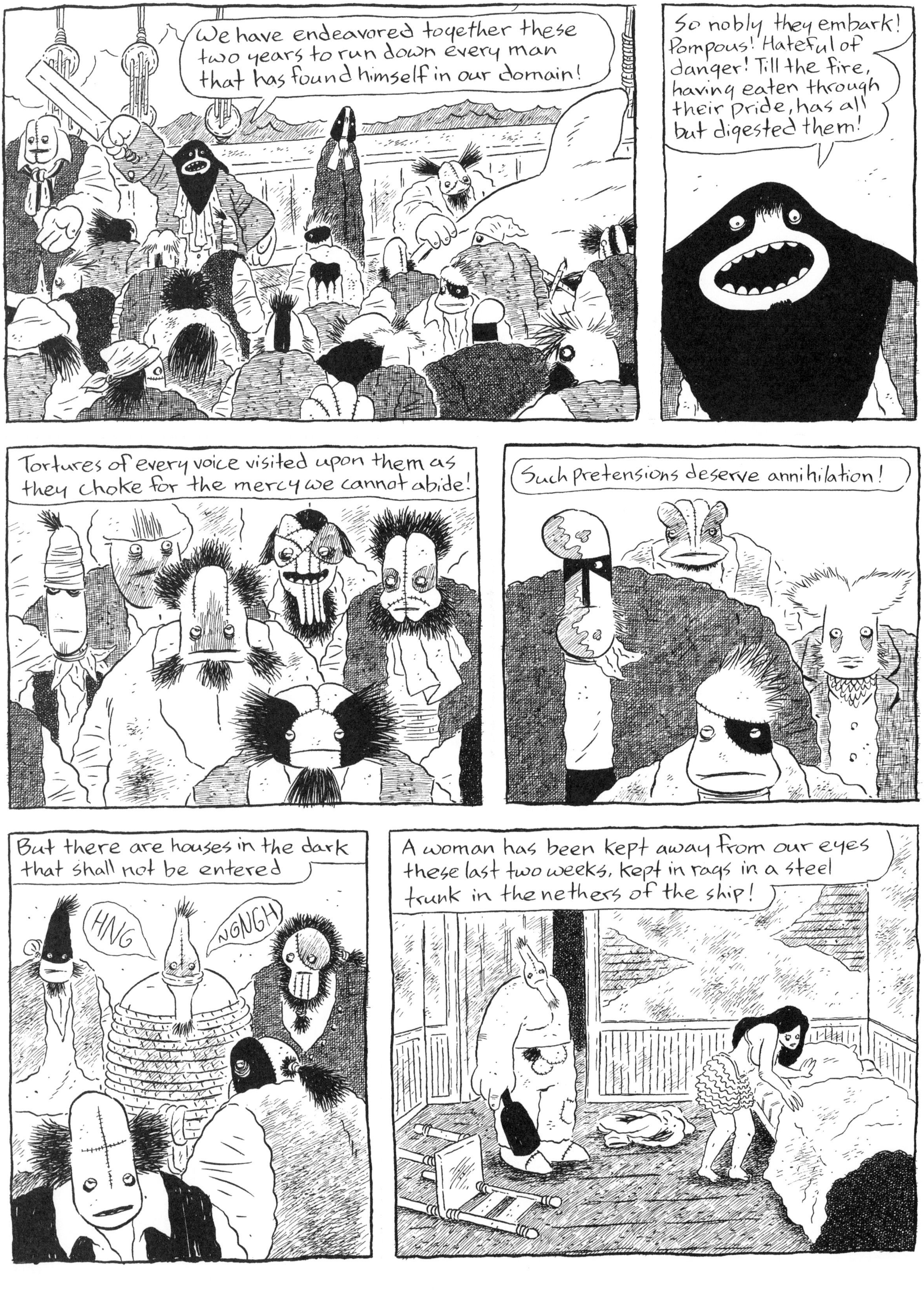
We have endeavored together these two years to run down every man that has found himself in our domain!
So nobly they embark! Pompous! Hateful of danger! Till the fire, having eaten through their pride, has all but digested them!
Tortures of every voice visited upon them as they choke for the mercy we cannot abide!
Such pretensions deserve annihilation!
But there are houses in the dark that shall not be entered
HNG
NGNGH
A woman has been kept away from our eyes these last two weeks, kept in rags in a steel trunk in the nethers of the ship!

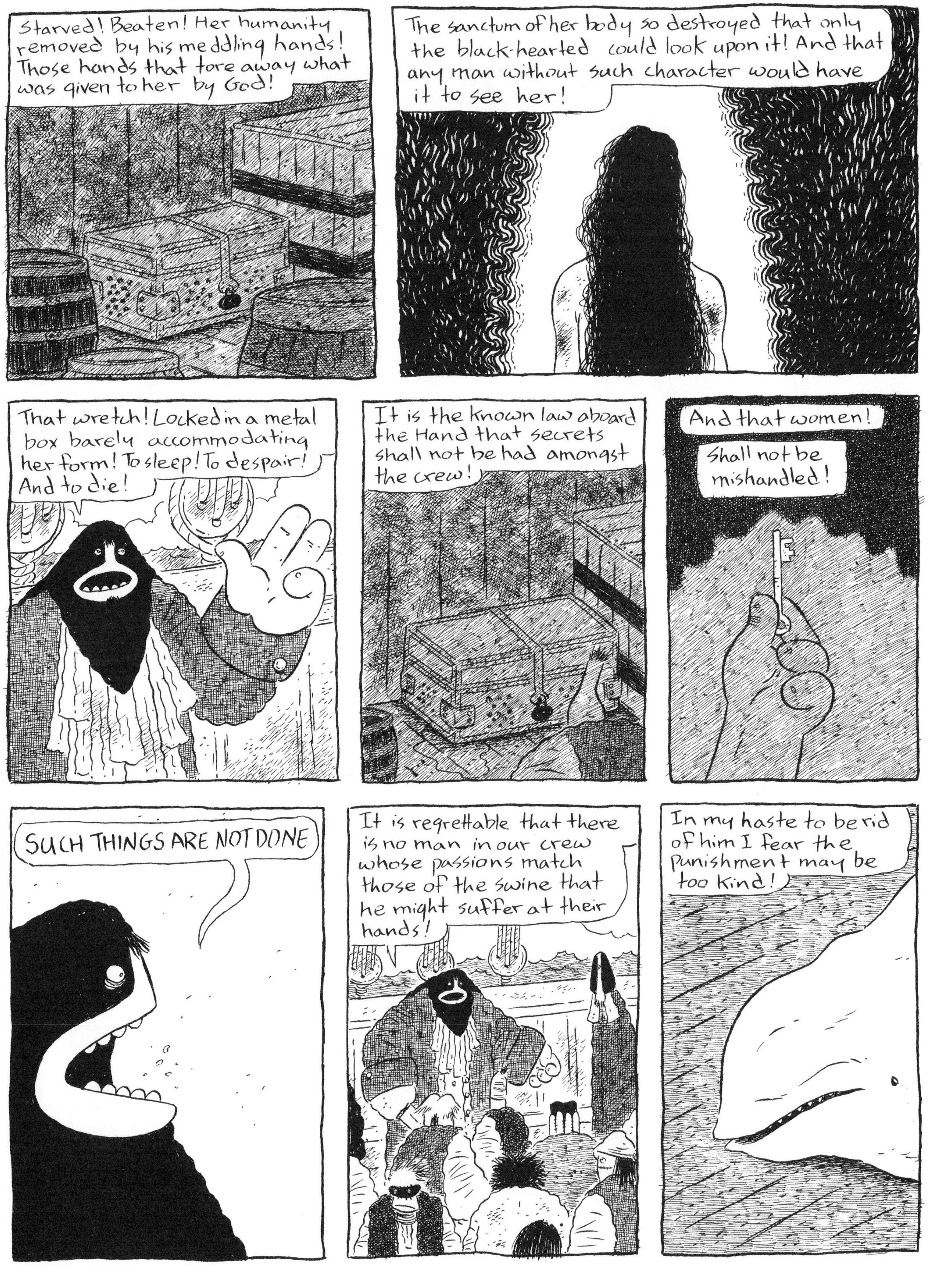
Starved! Beaten! Her humanity removed by his meddling hands! Those hands that tore away what was given to her by God!
The sanctum of her body so destroyed that only the black-hearted could look upon it! And that any man without such character would have it to see her!
That wretch! Locked in a metal box barely accommodating her form! To sleep! To despair! And to die!
It is the known law aboard the Hand that secrets shall not be had amongst the crew!
And that women!
Shall not be mishandled!
SUCH THINGS ARE NOT DONE
It is regrettable that there is no man in our crew whose passions match those of the swine that he might suffer at their hands!
In my haste to be rid of him I fear the punishment may be too kind!

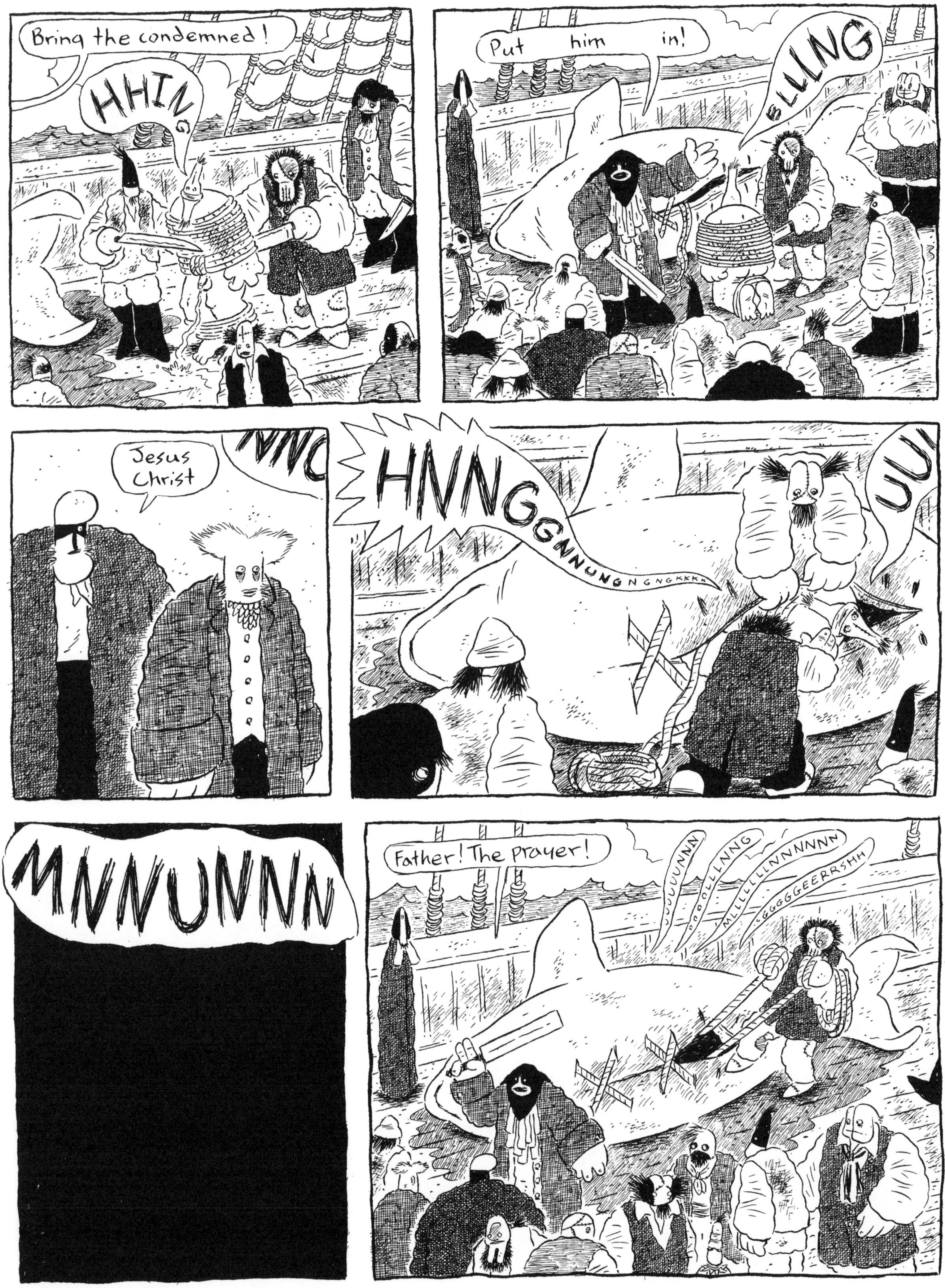
Bring the condemned!
HHING
Put him in!
BLLING
Jesus Christ
HNNGGNNUNGNGNGKKKK
MNNUNNN
Father! The prayer!
UUUUUNNN
OOOOLLLLNNG
MLLLLLLLNNNNNNN
GGGGGGEERRSHH

God gave! God held! God released! God torments! As you sink to the earthly depths to be raised and once again cast down, bear this in your heart!

Though your eyes may boil! Though your maggot-ridden skin may bloat and burn with unearthly gasses! Do not cry out lest the real horror be opened to you!

Amen!

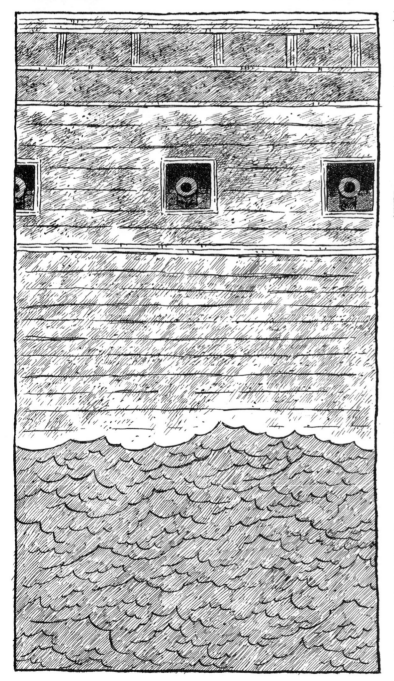

Steam in the hot sleeve
Feeling the demons investigate
Pressure near his crotch
His shoulder
Sure they are pulling him now
Why be aware of it?
Sudden gush
Furious Impotence
The mouth

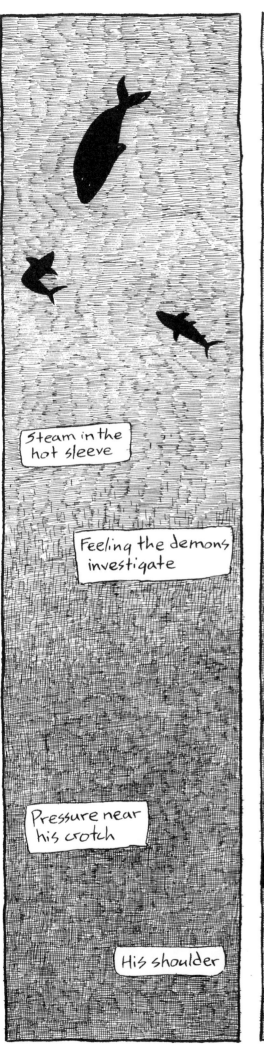

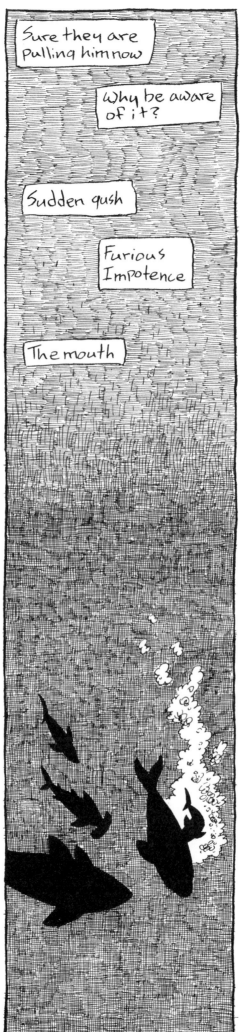

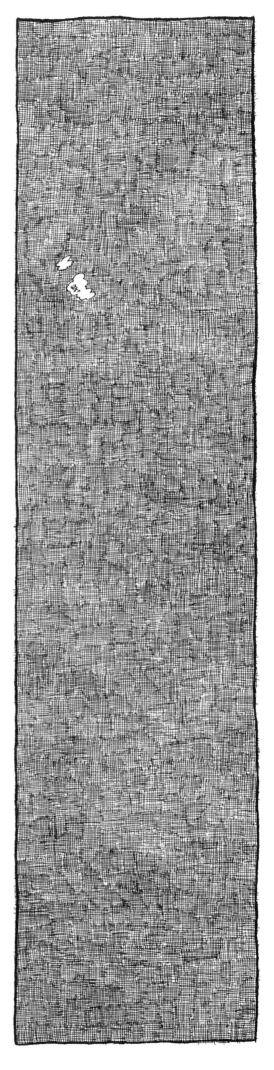

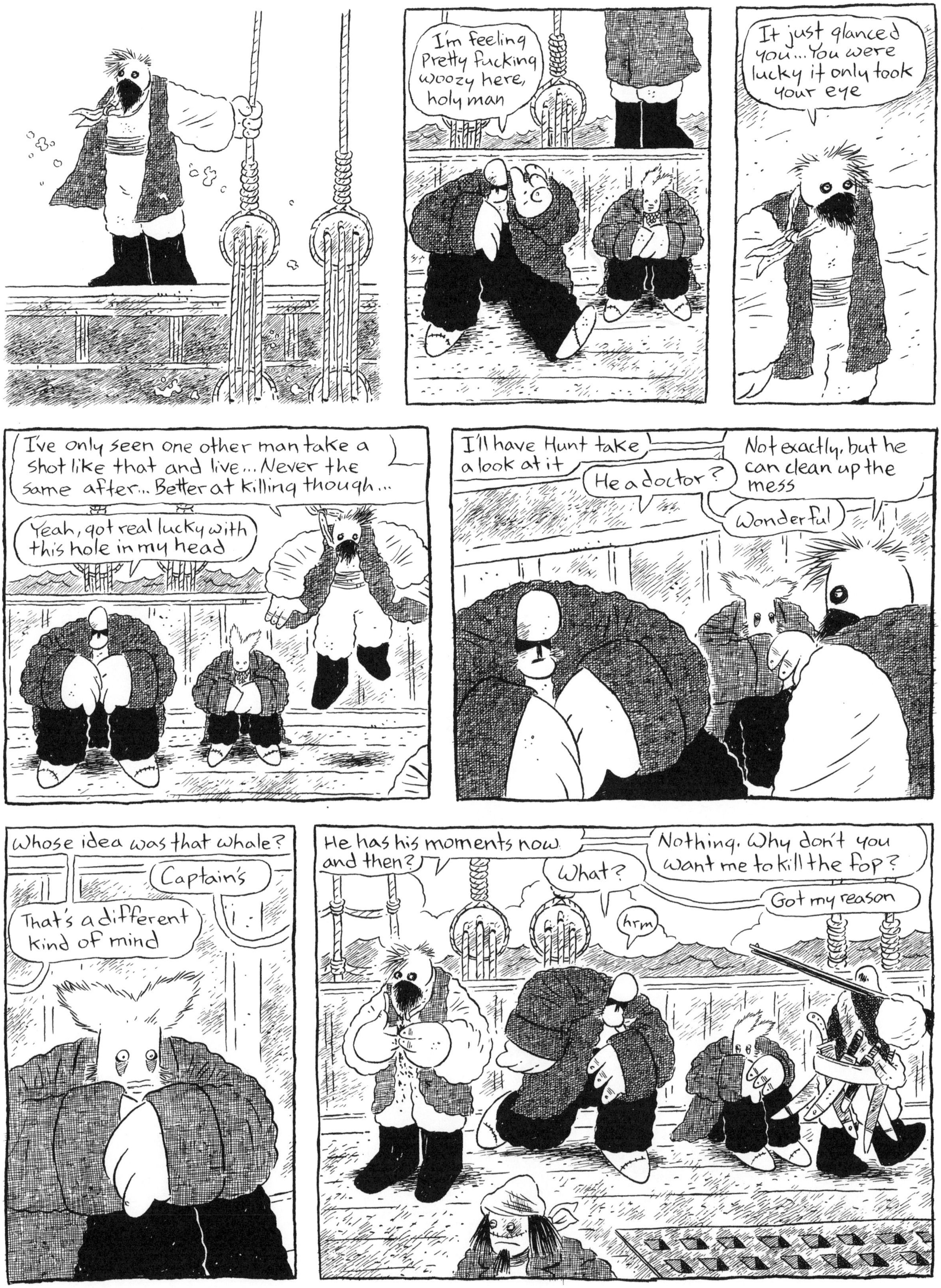
I'm feeling Pretty fucking woozy here, holy man
It just glanced you... You were lucky it only took your eye
I've only seen one other man take a shot like that and live... Never the same after... Better at killing though...
Yeah, got real lucky with this hole in my head
I'll have Hunt take a look at it
He a doctor?
Not exactly, but he can clean up the mess
Wonderful
Whose idea was that whale?
Captain's
That's a different kind of mind
He has his moments now and then?
What?
Nothing. Why don't you want me to kill the fop?
hrm
Got my reason

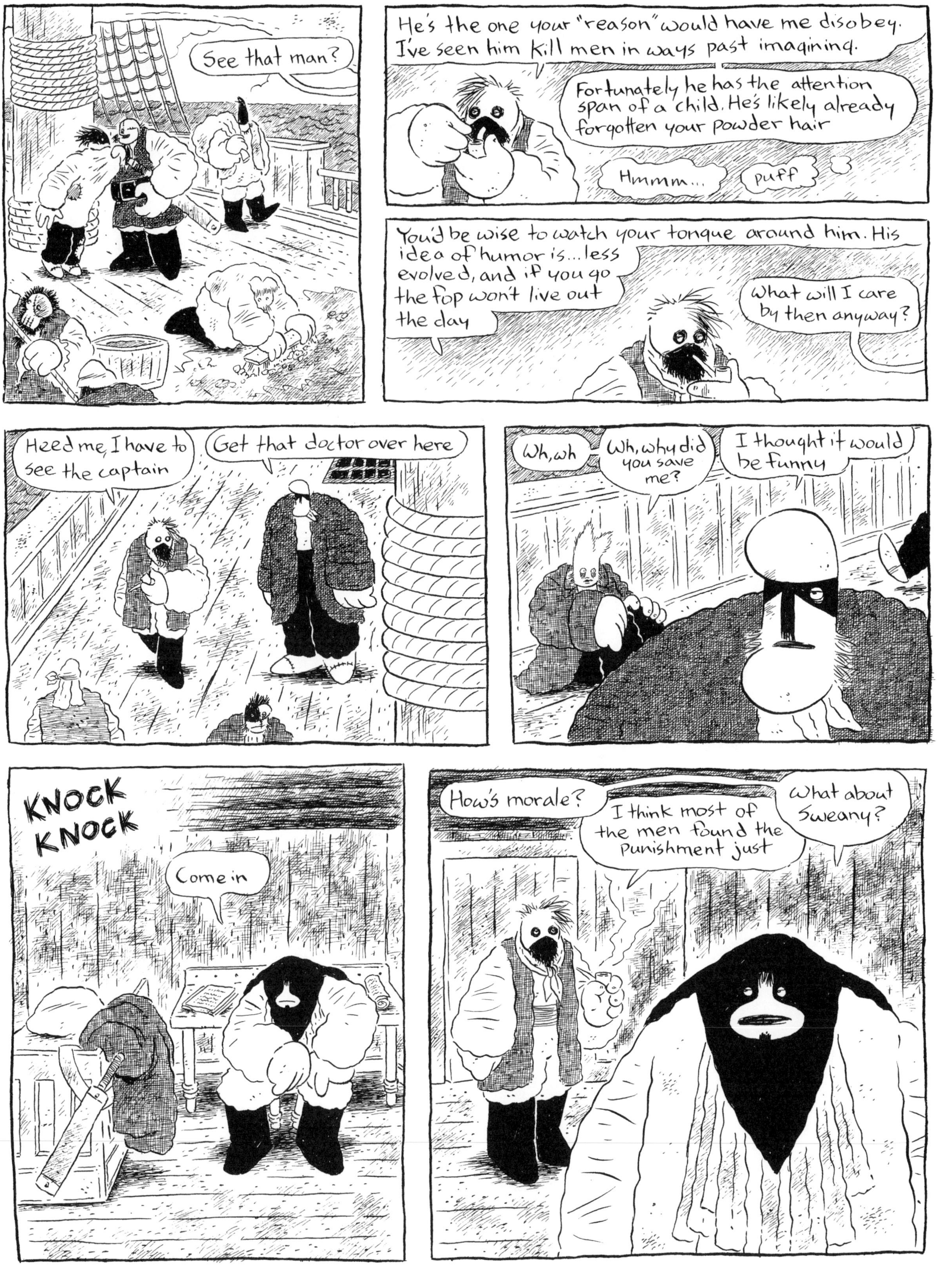
See that man?
He's the one your "reason" would have me disobey. I've seen him kill men in ways past imagining.
Fortunately he has the attention span of a child. He's likely already forgotten your powder hair
Hmmm...
puff
You'd be wise to watch your tongue around him. His idea of humor is... less evolved, and if you go the fop won't live out the day
What will I care by then anyway?
Heed me, I have to see the captain
Get that doctor over here
Wh, wh
Wh, why did you save me?
I thought it would be funny
KNOCK KNOCK
Come in
How's morale?
I think most of the men found the punishment just
What about Sweany?

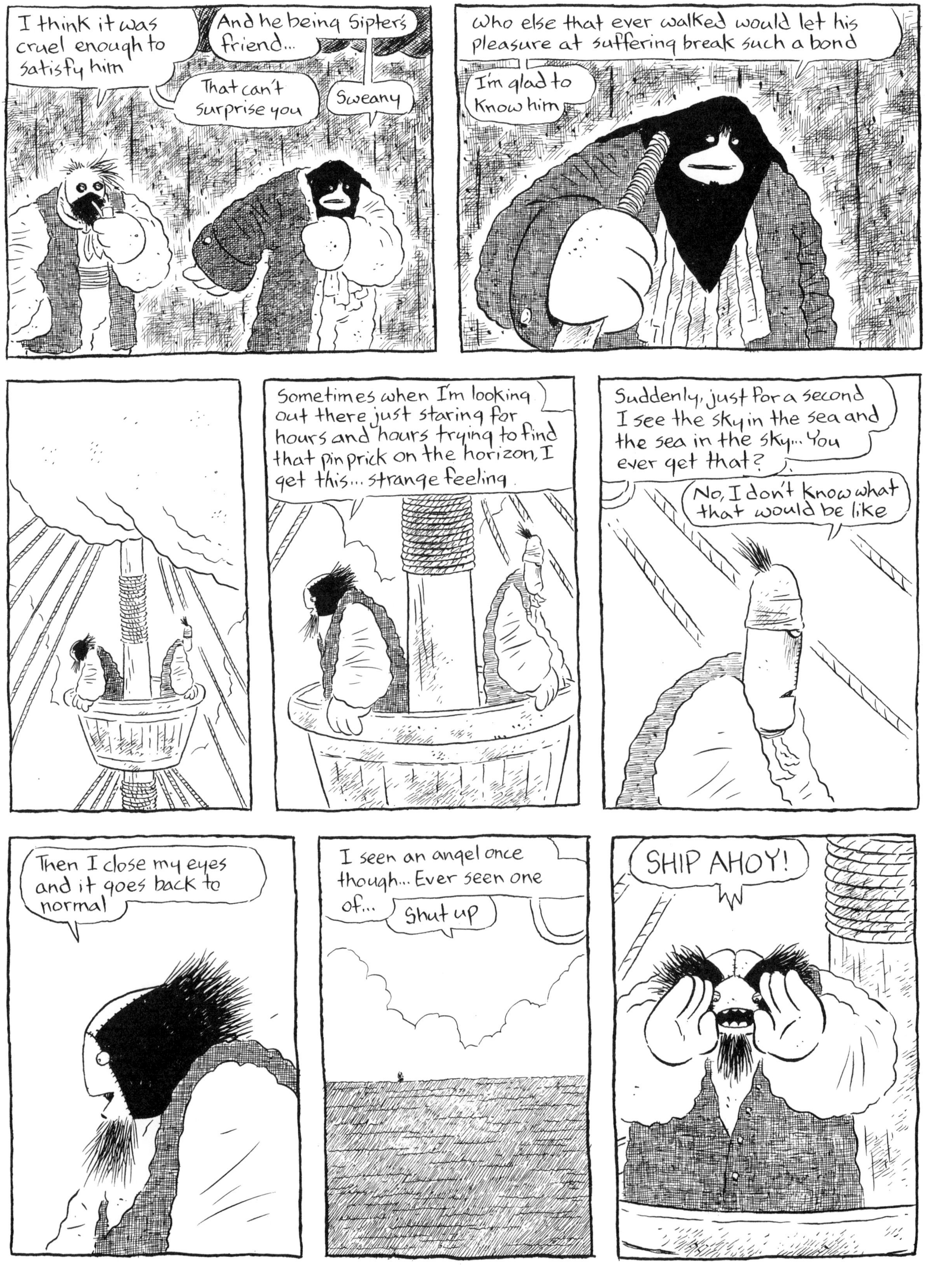
I think it was cruel enough to satisfy him
And he being Sipter's friend...
That can't surprise you
Sweany
Who else that ever walked would let his pleasure at suffering break such a bond
I'm glad to know him
Sometimes when I'm looking out there just staring for hours and hours trying to find that pin prick on the horizon, I get this... strange feeling
Suddenly, just for a second I see the sky in the sea and the sea in the sky... You ever get that?
No, I don't know what that would be like
Then I close my eyes and it goes back to normal
I seen an angel once though... Ever seen one of...
Shut up
SHIP AHOY!

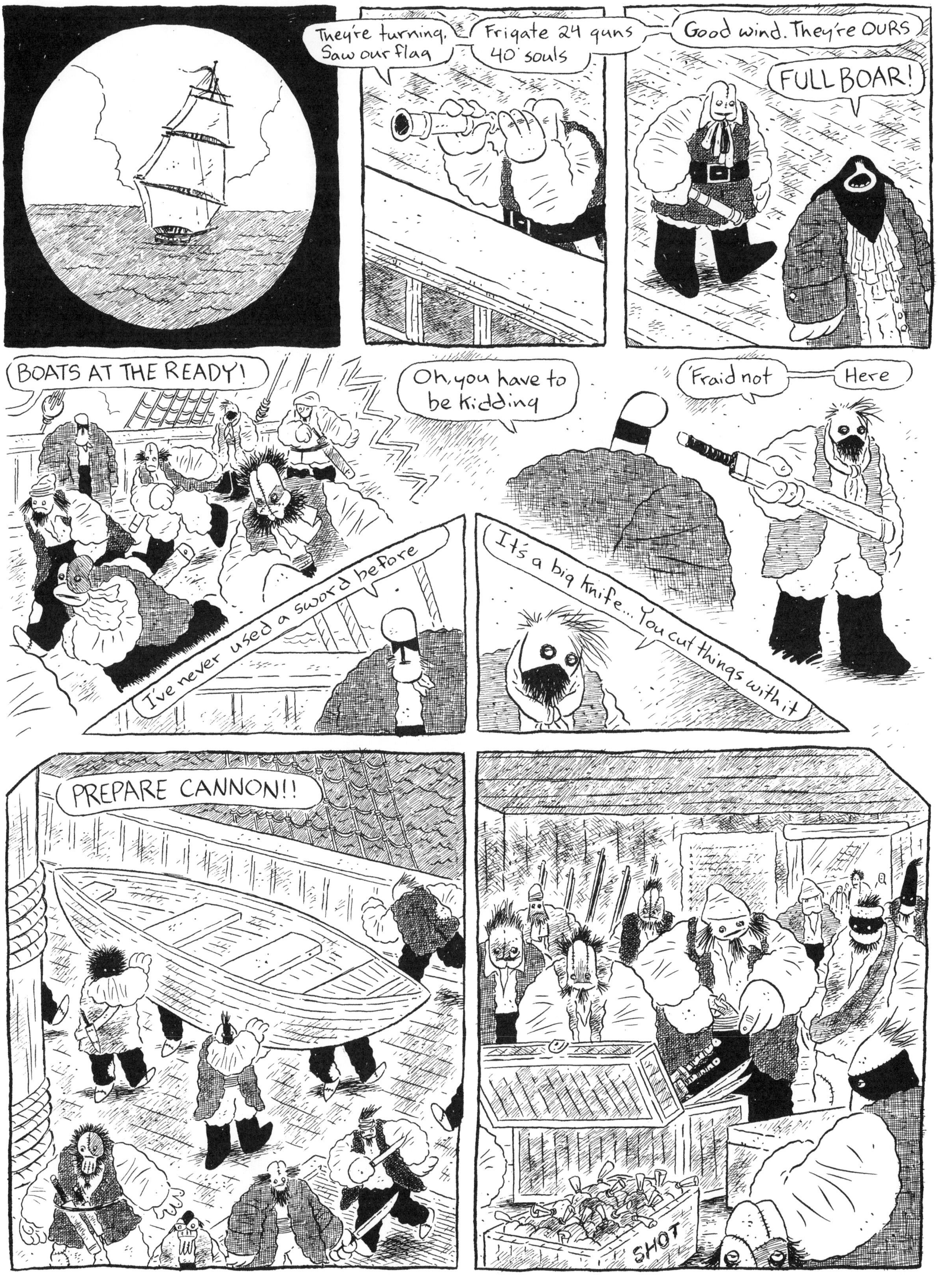
They're turning. Saw our flag
Frigate 24 guns 40 souls
Good wind. They're OURS
FULL BOAR!
BOATS AT THE READY!
Oh, you have to be kidding
I've never used a sword before
It's a big knife... You cut things with it
'Fraid not
Here
PREPARE CANNON!!
SHOT

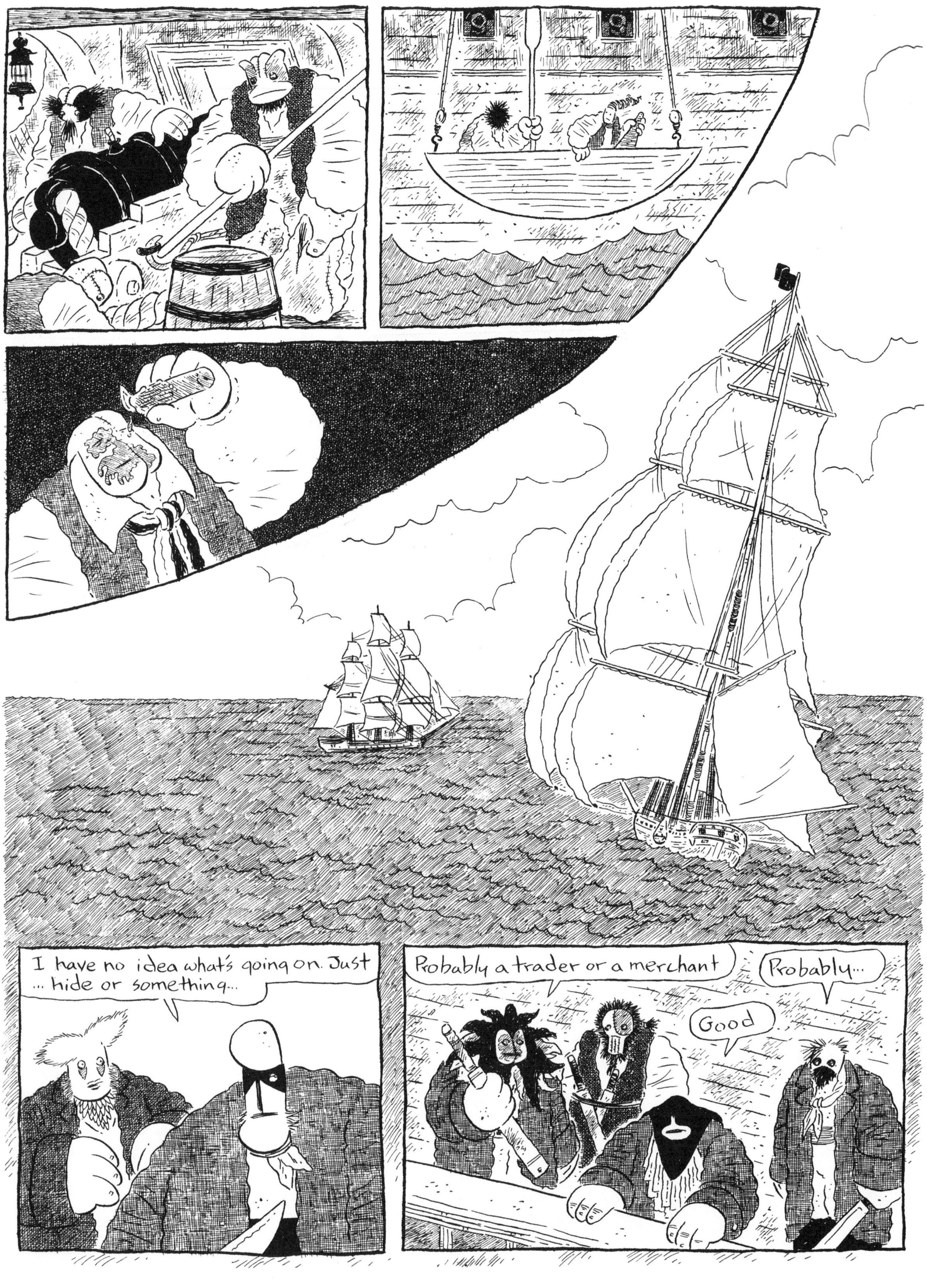
I have no idea what's going on. Just ... hide or something...
Probably a trader or a merchant
Probably...
Good

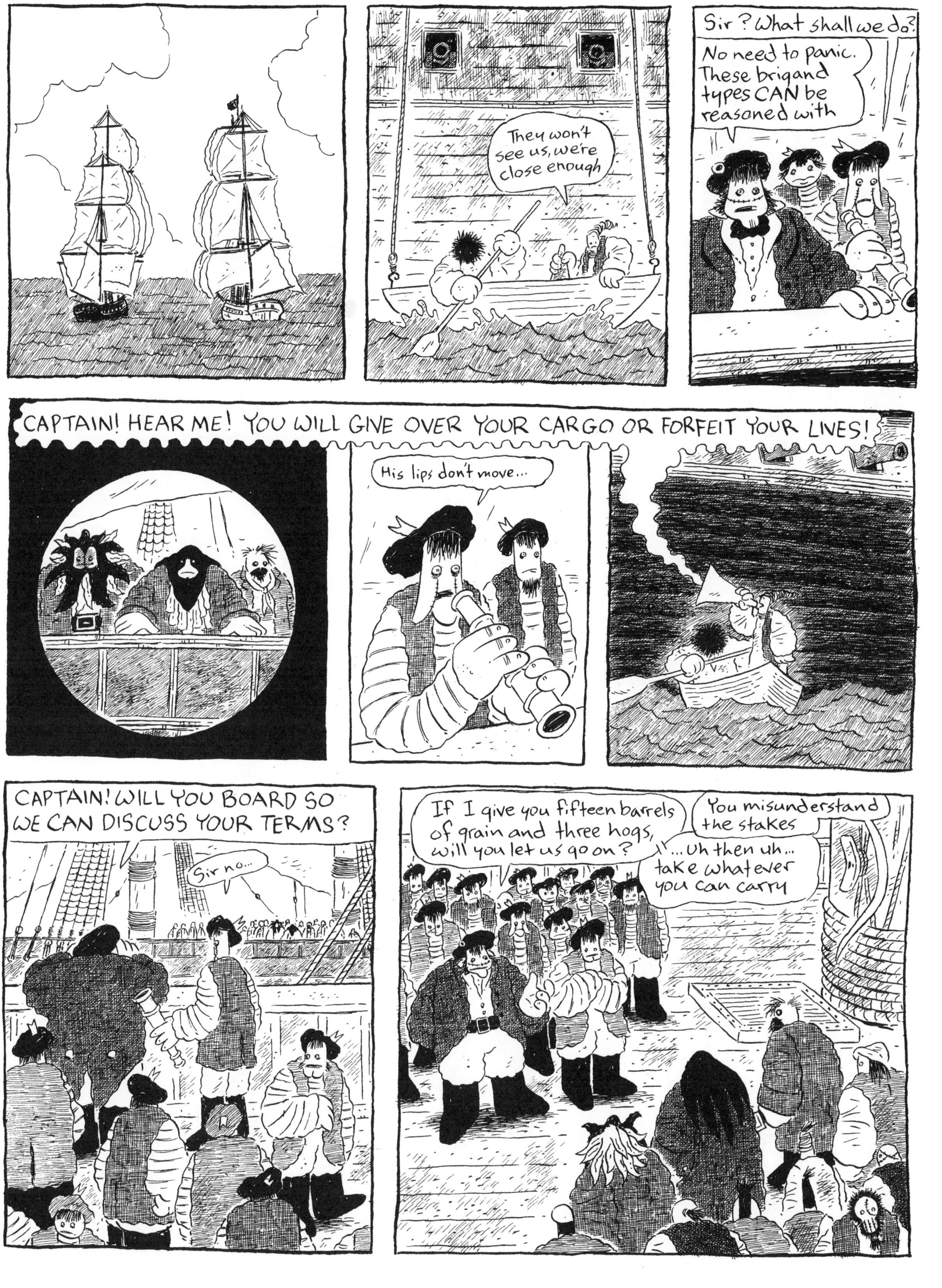
They won't see us, we're close enough
Sir? What shall we do?
No need to panic. These brigand types CAN be reasoned with
CAPTAIN! HEAR ME! YOU WILL GIVE OVER YOUR CARGO OR FORFEIT YOUR LIVES!
His lips don't move...
CAPTAIN! WILL YOU BOARD SO WE CAN DISCUSS YOUR TERMS?
Sir no...
If I give you fifteen barrels of grain and three hogs, will you let us go on?
You misunderstand the stakes
...uh then uh... take whatever you can carry

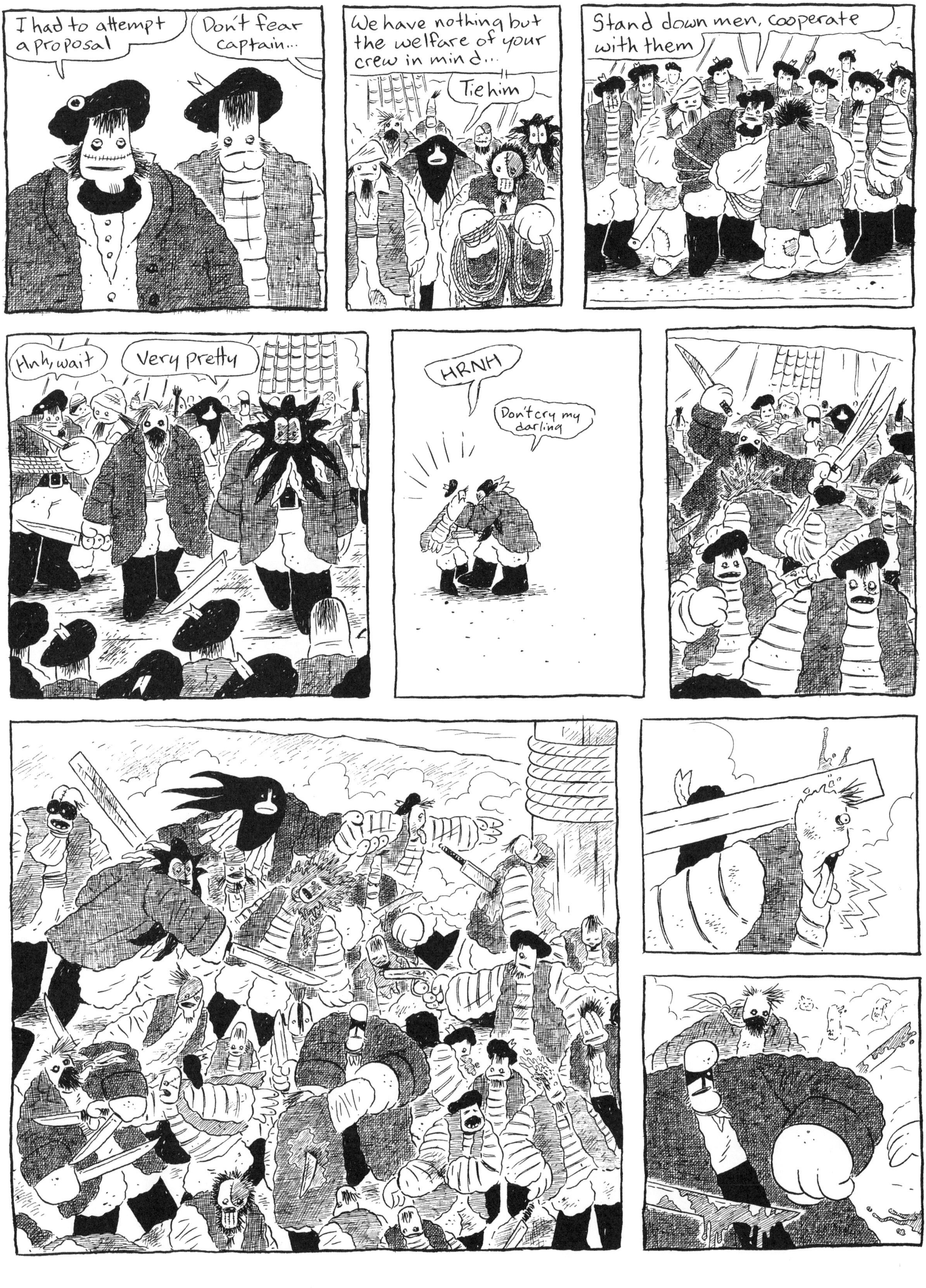

I had to attempt a proposal
Don't fear captain...
We have nothing but the welfare of your crew in mind...
Tie him
Stand down men, cooperate with them
Hnh, wait
Very pretty
HRNH
Don't cry my darling

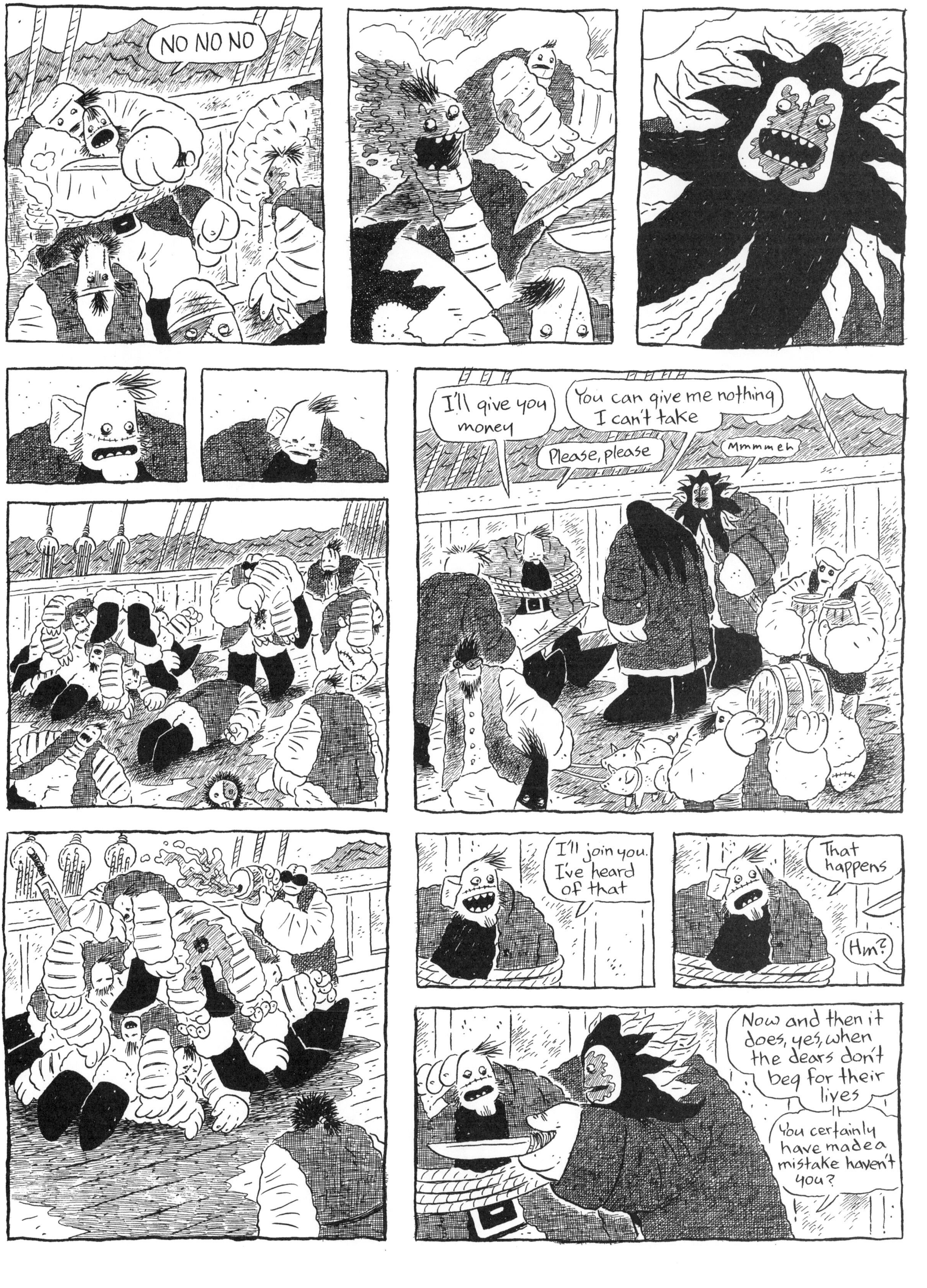
NO NO NO
I'll give you money
You can give me nothing I can't take
Please, please
Mmmmeh
I'll join you. I've heard of that
That happens
Hm?
Now and then it does, yes, when the dears don't beg for their lives
You certainly have made a mistake haven't you?

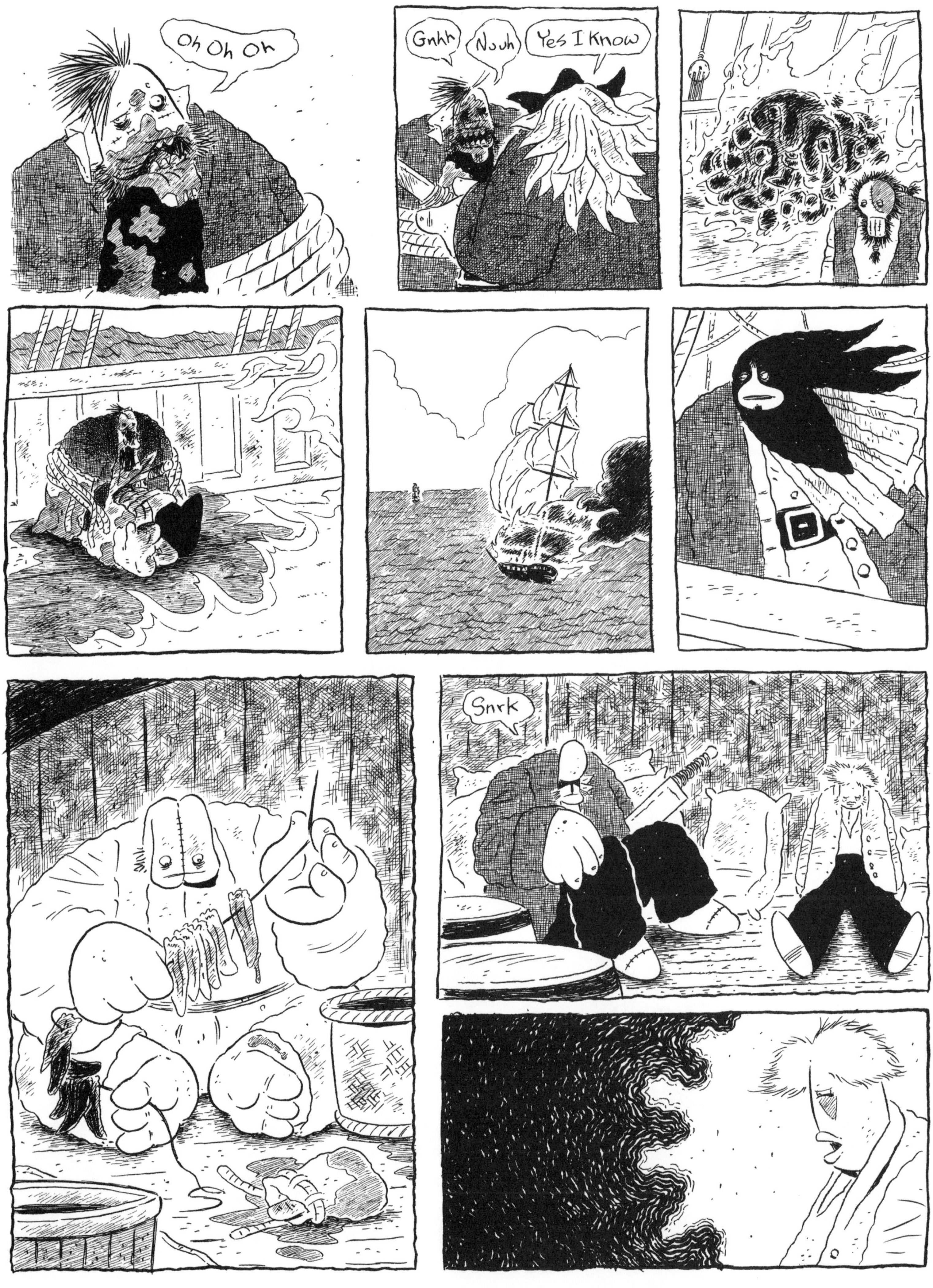

Oh Oh Oh
Gnhh
Nouh
Yes I Know
Snrk

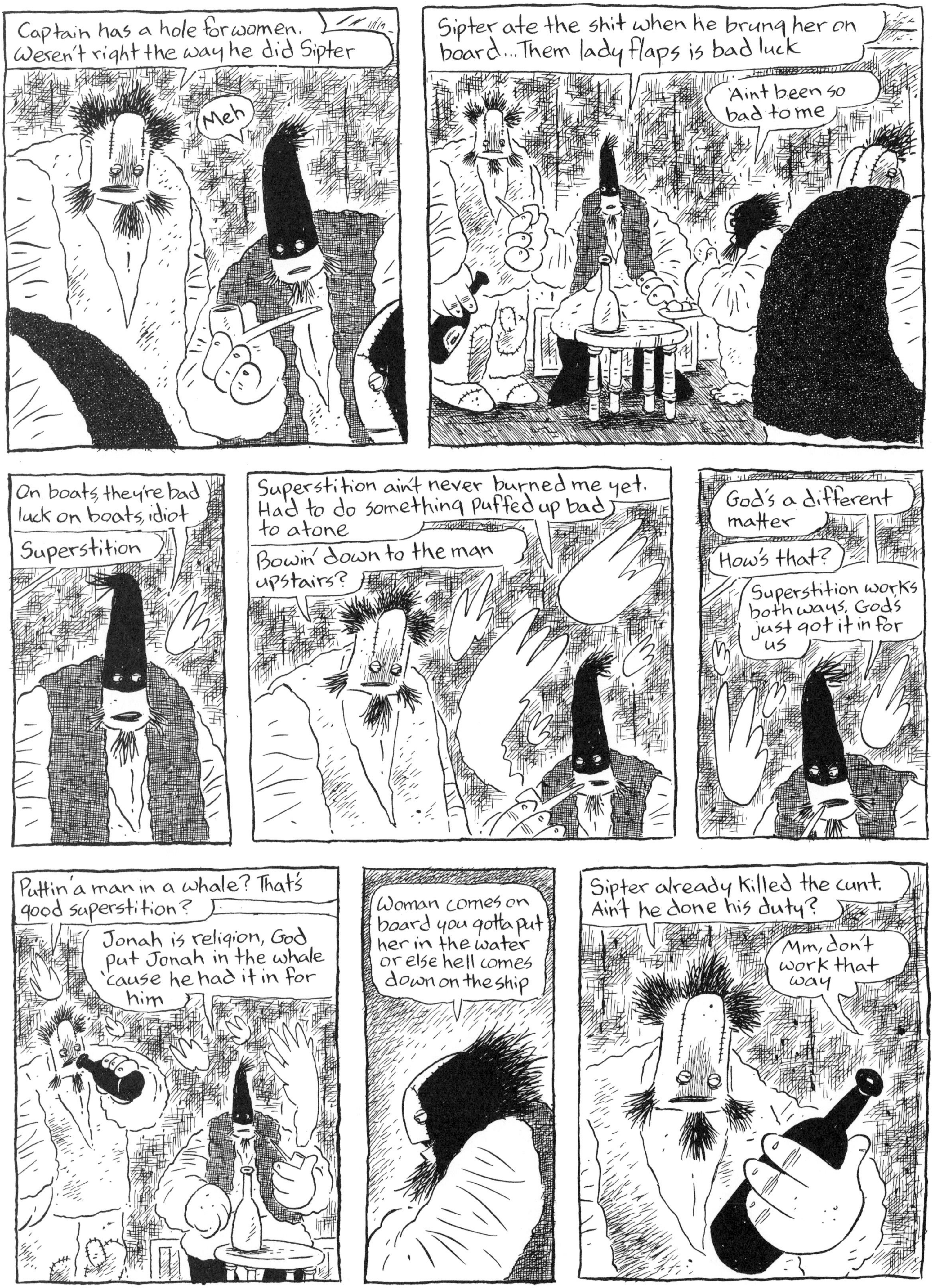
Captain has a hole for women. Weren't right the way he did Sipter
Meh
Sipter ate the shit when he brung her on board... Them lady flaps is bad luck
'Aint been so bad to me
On boats, they're bad luck on boats, idiot
Superstition
Superstition ain't never burned me yet. Had to do something puffed up bad to atone
Bowin' down to the man upstairs?
God's a different matter
How's that?
Superstition works both ways. God's just got it in for us
Puttin' a man in a whale? That's good superstition?
Jonah is religion, God put Jonah in the whale 'cause he had it in for him
Woman comes on board you gotta put her in the water or else hell comes down on the ship
Sipter already killed the cunt. Ain't he done his duty?
Mm, don't work that way

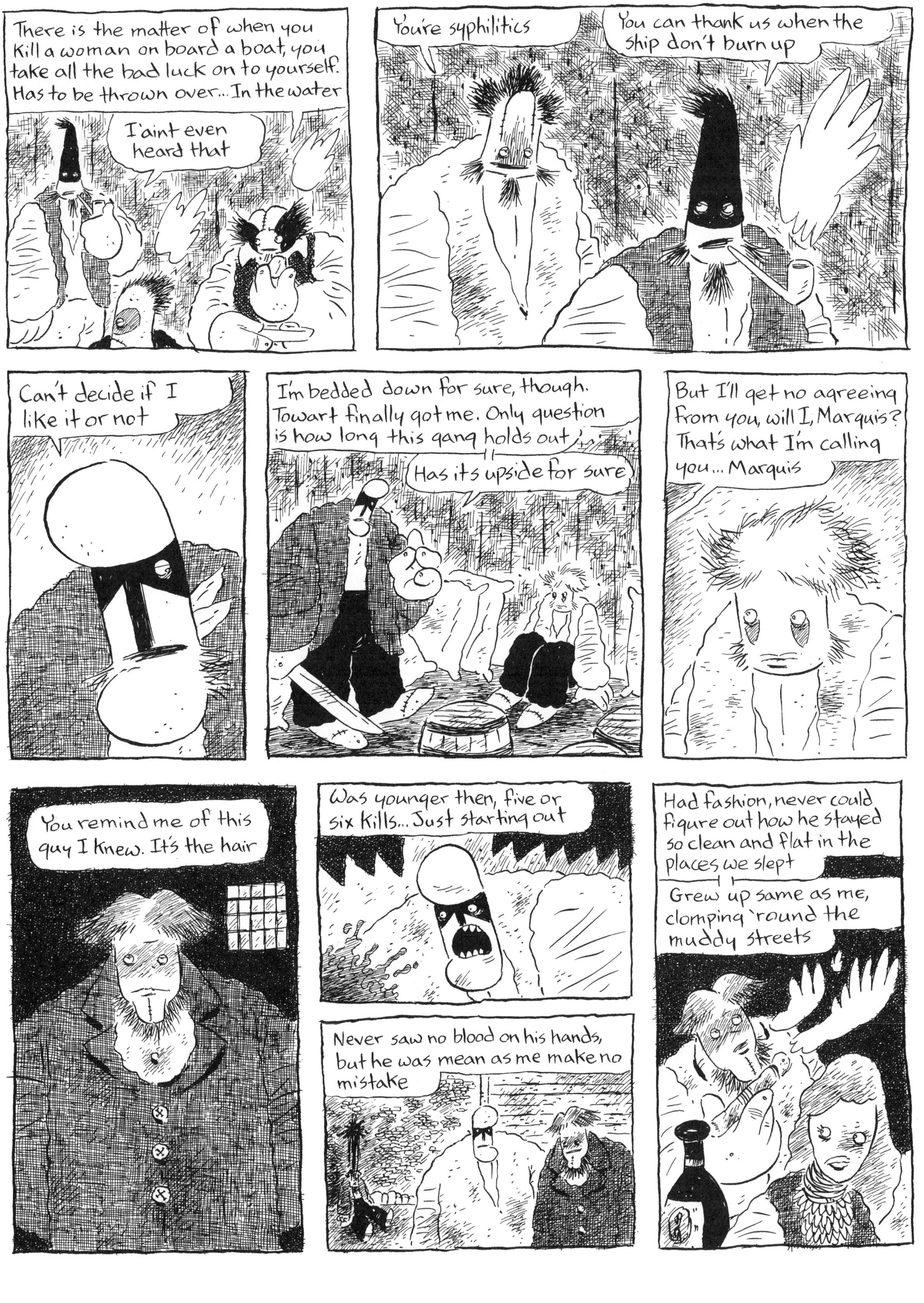
There is the matter of when you kill a woman on board a boat, you take all the bad luck on to yourself. Has to be thrown over... In the water
I'aint even heard that
You're syphilitics
You can thank us when the ship don't burn up
Can't decide if I like it or not
I'm bedded down for sure, though. Towart finally got me. Only question is how long this gang holds out
Has its upside for sure
But I'll get no agreeing from you, will I, Marquis? That's what I'm calling you... Marquis
You remind me of this guy I knew. It's the hair
Was younger then, five or six kills... Just starting out
Never saw no blood on his hands, but he was mean as me make no mistake
Had fashion, never could figure out how he stayed so clean and flat in the places we slept
Grew up same as me, clomping 'round the muddy streets

Six foot tall, silver face, had a tongue for words, but I never seen him with a woman

Truth is, where we come from, he scared 'em

Different kind of creature to them

No idea if he ever stuffed it in

Old Jaques called him Marquis. No idea why. You ain't nothing like him in the heart, but you got that hair part

You not make with ze threats eh Marquis?

Woke up one morning, his back was cold against mine. Corpsed himself with drink

Nattiest coffin helping I ever seen

You don't gotta talk, Better if you don't

I'm bedded in here...

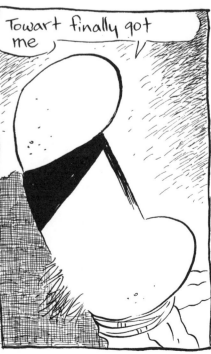
Towart finally got me

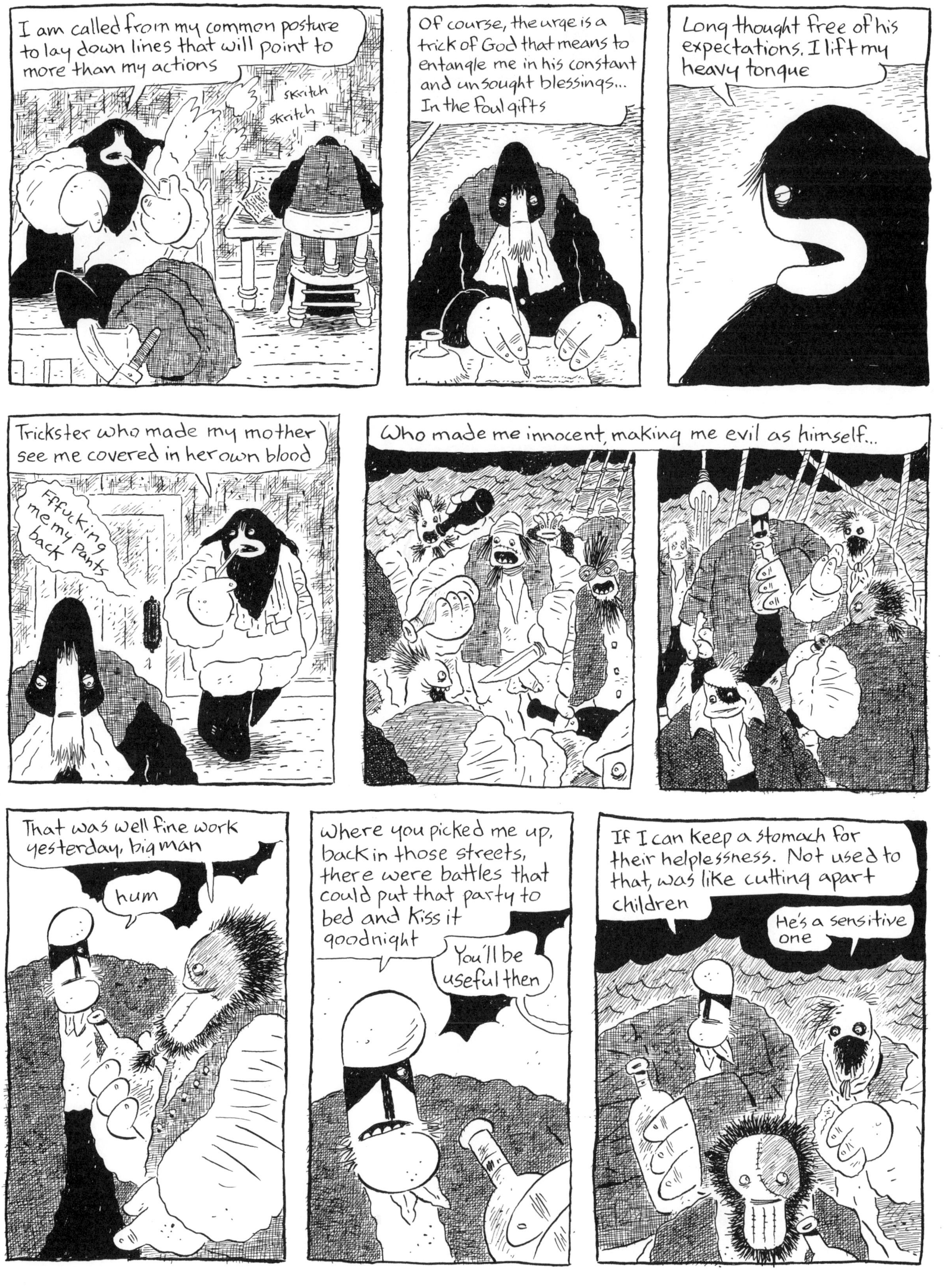

I am called from my common posture to lay down lines that will point to more than my actions
skritch
skritch
Of course, the urge is a trick of God that means to entangle me in his constant and unsought blessings...
In the foul gifts
Long thought free of his expectations. I lift my heavy tongue
Trickster who made my mother see me covered in her own blood
Ffffucking me my pants back
Who made me innocent, making me evil as himself...
That was well fine work yesterday, big man
hum
Where you picked me up, back in those streets, there were battles that could put that party to bed and kiss it goodnight
You'll be useful then
If I can keep a stomach for their helplessness. Not used to that, was like cutting apart children
He's a sensitive one

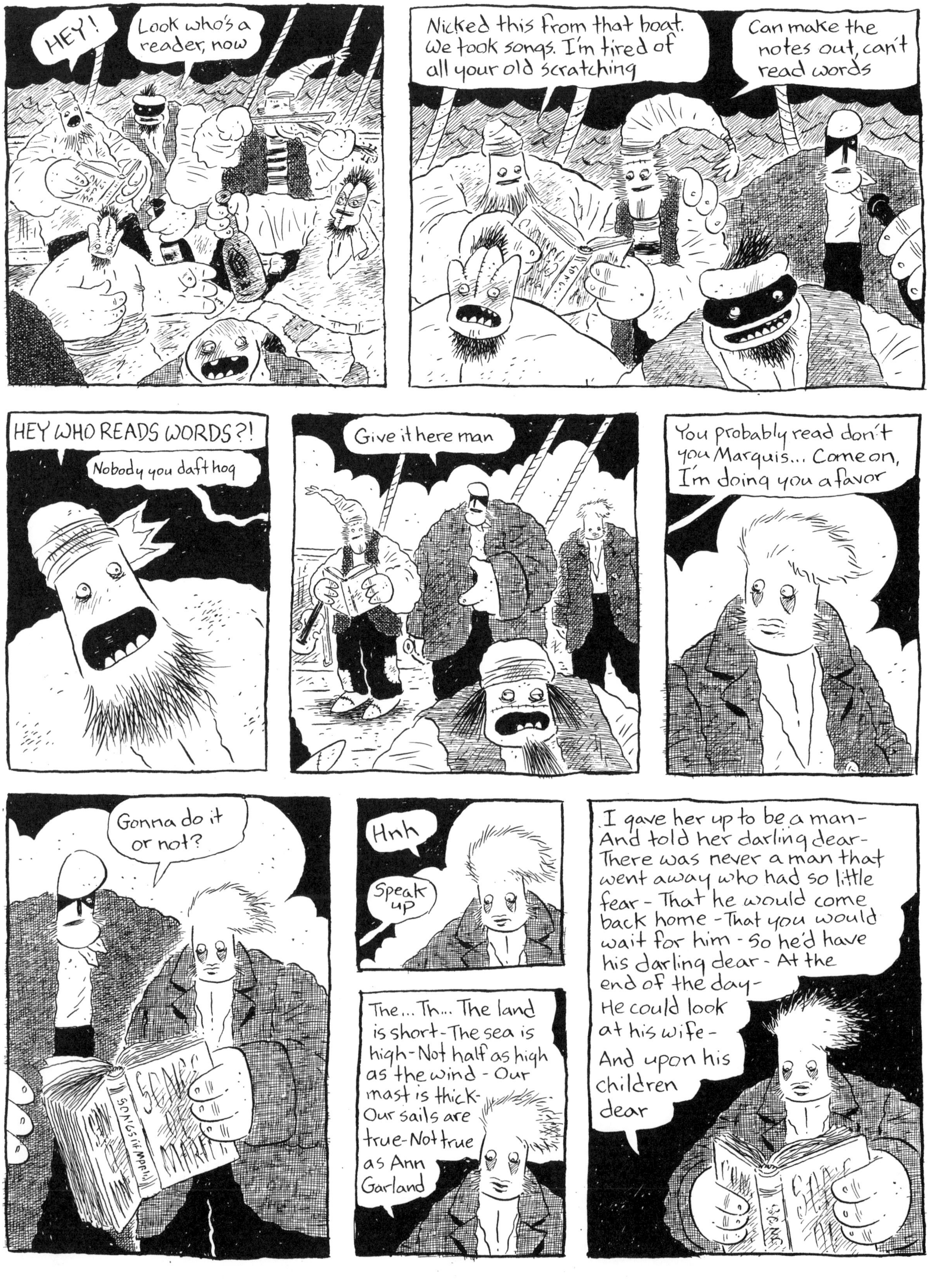
HEY!
Look who's a reader, now
Nicked this from that boat. We took songs. I'm tired of all your old scratching
Can make the notes out, can't read words
HEY WHO READS WORDS?!
Nobody you daft hog
Give it here man
You probably read don't you Marquis... Come on, I'm doing you a favor
Gonna do it or not?
Hnh
Speak up
The... Th... The land is short - The sea is high - Not half as high as the wind - Our mast is thick - Our sails are true - Not true as Ann Garland
I gave her up to be a man - And told her darling dear - There was never a man that went away who had so little fear - That he would come back home - That you would wait for him - So he'd have his darling dear - At the end of the day -
He could look at his wife -
And upon his children dear

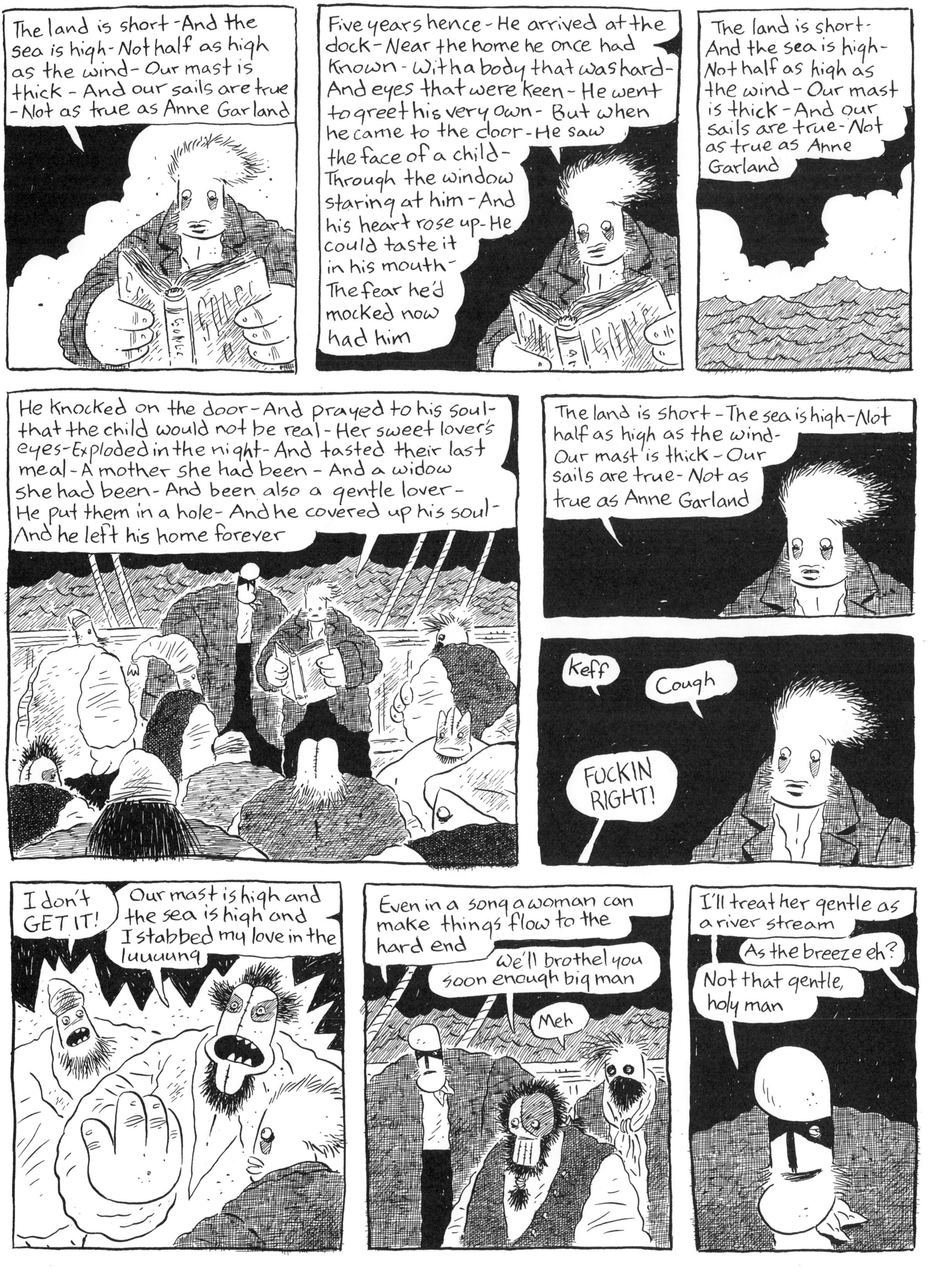

The land is short - And the sea is high - Not half as high as the wind - Our mast is thick - And our sails are true - Not as true as Anne Garland
Five years hence - He arrived at the dock - Near the home he once had Known - With a body that was hard - And eyes that were keen - He went to greet his very own - But when he came to the door - He saw the face of a child - Through the window staring at him - And his heart rose up - He could taste it in his mouth - The fear he'd mocked now had him
The land is short - And the sea is high - Not half as high as the wind - Our mast is thick - And our sails are true - Not as true as Anne Garland
He knocked on the door - And prayed to his soul - that the child would not be real - Her sweet lover's eyes - Exploded in the night - And tasted their last meal - A mother she had been - And a widow she had been - And been also a gentle lover - He put them in a hole - And he covered up his soul - And he left his home forever
The land is short - The sea is high - Not half as high as the wind - Our mast is thick - Our sails are true - Not as true as Anne Garland
Keff
Cough
FUCKIN RIGHT!
I don't GET IT!
Our mast is high and the sea is high and I stabbed my love in the luuuung
Even in a song a woman can make things flow to the hard end
We'll brothel you soon enough big man
Meh
I'll treat her gentle as a river stream
As the breeze eh?
Not that gentle, holy man

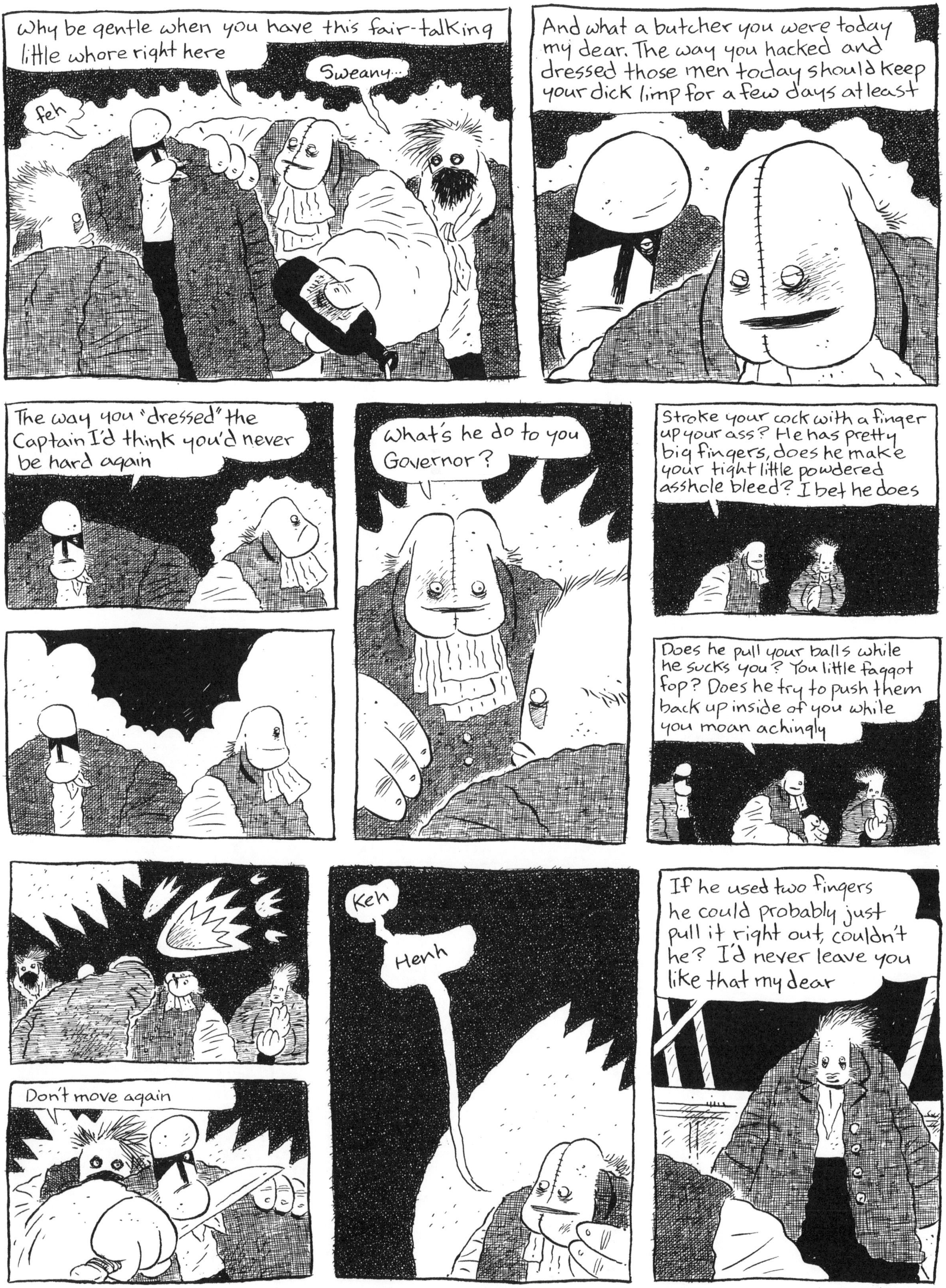
Why be gentle when you have this fair-talking little whore right here
feh
Sweany...
And what a butcher you were today my dear. The way you hacked and dressed those men today should keep your dick limp for a few days atleast
The way you "dressed" the Captain I'd think you'd never be hard again
What's he do to you Governor?
Stroke your cock with a finger up your ass? He has pretty big fingers, does he make your tight little powdered asshole bleed? I bet he does
Does he pull your balls while he sucks you? You little faggot fop? Does he try to push them back up inside of you while you moan achingly
Keh
Henh
If he used two fingers he could probably just pull it right out, couldn't he? I'd never leave you like that my dear
Don't move again

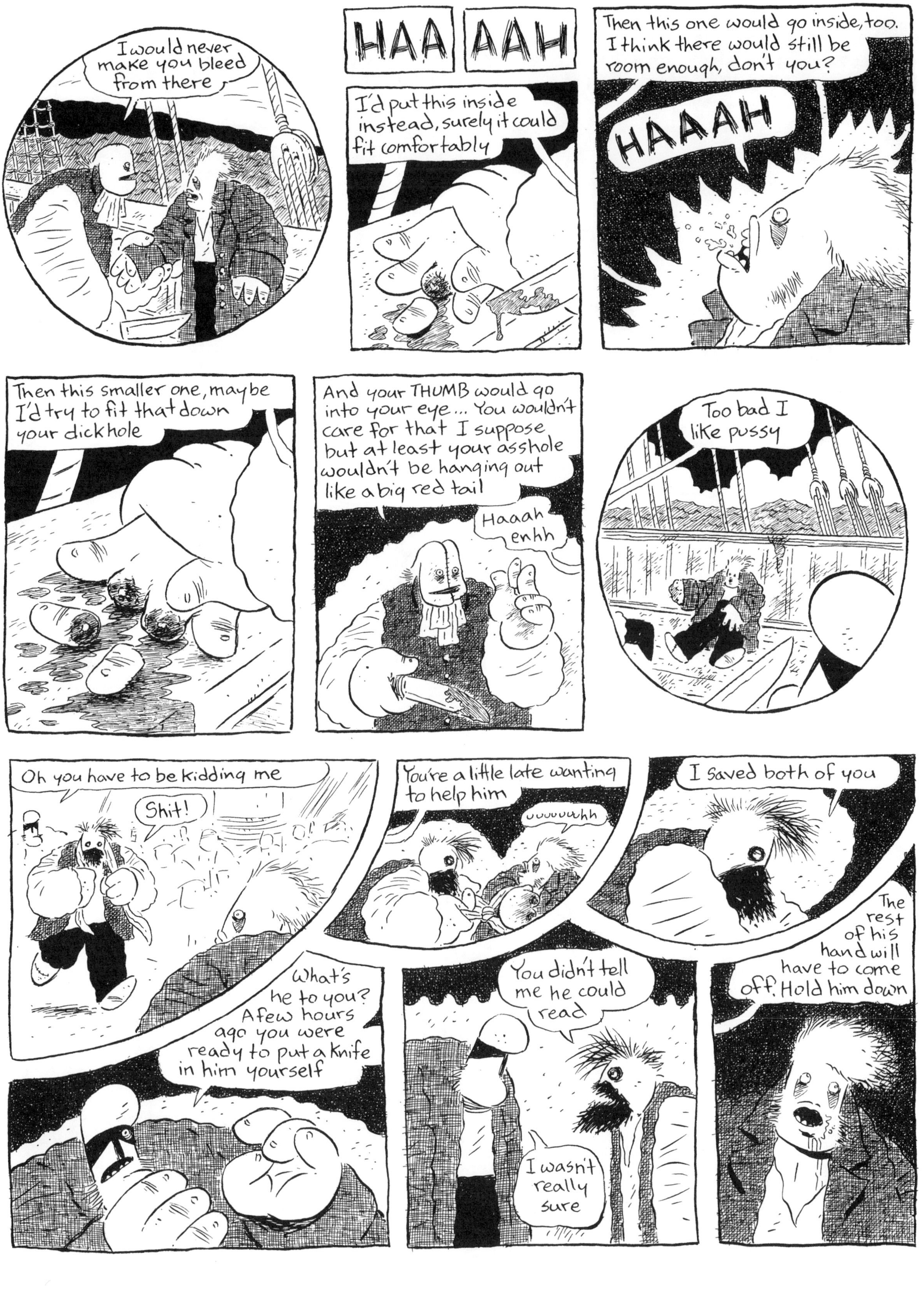

I would never make you bleed from there
HAA
AAH
I'd put this inside instead, surely it could fit comfortably
Then this one would go inside, too. I think there would still be room enough, don't you?
HAAAH
Then this smaller one, maybe I'd try to fit that down your dickhole
And your THUMB would go into your eye... You wouldn't care for that I suppose but at least your asshole wouldn't be hanging out like a big red tail
Haaah enhh
Too bad I like pussy
Oh you have to be kidding me
Shit!
You're a little late wanting to help him
uuuuuuhh
I saved both of you
What's he to you? A few hours ago you were ready to put a knife in him yourself
You didn't tell me he could read
I wasn't really sure
The rest of his hand will have to come off. Hold him down

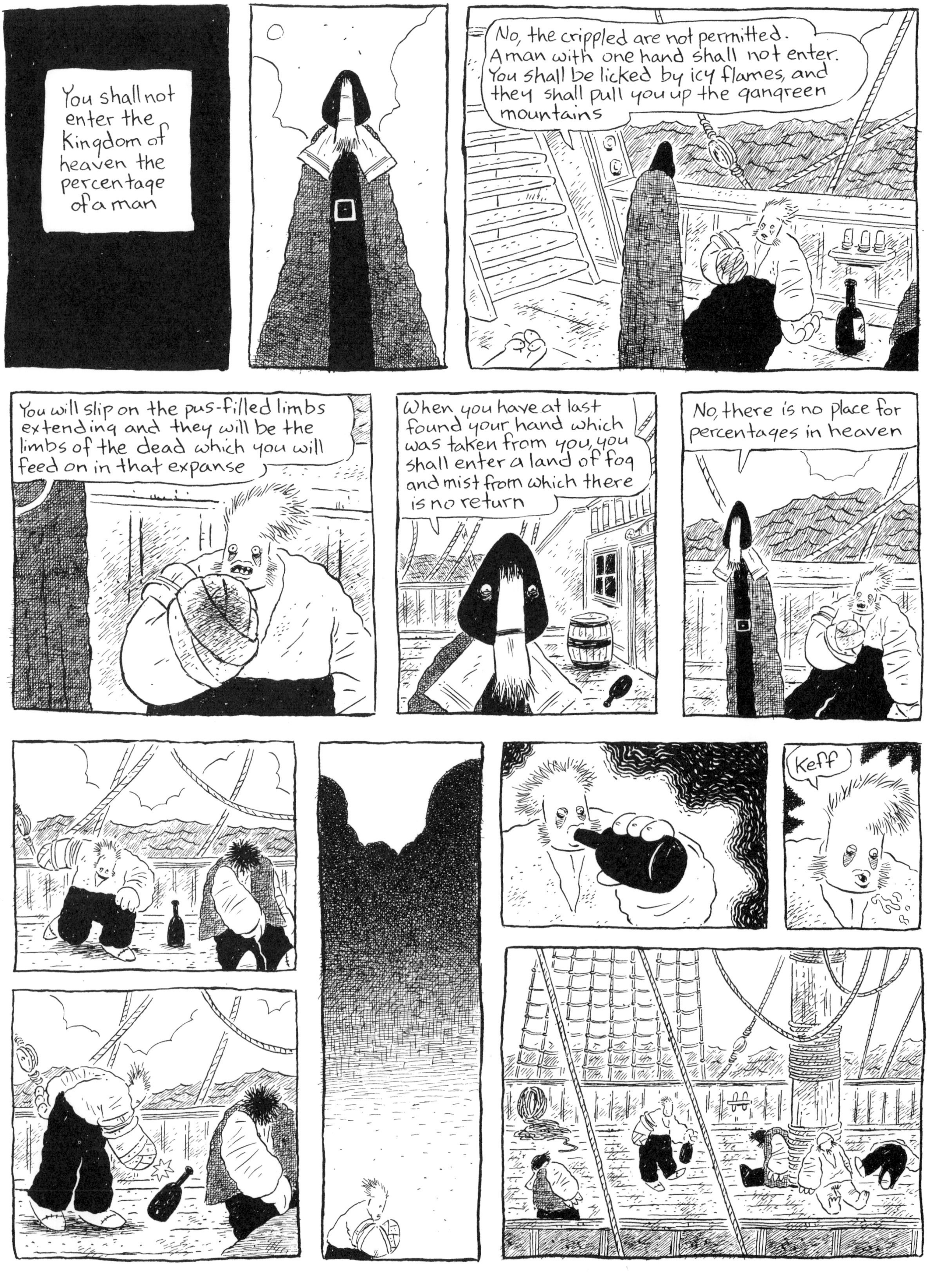

You shall not enter the Kingdom of heaven the percentage of a man
No, the crippled are not permitted. A man with one hand shall not enter. You shall be licked by icy flames, and they shall pull you up the gangreen mountains
You will slip on the pus-filled limbs extending and they will be the limbs of the dead which you will feed on in that expanse
When you have at last found your hand which was taken from you, you shall enter a land of fog and mist from which there is no return
No, there is no place for percentages in heaven
Keff

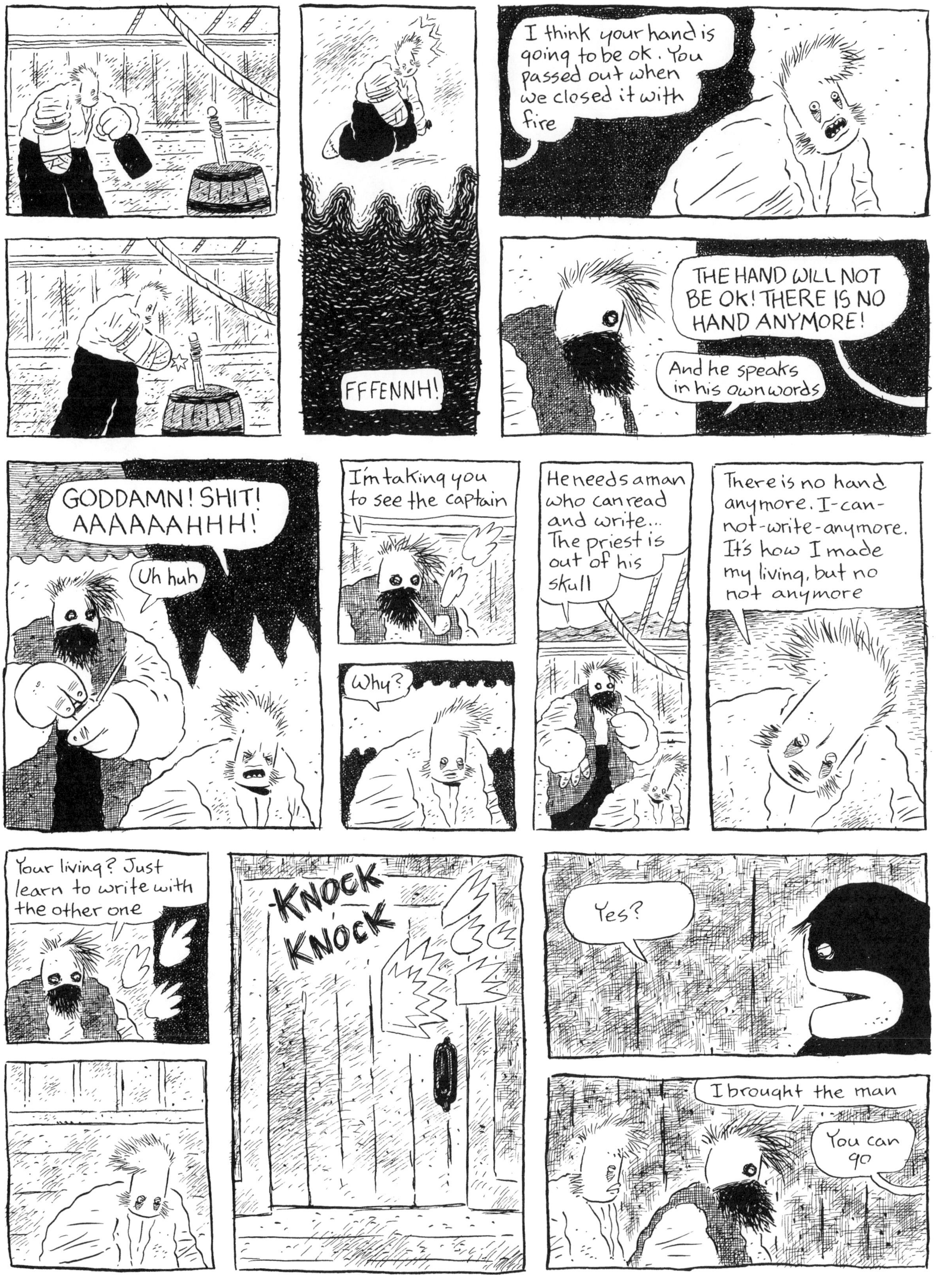
I think your hand is going to be ok. You passed out when we closed it with fire
FFFENNH!
THE HAND WILL NOT BE OK! THERE IS NO HAND ANYMORE!
And he speaks in his own words
GODDAMN! SHIT! AAAAAAHHH!
Uh huh
I'm taking you to see the captain
Why?
He needs a man who can read and write... The priest is out of his skull
There is no hand anymore. I-can-not-write-anymore. It's how I made my living, but no not anymore
Your living? Just learn to write with the other one
KNOCK KNOCK
Yes?
I brought the man
You can go

You read and write?

Read

This

Yes, I see, I heard

Jericho Sweany is a miserable creature with a distinguished lack of self-control. All the demons blush with envy

He is always on the half boundary of my control. Outwater keeps him in view. He is small, Outwater, but his knife is fast in dire places

Even Sweany fears him. Their fellowship is taut, and fraught, though neither will speak to it. Sweany is kept calm

He is an evil creature, yes, but he serves my purposes

As you must

The priest, he has been writing down my words

I say them out loud and he writes them down

I cannot write or read

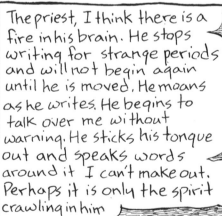

The priest, I think there is a fire in his brain. He stops writing for strange periods and will not begin again until he is moved. He moans as he writes. He begins to talk over me without warning. He sticks his tongue out and speaks words around it I can't make out. Perhaps it is only the spirit crawling in him

But I feel he may be cheating my words

I need eyes that can recognize the cheat

Where is it?

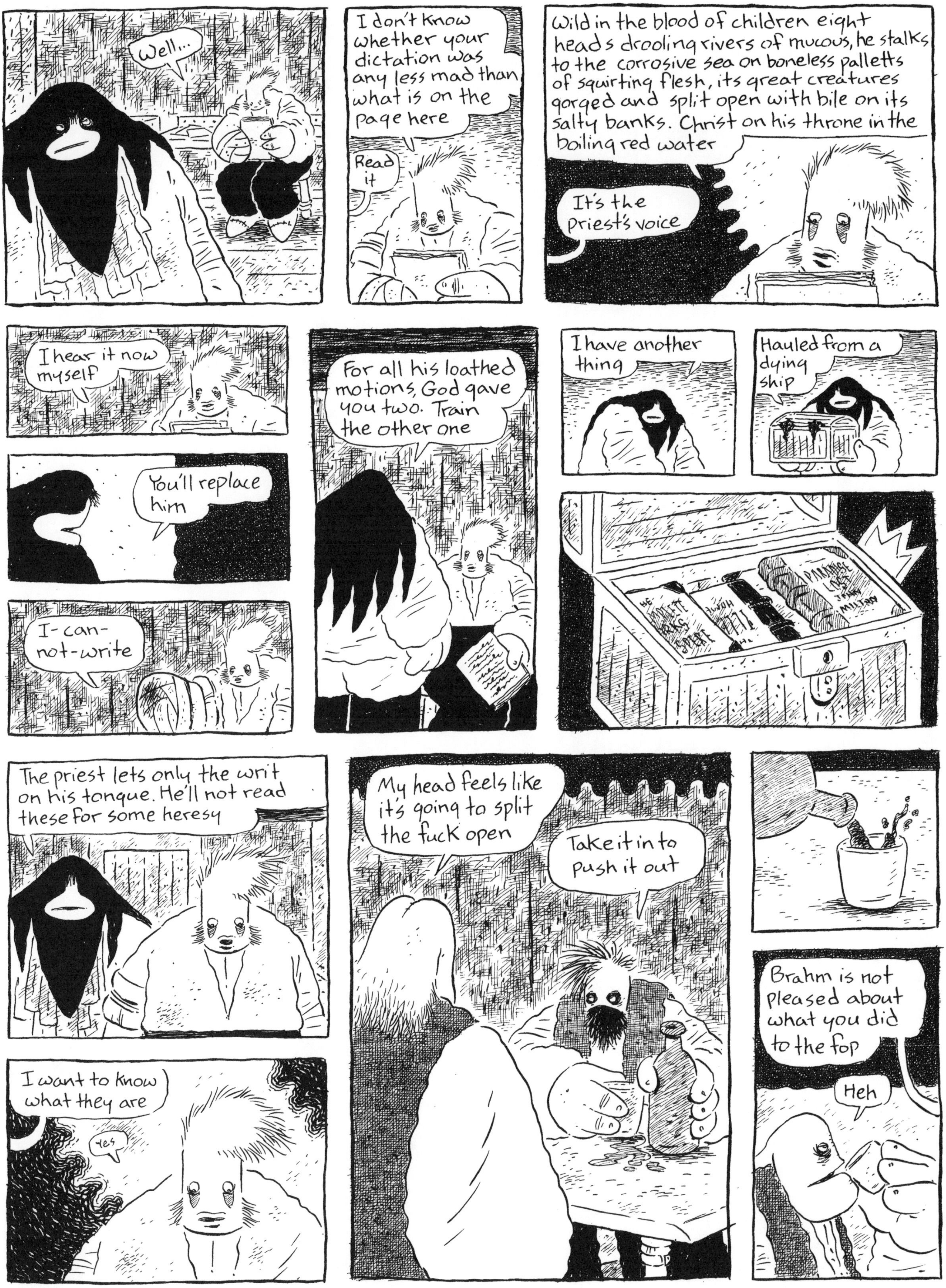
Well...
I don't know whether your dictation was any less mad than what is on the page here
Read it
Wild in the blood of children eight heads drooling rivers of mucous, he stalks to the corrosive sea on boneless palletts of squirting flesh, its great creatures gorged and split open with bile on its salty banks. Christ on his throne in the boiling red water
It's the priest's voice
I hear it now myself
You'll replace him
I-can-not-write
For all his loathed motions, God gave you two. Train the other one
I have another thing
Hauled from a dying ship
The priest lets only the writ on his tongue. He'll not read these for some heresy
I want to know what they are
Yes
My head feels like it's going to split the fuck open
Take it in to push it out
Brahm is not pleased about what you did to the fop
Heh

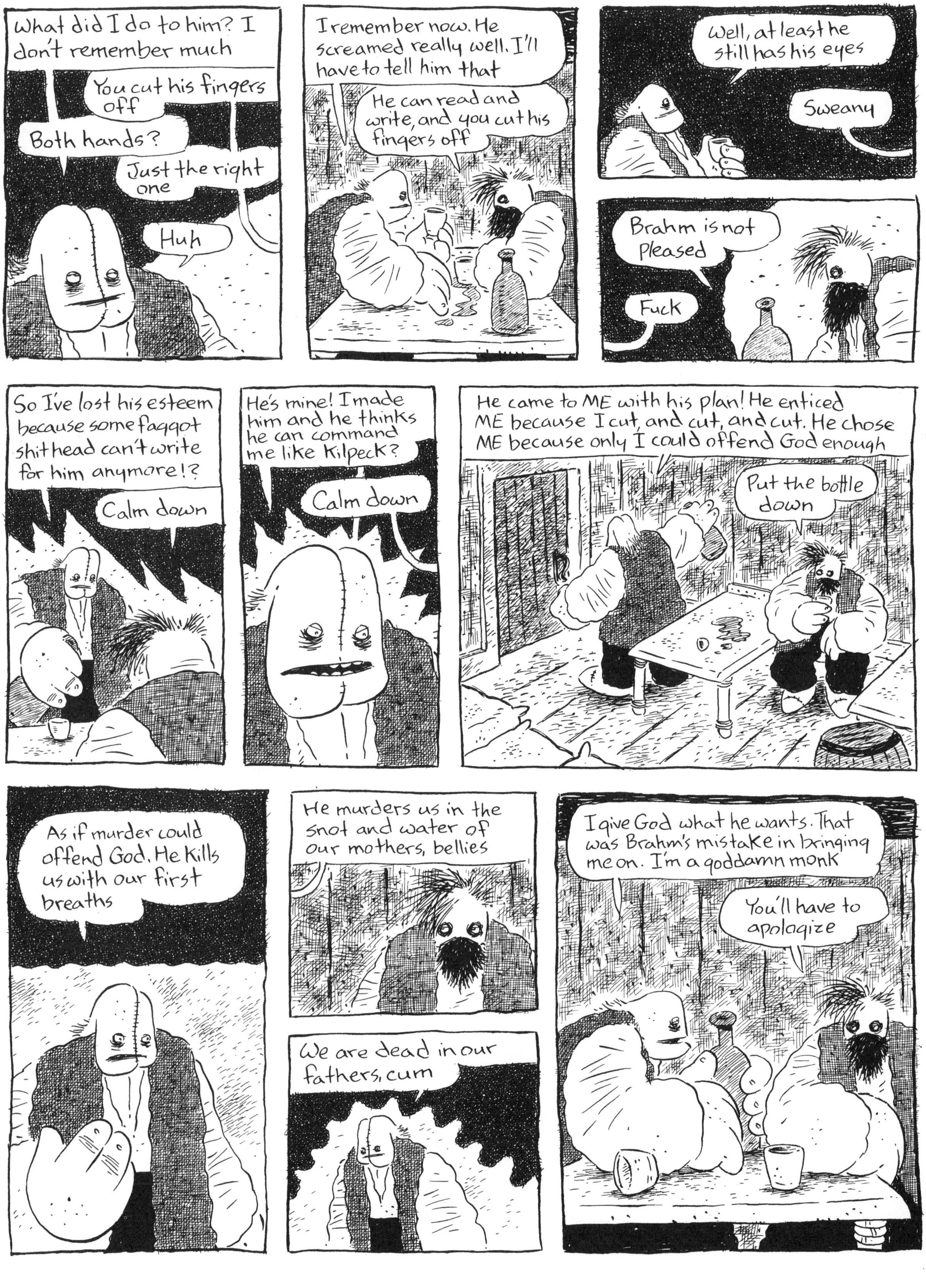
What did I do to him? I don't remember much
You cut his fingers off
Both hands?
Just the right one
Huh
I remember now. He screamed really well. I'll have to tell him that
He can read and write, and you cut his fingers off
Well, at least he still has his eyes
Sweany
Brahm is not pleased
Fuck
So I've lost his esteem because some faggot shithead can't write for him anymore!?
Calm down
He's mine! I made him and he thinks he can command me like Kilpeck?
Calm down
He came to ME with his plan! He enticed ME because I cut, and cut, and cut. He chose ME because only I could offend God enough
Put the bottle down
As if murder could offend God. He kills us with our first breaths
He murders us in the snot and water of our mothers, bellies
We are dead in our fathers, cum
I give God what he wants. That was Brahm's mistake in bringing me on. I'm a goddamn monk
You'll have to apologize

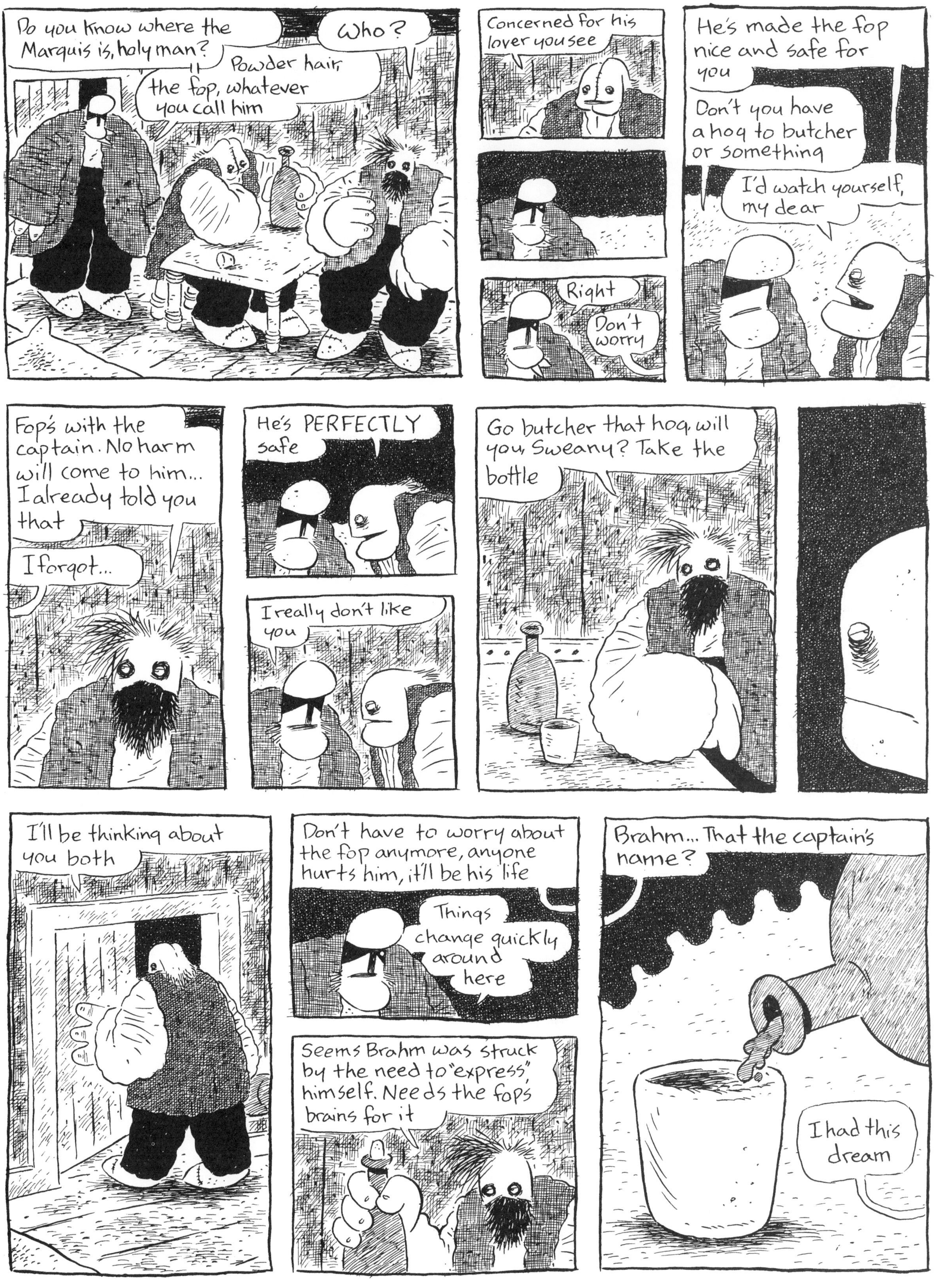
Do you know where the Marquis is, holy man?
Who?
Powder hair, the fop, whatever you call him
Concerned for his lover you see
He's made the fop nice and safe for you
Don't you have a hog to butcher or something
I'd watch yourself, my dear
Right
Don't worry
Fop's with the captain. No harm will come to him... I already told you that
I forgot...
He's PERFECTLY safe
I really don't like you
Go butcher that hog, will you, Sweany? Take the bottle
I'll be thinking about you both
Don't have to worry about the fop anymore, anyone hurts him, it'll be his life
Things change quickly around here
Seems Brahm was struck by the need to "express," himself. Needs the fop's brains for it
Brahm... That the captain's name?
I had this dream

There were a million birds still in the sky, as if it were reflecting this huge lake where they were at rest

I just saw one huge shape that shuddered and moved and then began to break apart as they flew up into something else

Then there were angels at my sides like in paintings I've seen. They carried me awhile

Then I was climbing a stony hill and I thought my heart was just going to burst

Then I was at the top. There were huge gray statues in the distance

And there was a very thin man climbing a flaming cable and he was on fire, too

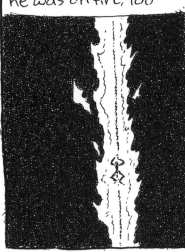

And I stood watching as the flames spread out in front of me

Why tell me about that?

I've been doing this madness for four years on different ships, and my legs are kicking in the wind

I had another dream I won't speak of... I've been resisting the demand that my bad dreams become good dreams

I tell you because of the tone of your voice. It's uncommon

Mm, don't think I've forgotten that you killed Hollows

Hen

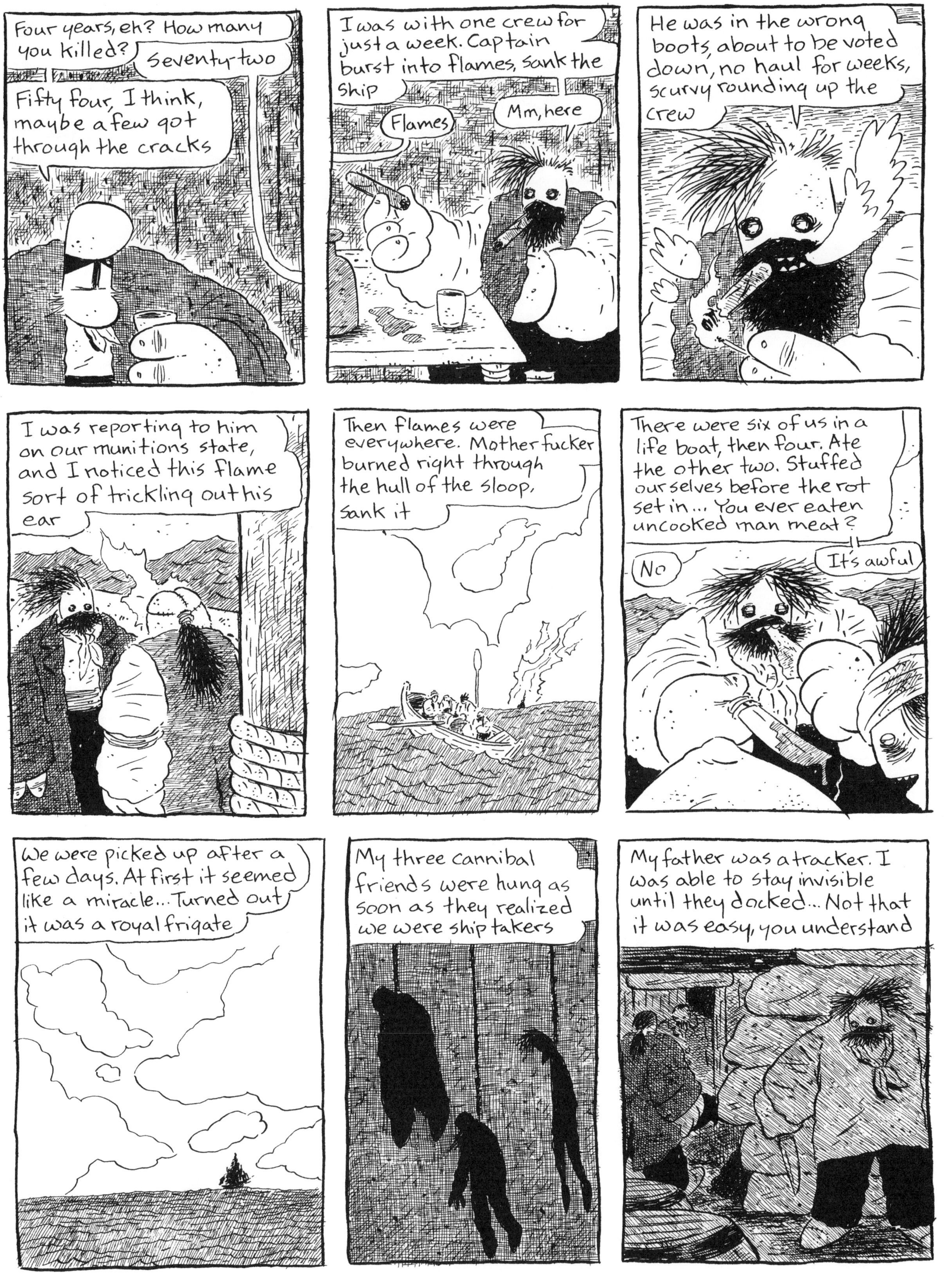
Four years, eh? How many you killed?
Seventy-two
Fifty four, I think, maybe a few got through the cracks
I was with one crew for just a week. Captain burst into flames, sank the ship
Flames
Mm, here
He was in the wrong boots, about to be voted down, no haul for weeks, scurvy rounding up the crew
I was reporting to him on our munitions state, and I noticed this flame sort of trickling out his ear
Then flames were everywhere. Mother fucker burned right through the hull of the sloop, sank it
There were six of us in a life boat, then four. Ate the other two. Stuffed ourselves before the rot set in... You ever eaten uncooked man meat?
No
It's awful
We were picked up after a few days. At first it seemed like a miracle... Turned out it was a royal frigate
My three cannibal friends were hung as soon as they realized we were ship takers
My father was a tracker. I was able to stay invisible until they docked... Not that it was easy, you understand

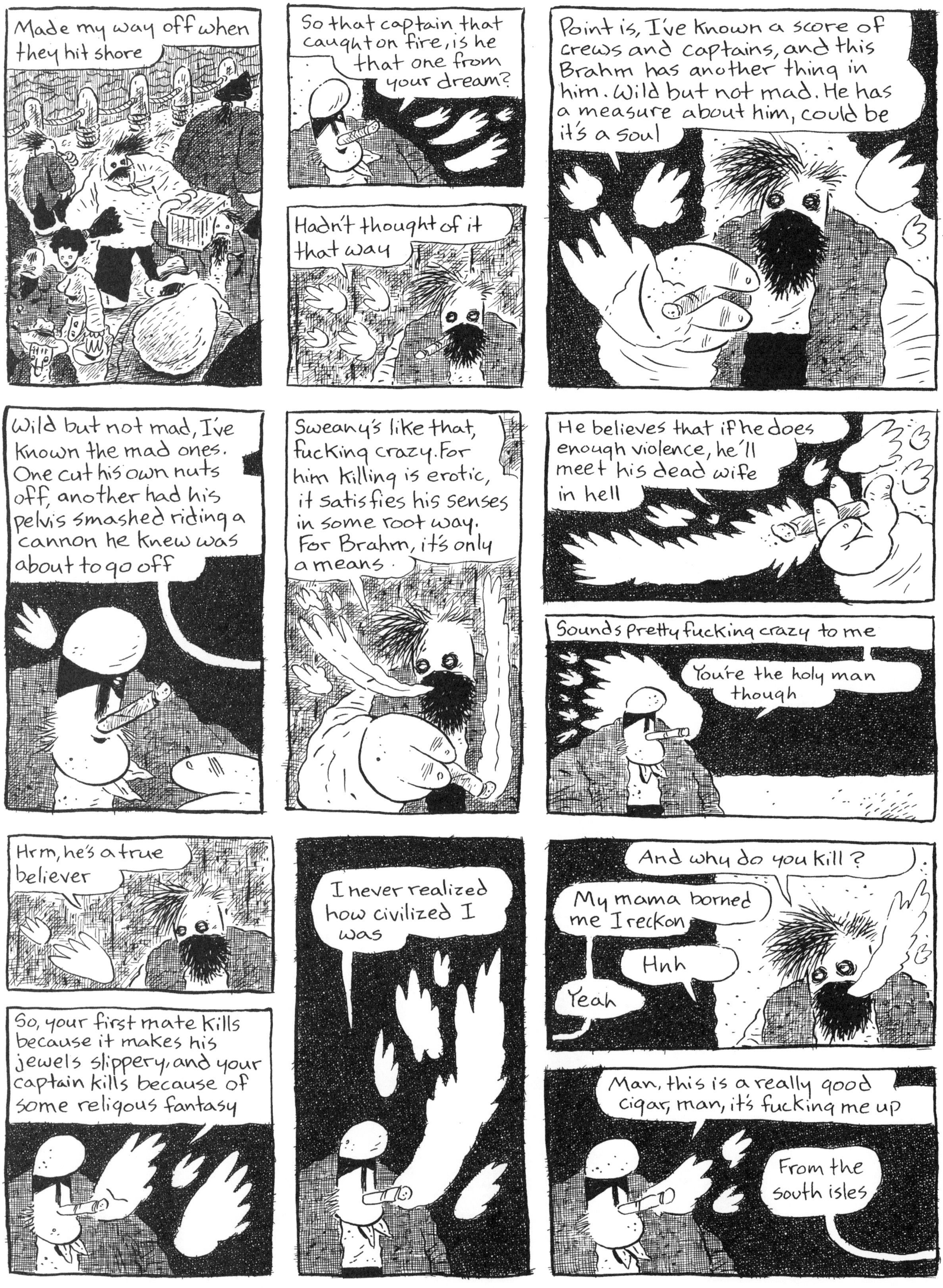

Made my way off when they hit shore
So that captain that caught on fire, is he that one from your dream?
Hadn't thought of it that way
Point is, I've known a score of crews and captains, and this Brahm has another thing in him. Wild but not mad. He has a measure about him, could be it's a soul
Wild but not mad, I've known the mad ones. One cut his own nuts off, another had his pelvis smashed riding a cannon he knew was about to go off
Sweany's like that, fucking crazy. For him killing is erotic, it satisfies his senses in some root way. For Brahm, it's only a means
He believes that if he does enough violence, he'll meet his dead wife in hell
Sounds pretty fucking crazy to me
You're the holy man though
Hrm, he's a true believer
So, your first mate kills because it makes his jewels slippery, and your captain kills because of some religous fantasy
I never realized how civilized I was
And why do you kill?
My mama borned me I reckon
Hnh
Yeah
Man, this is a really good cigar, man, it's fucking me up
From the south isles

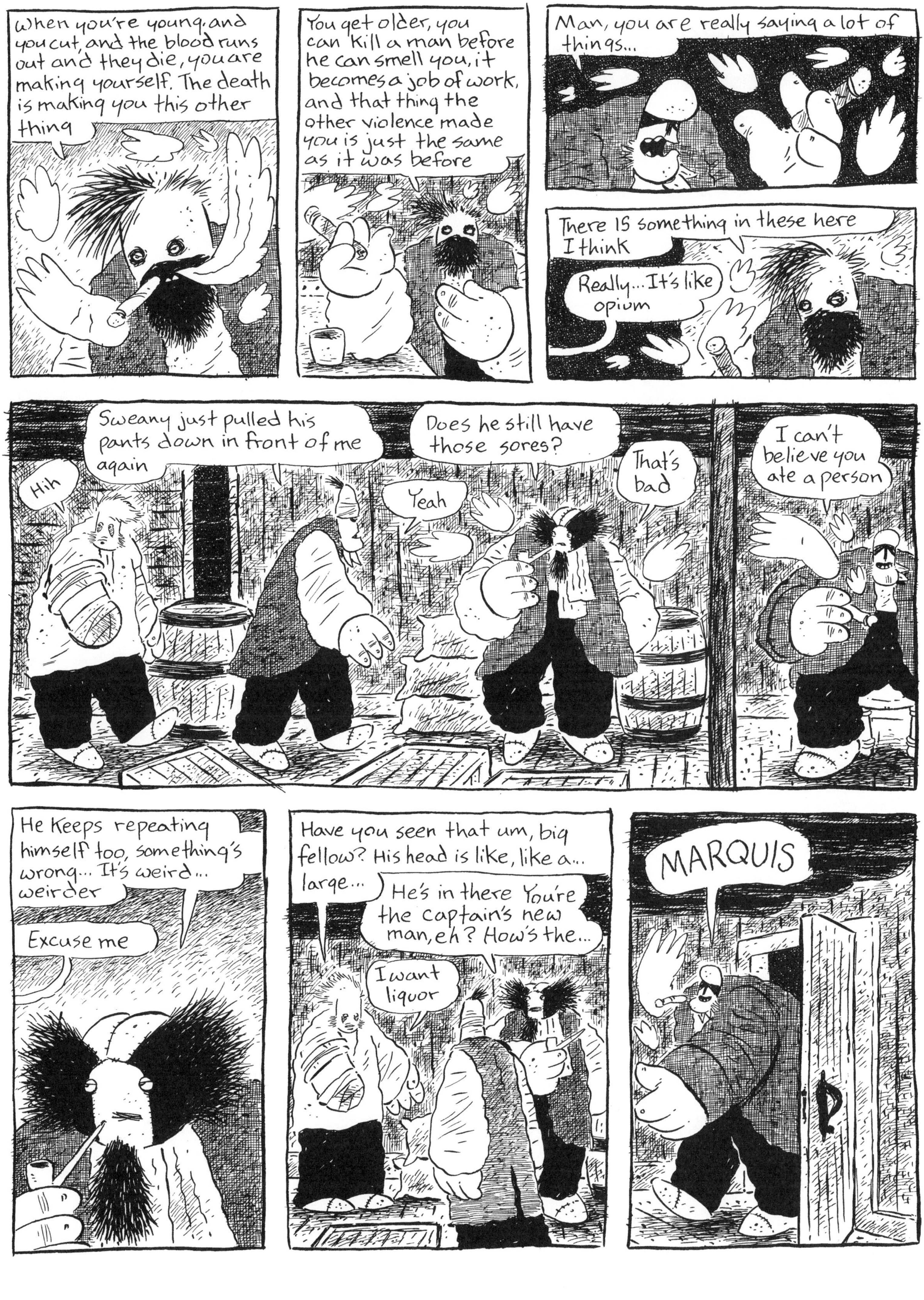
when you're young, and you cut, and the blood runs out and they die, you are making yourself. The death is making you this other thing
You get older, you can kill a man before he can smell you, it becomes a job of work, and that thing the other violence made you is just the same as it was before
Man, you are really saying a lot of things...
There IS something in these here I think
Really... It's like opium
Hih
Sweany just pulled his pants down in front of me again
Yeah
Does he still have those sores?
That's bad
I can't believe you ate a person
He Keeps repeating himself too, something's wrong... It's weird... weirder
Excuse me
Have you seen that um, big fellow? His head is like, like a... large...
He's in there You're the captain's new man, eh? How's the...
I want liquor
MARQUIS

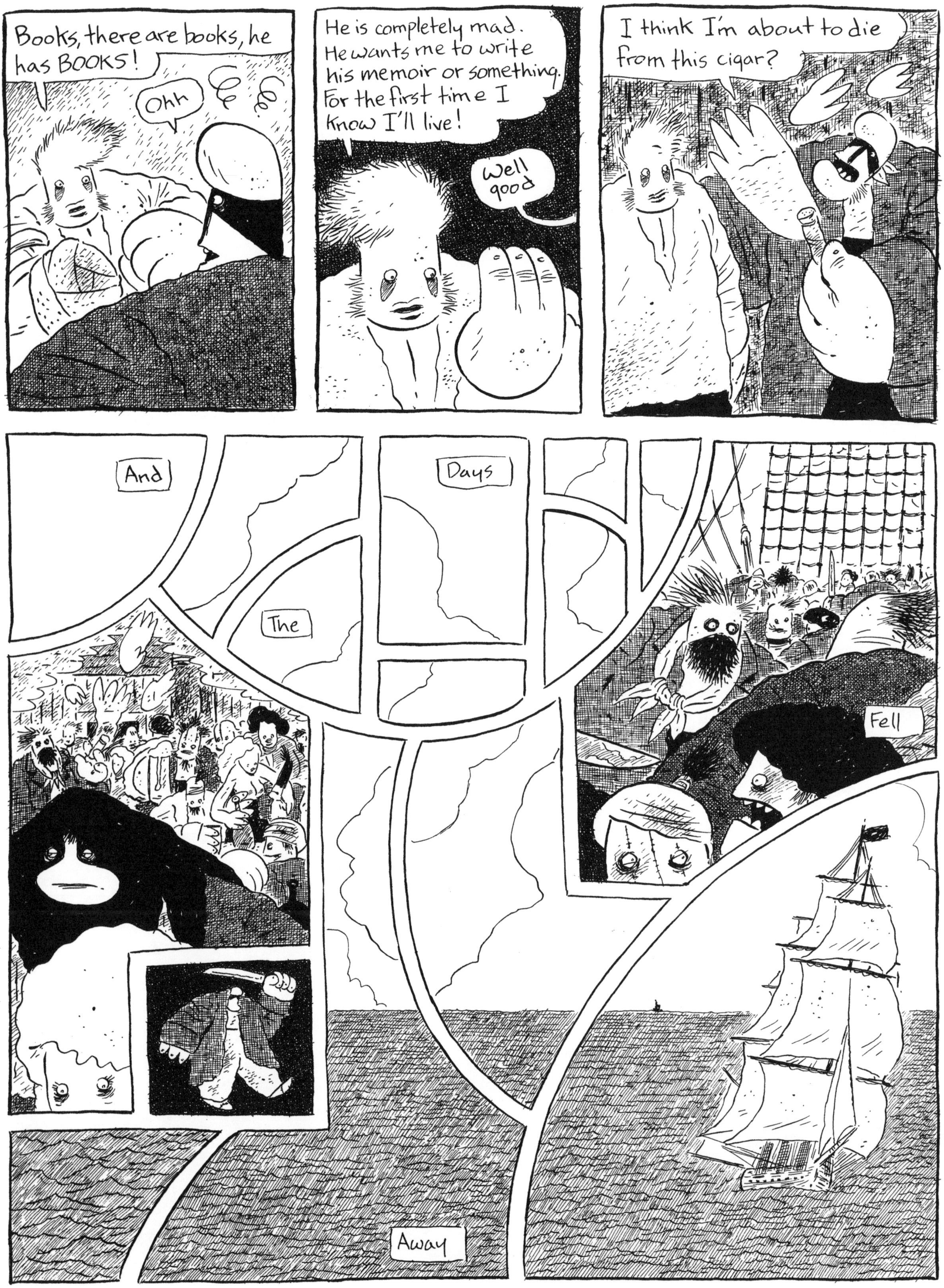
Books, there are books, he has BOOKS!
Ohh
He is completely mad. He wants me to write his memoir or something. For the first time I know I'll live!
Well good
I think I'm about to die from this cigar?
And
The
Days
Fell
Away

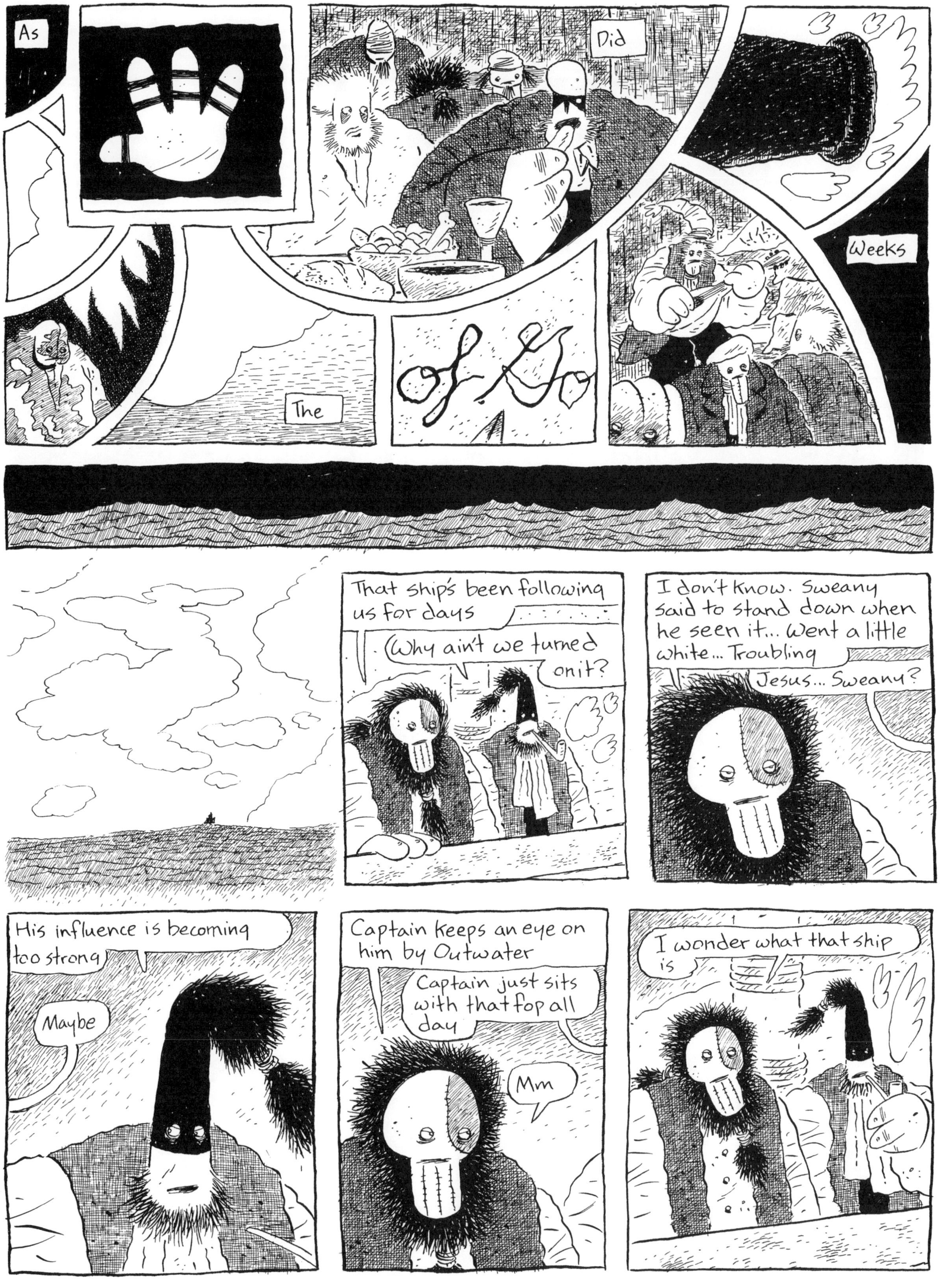
As
Did
Weeks
The
Of. Go
That ship's been following us for days
Why ain't we turned onit?
I don't know. Sweany said to stand down when he seen it... Went a little white... Troubling
Jesus... Sweany?
His influence is becoming too strong
Maybe
Captain keeps an eye on him by Outwater
Captain just sits with that fop all day
Mm
I wonder what that ship is

Back back she's back she's back back back back nnnnnnnqq back back nnnqqnn back back KNOCK KNOCK

KNOCK KNOCK

Sweany...

Shit... What are you...

Mmmenhh

"Though changed in outward lustre, that fixed mind / And high disdain from sense of injured merit / That with the Mightiest raised me to contend, / And to the fierce contention brought along Innumerable force of spirits armed..."

Fuck

"...That durst dislike his reign, / And, me preferring / His utmost power with adverse power opposed / In dubious battle on the plains of Heaven, / And shook His throne. What though the field be lost?..."

Oh Teasley, I am sorry

"...All is not lost; the unconquerable will, / And study of revenge, immortal hate, / And courage never to submit or yield, / And what else not to be overcome, / That glory never shall his wrath or might / Exort from me..."

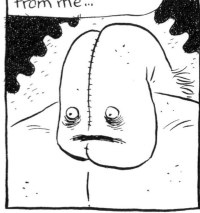

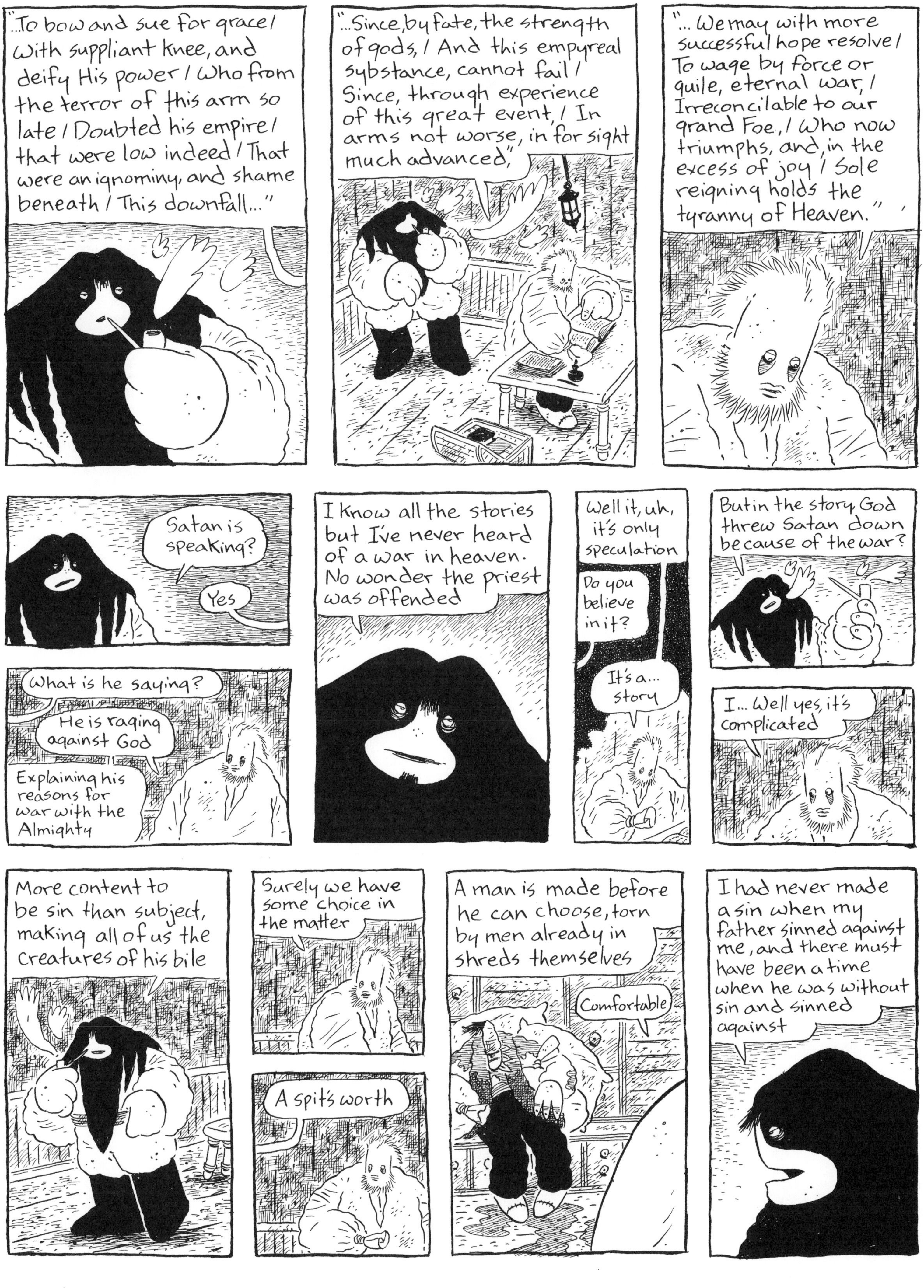
"...To bow and sue for grace / With suppliant knee, and deify His power / Who from the terror of this arm so late / Doubted his empire / that were low indeed / That were an ignominy, and shame beneath / This downfall..."
"...Since, by fate, the strength of gods, / And this empyreal substance, cannot fail / Since, through experience of this great event, / In arms not worse, in for sight much advanced,"
"... We may with more successful hope resolve / To wage by force or guile, eternal war, / Irreconcilable to our grand Foe, / Who now triumphs, and, in the excess of joy / Sole reigning holds the tyranny of Heaven."
Satan is speaking?
Yes
What is he saying?
He is raging against God
Explaining his reasons for war with the Almighty
I know all the stories but I've never heard of a war in heaven. No wonder the priest was offended
Well it, uh, it's only speculation
Do you believe in it?
It's a... story
But in the story, God threw Satan down because of the war?
I... Well yes, it's complicated
More content to be sin than subject, making all of us the creatures of his bile
Surely we have some choice in the matter
A spit's worth
A man is made before he can choose, torn by men already in shreds themselves
Comfortable
I had never made a sin when my father sinned against me, and there must have been a time when he was without sin and sinned against

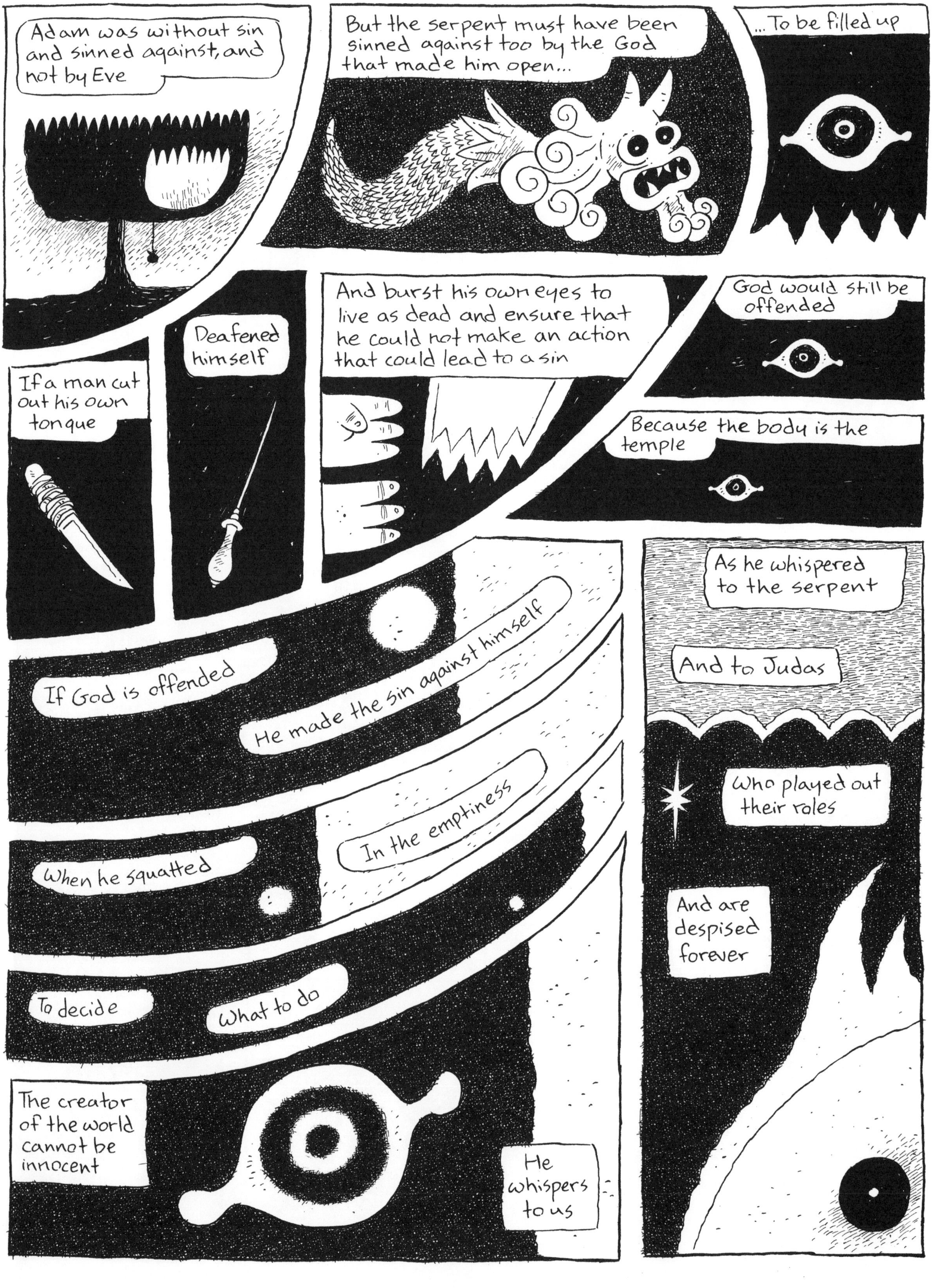
Adam was without sin and sinned against, and not by Eve
But the serpent must have been sinned against too by the God that made him open...
...To be filled up
If a man cut out his own tongue
Deafened himself
And burst his own eyes to live as dead and ensure that he could not make an action that could lead to a sin
God would still be offended
Because the body is the temple
If God is offended
He made the sin against himself
When he squatted
In the emptiness
To decide
What to do
The creator of the world cannot be innocent
He whispers to us
As he whispered to the serpent
And to Judas
Who played out their roles
And are despised forever

Why not a war in heaven?

You've considered this

He comes in the darkness

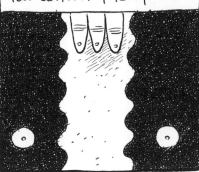

A thing like water rushing through my outstretched hands. I feel that I want to pour out of my eyes and join with it. My heart is seized, my throat is choked fat with my tongue...

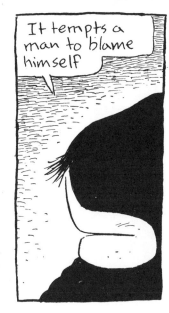

Which can only wag with silent curses

I'm full already, you bastard,

of all you've had to offer me

Surely there is more than sin to be offered

Name it

Love... I suppose

So much of the filth in history can be pulled back into love. It is His masterpiece

It tempts a man to blame himself

And to think that he will be something other, when the sin has left him

Then you give everything away?

It may be...

It may be that a man can gather the dangling ends of his grievous acts and weave them into some crude pattern he doesn't desire... But which God doesn't either

Why do you know about these things? The books?

Uh... University

I uh, read as a child and didn't understand. I got older and, uh, started solving some of the mysteries

I felt a, uh, well-deserved intimacy. I went to university, studied, wrote, published. I had actually published twelve articles and a book

I got my master's, became a professor... What I always wanted... Then there was an affair, my first of any kind, a student. I couldn't refuse her. I had only ever touched my mother

Hnf

I was dismissed... I had to begin teaching children. Their, uh... enthusiasms were... not like mine had been

But my unhappiness was tempered by Vivian... Hardly feels real to say her name. Can I claim her as the love of my life when I've only loved twice?

I drove her away

Then I was cruel

Thinking it would rouse her to defend her love for me

I didn't mean to speak so much

All right

Vivian...

Was there a woman?

Not now

My own name hardly sounds real to me

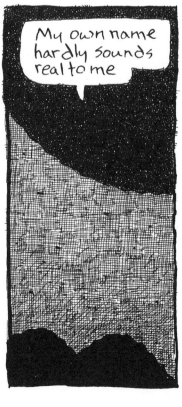

Anymore

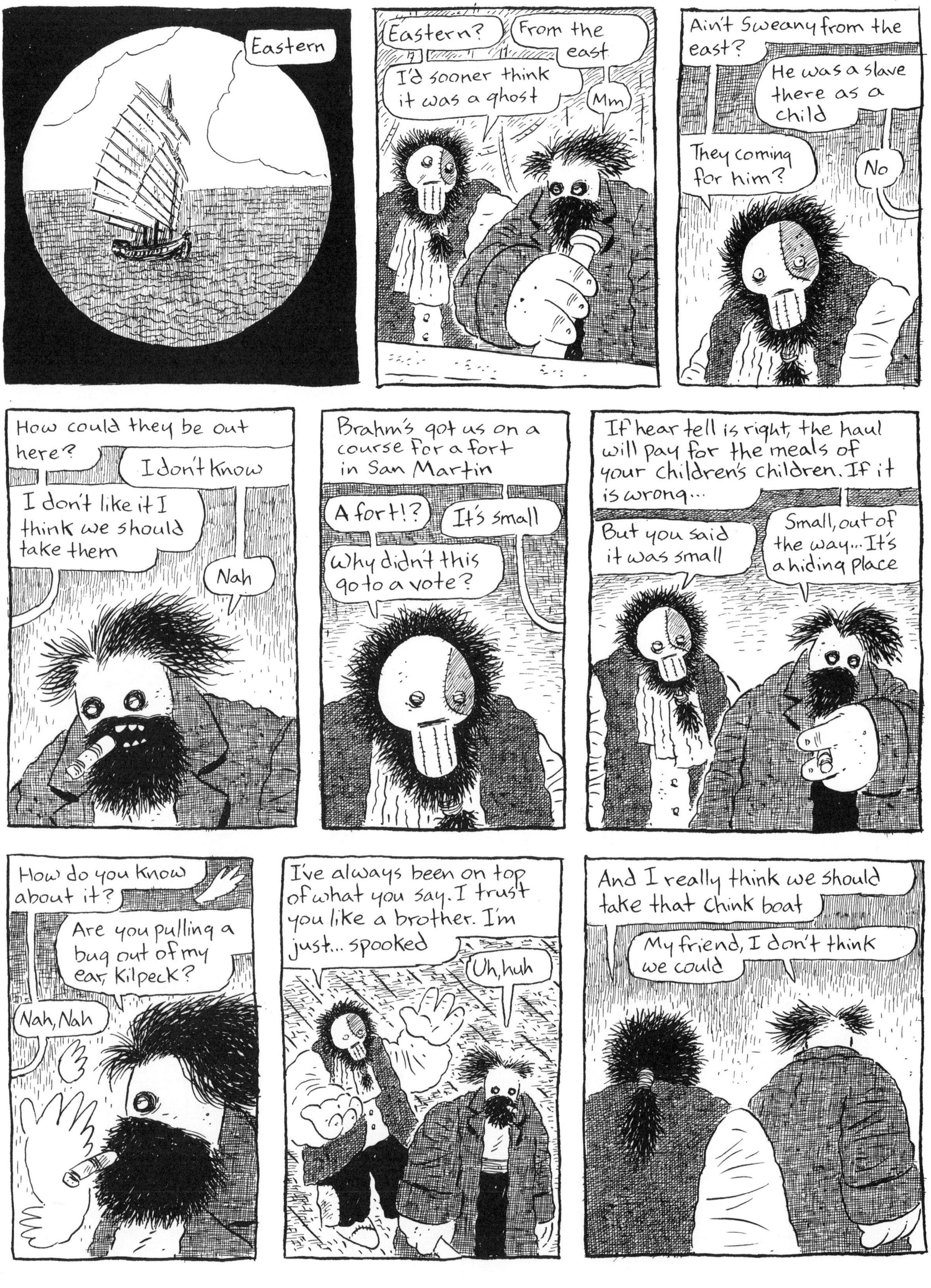
Eastern
Eastern?
From the east
I'd sooner think it was a ghost
Mm
Ain't Sweany from the east?
He was a slave there as a child
They coming for him?
No
How could they be out here?
I don't know
I don't like it I think we should take them
Nah
Brahm's got us on a course for a fort in San Martin
A fort!?
It's small
Why didn't this go to a vote?
If hear tell is right, the haul will pay for the meals of your children's children. If it is wrong...
But you said it was small
Small, out of the way... It's a hiding place
How do you know about it?
Are you pulling a bug out of my ear, Kilpeck?
Nah, Nah
I've always been on top of what you say. I trust you like a brother. I'm just... spooked
Uh, huh
And I really think we should take that Chink boat
My friend, I don't think we could

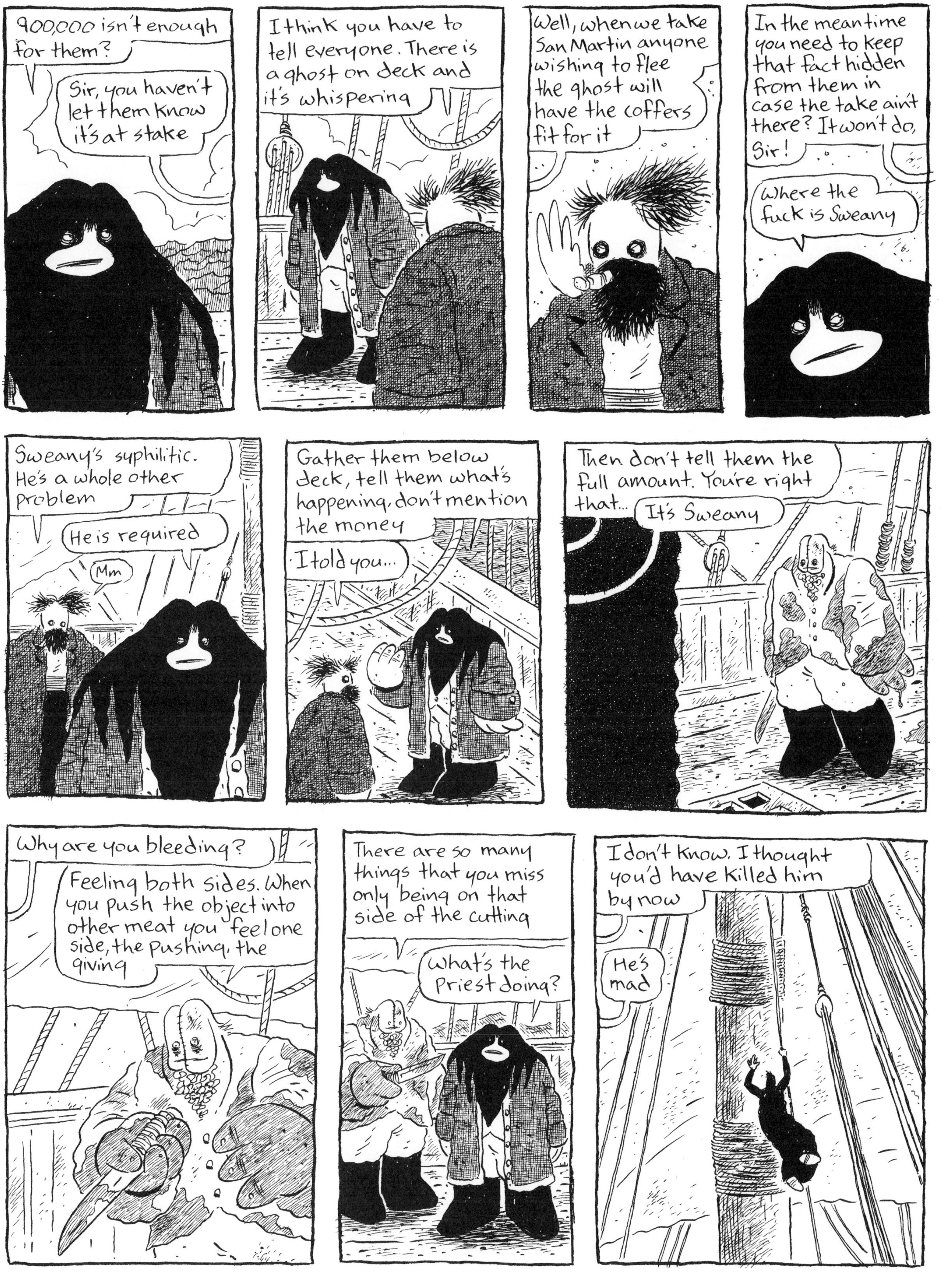
900,000 isn't enough for them?
Sir, you haven't let them know it's at stake
I think you have to tell everyone. There is a ghost on deck and it's whispering
Well, when we take San Martin anyone wishing to flee the ghost will have the coffers fit for it
In the mean time you need to keep that fact hidden from them in case the take ain't there? It won't do, Sir!
Where the fuck is Sweany
Sweany's syphilitic. He's a whole other problem
He is required
Mm
Gather them below deck, tell them what's happening, don't mention the money
I told you...
Then don't tell them the full amount. You're right that...
It's Sweany
Why are you bleeding?
Feeling both sides. When you push the object into other meat you feel one side, the pushing, the giving
There are so many things that you miss only being on that side of the cutting
What's the Priest doing?
I don't know. I thought you'd have killed him by now
He's mad

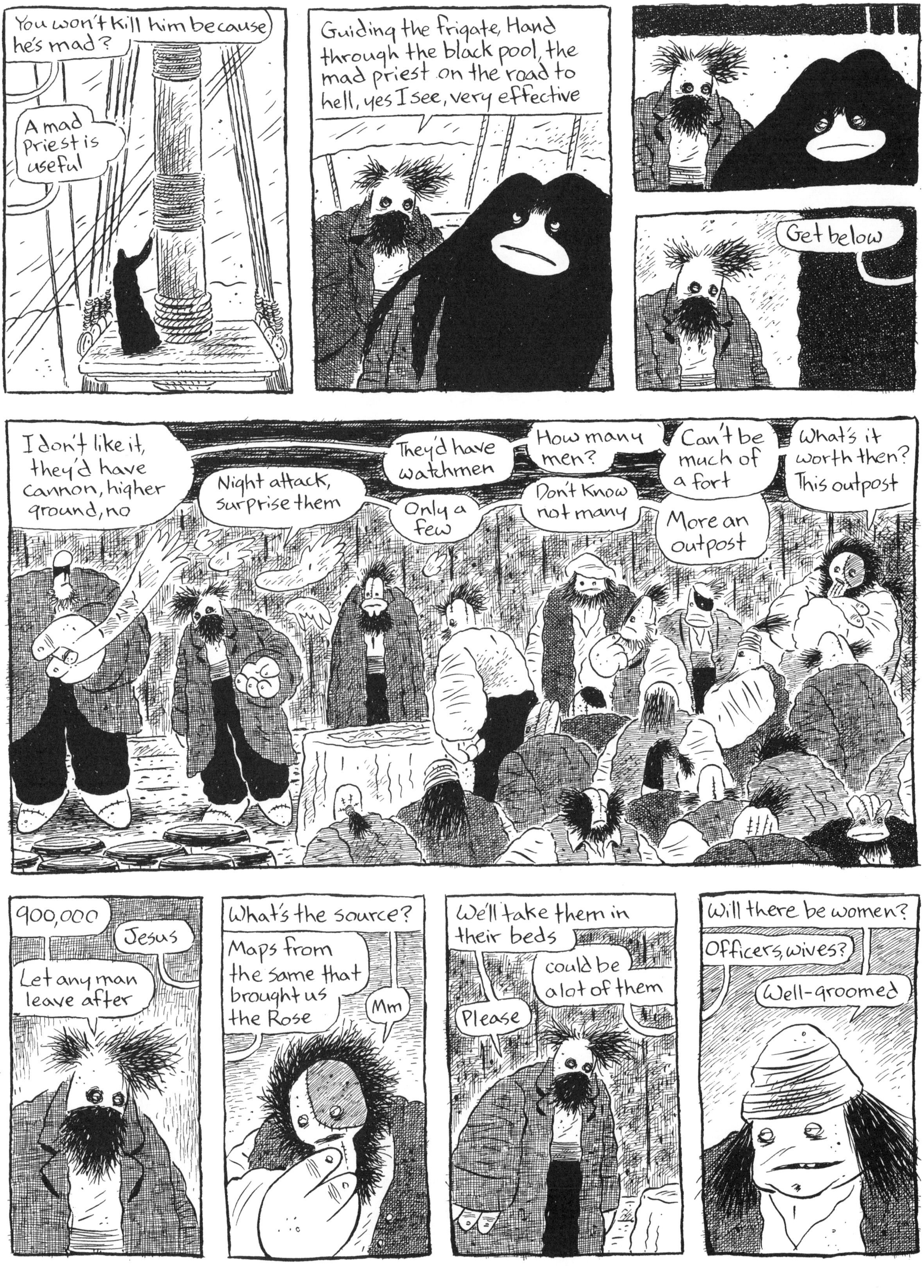
You won't kill him because he's mad?
A mad Priest is useful
Guiding the frigate, Hand through the black pool, the mad priest on the road to hell, yes I see, very effective
Get below
I don't like it, they'd have cannon, higher ground, no
Night attack, surprise them
They'd have watchmen
Only a few
How many men?
Don't Know not many
Can't be much of a fort
More an outpost
What's it worth then? This outpost
900,000
Jesus
Let any man leave after
What's the source?
Maps from the same that brought us the Rose
Mm
We'll take them in their beds
could be a lot of them
Please
Will there be women?
Officers, wives?
Well-groomed

Maybe a whore camp too... soldiers can't be far away from whores for long

900,000, Women, silver, livestock, everything else... We go tonight

If you don't want to fight, you won't be forced, but you'll have no say in the gains

We'll vote anyway

... Aye

Aye

Aye

Aye

Nay Aye

Aye

Aye Oh?

If I can make two arms' worth AND get the fuck off this wreck? COURSE

Nay

Aye

Aye Aye

Aye

Hrm

We fight at San Martin then

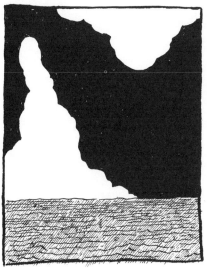

You're an ignorant man

What?

I said, you're ignorant

I, uh

You make a claim for your books. The stakes of war, old man and his dead daughters, man dying of poison, woman carving her own gut

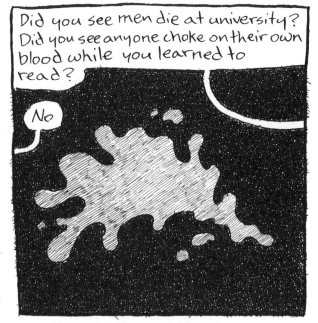

Did you see men die at university? Did you see anyone choke on their own blood while you learned to read?

No

Tonight will be your other university

What?

I won't put you in the thick of it. You'll have a survey at the end

You'll land with us

Come

Thanks for the knives

They're nothing special

Anyone know where Teasley is?

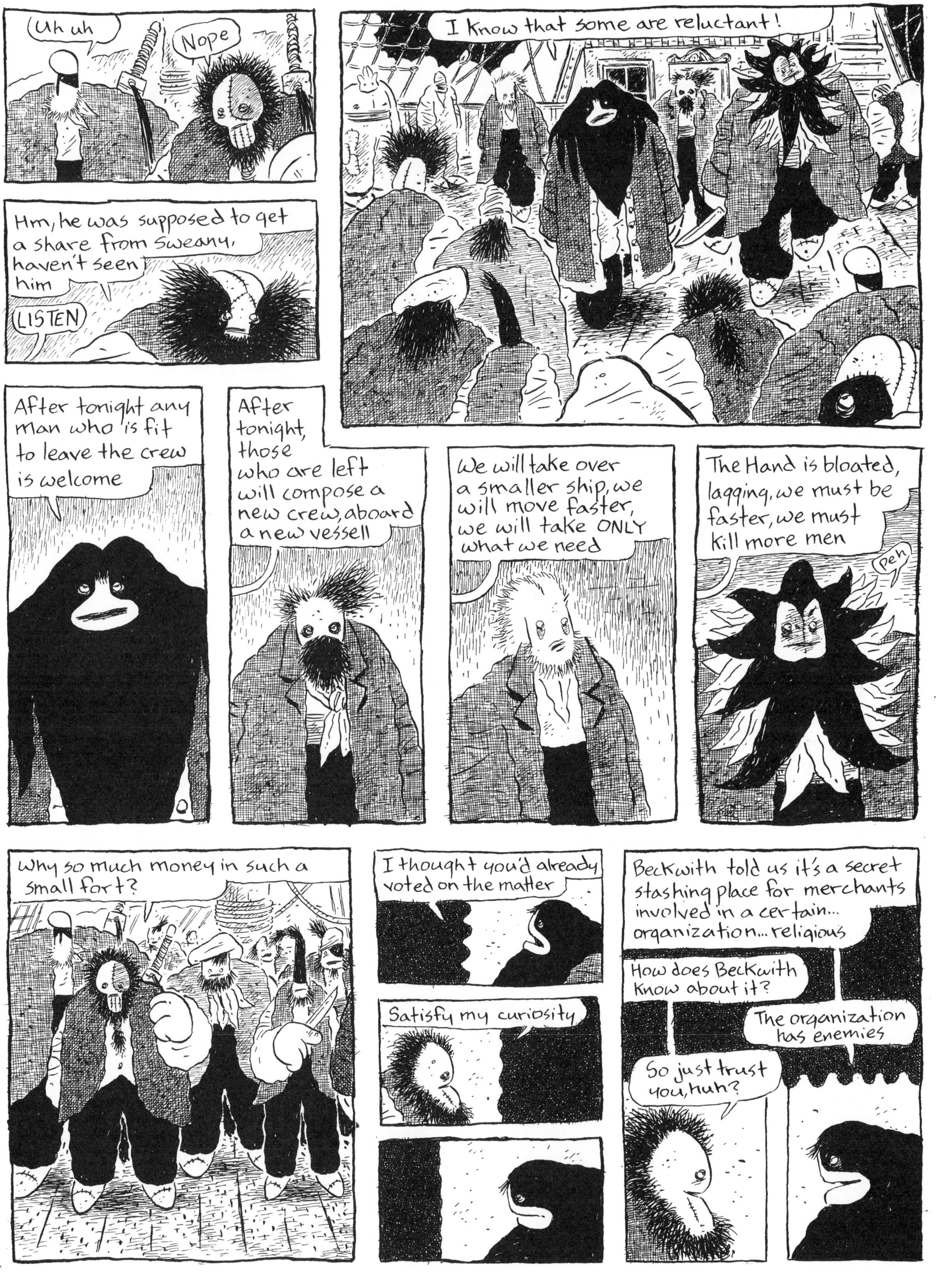
Uh uh
Nope
I know that some are reluctant!
Hm, he was supposed to get a share from Sweany, haven't seen him
LISTEN
After tonight any man who is fit to leave the crew is welcome
After tonight, those who are left will compose a new crew, aboard a new vessell
We will take over a smaller ship, we will move faster, we will take ONLY what we need
The Hand is bloated, lagging, we must be faster, we must kill more men
peh
Why so much money in such a small fort?
I thought you'd already voted on the matter
Satisfy my curiosity
Beckwith told us it's a secret stashing place for merchants involved in a certain... organization... religious
How does Beckwith know about it?
The organization has enemies
So just trust you, huh?

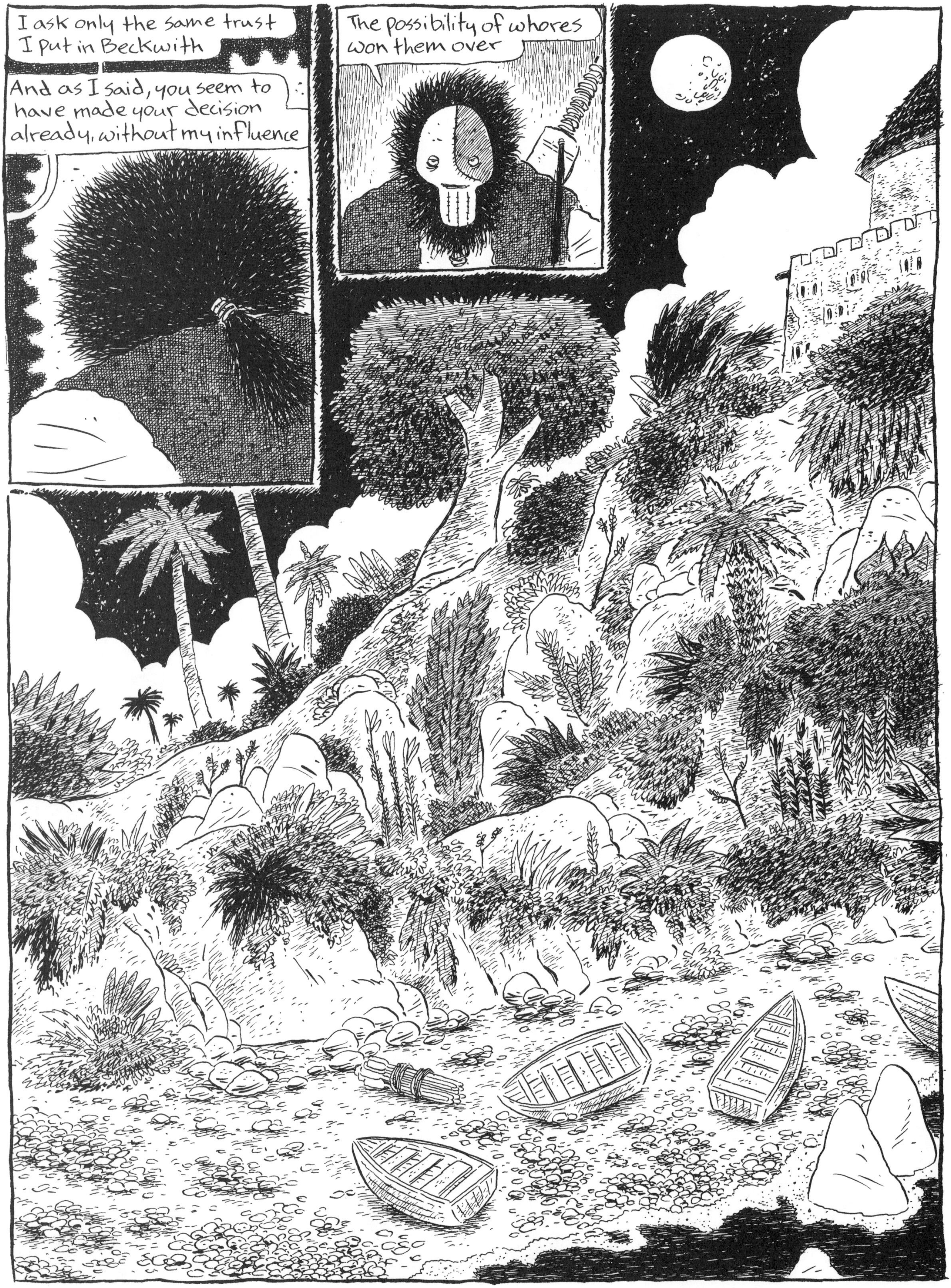

I ask only the same trust I put in Beckwith
And as I said, you seem to have made your decision already, without my influence
The possibility of whores won them over

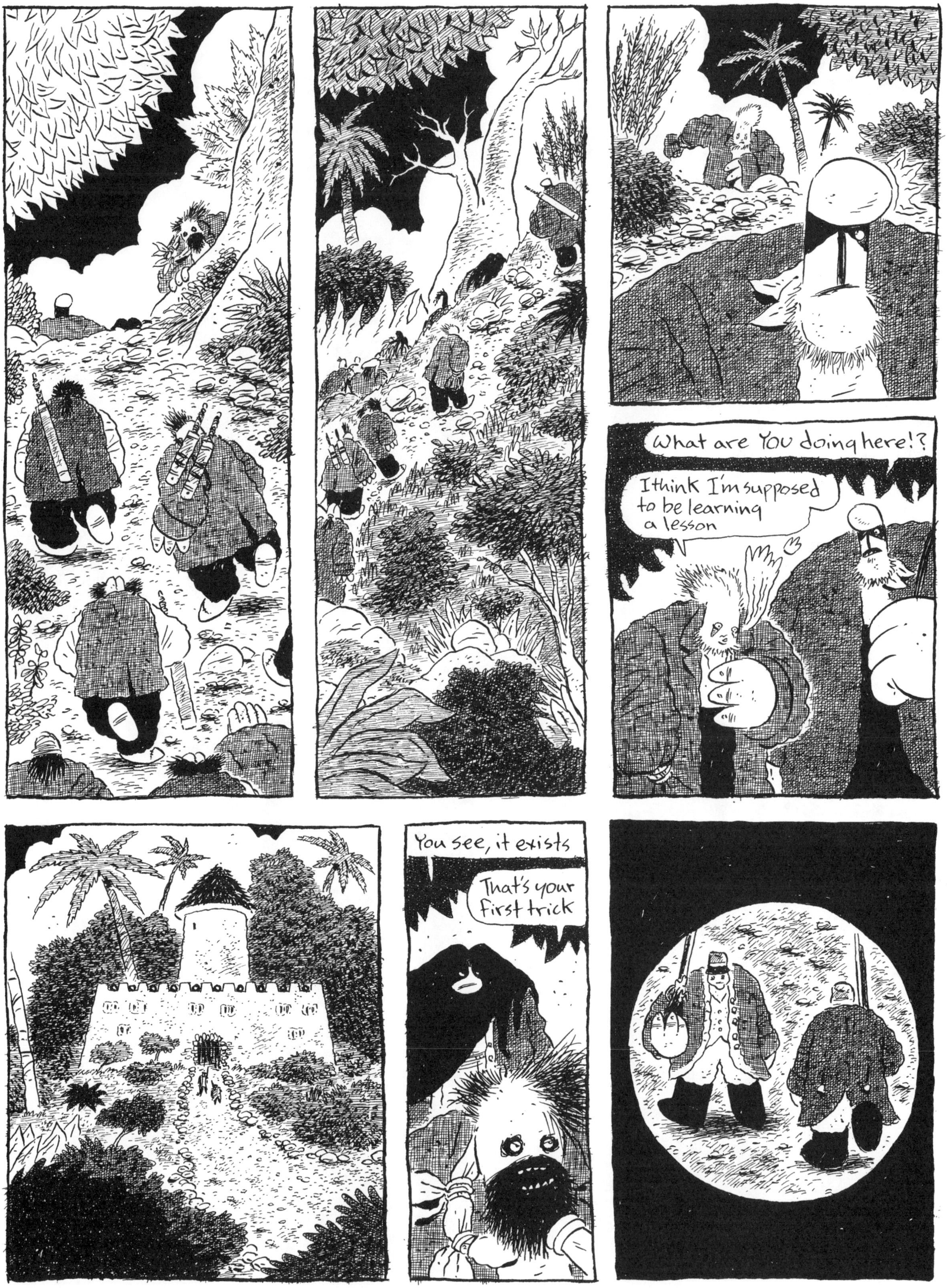
What are YOU doing here!?
I think I'm supposed to be learning a lesson
You see, it exists
That's your first trick

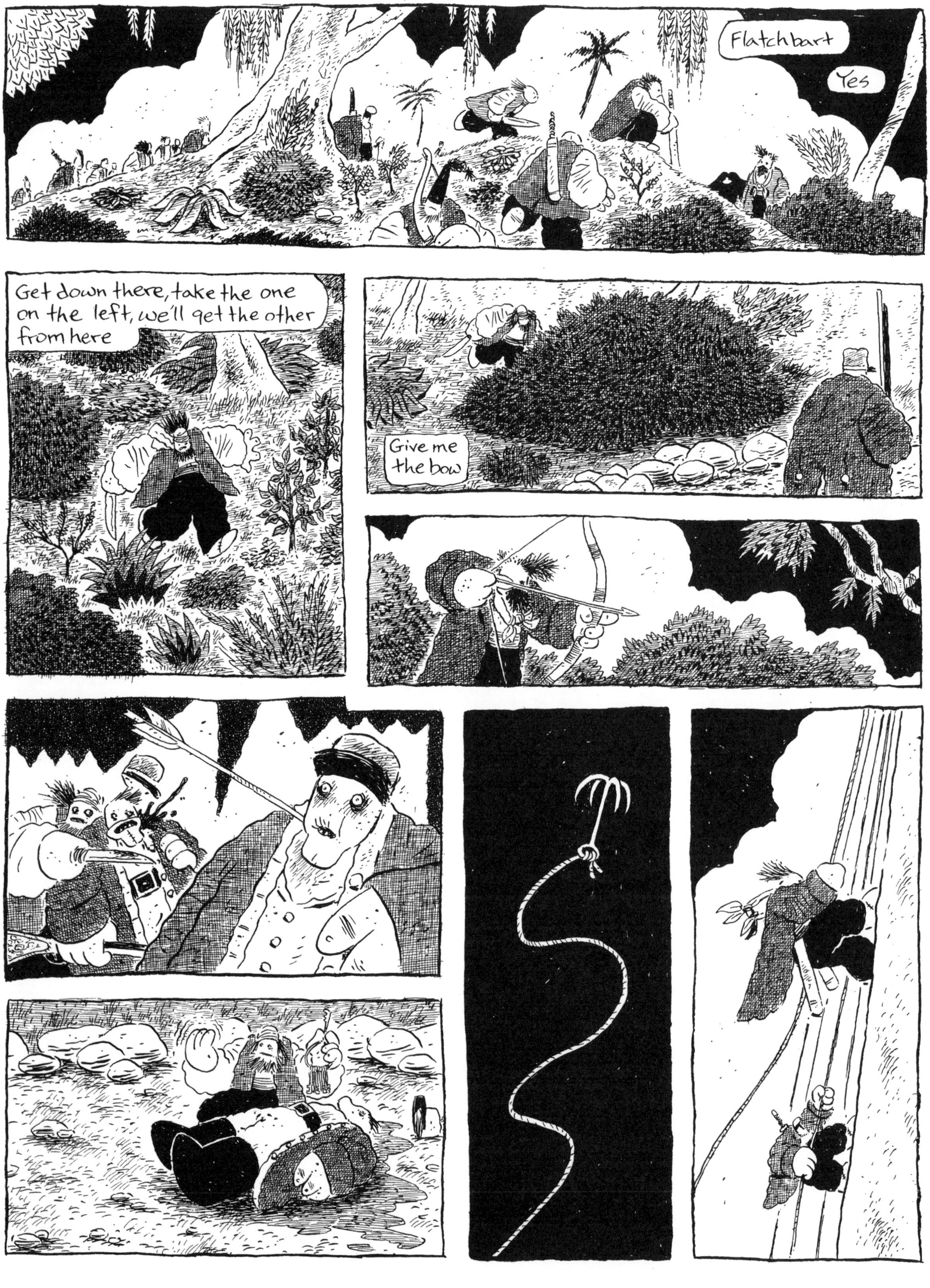
Flatchbart
Yes
Get down there, take the one on the left, we'll get the other from here
Give me the bow

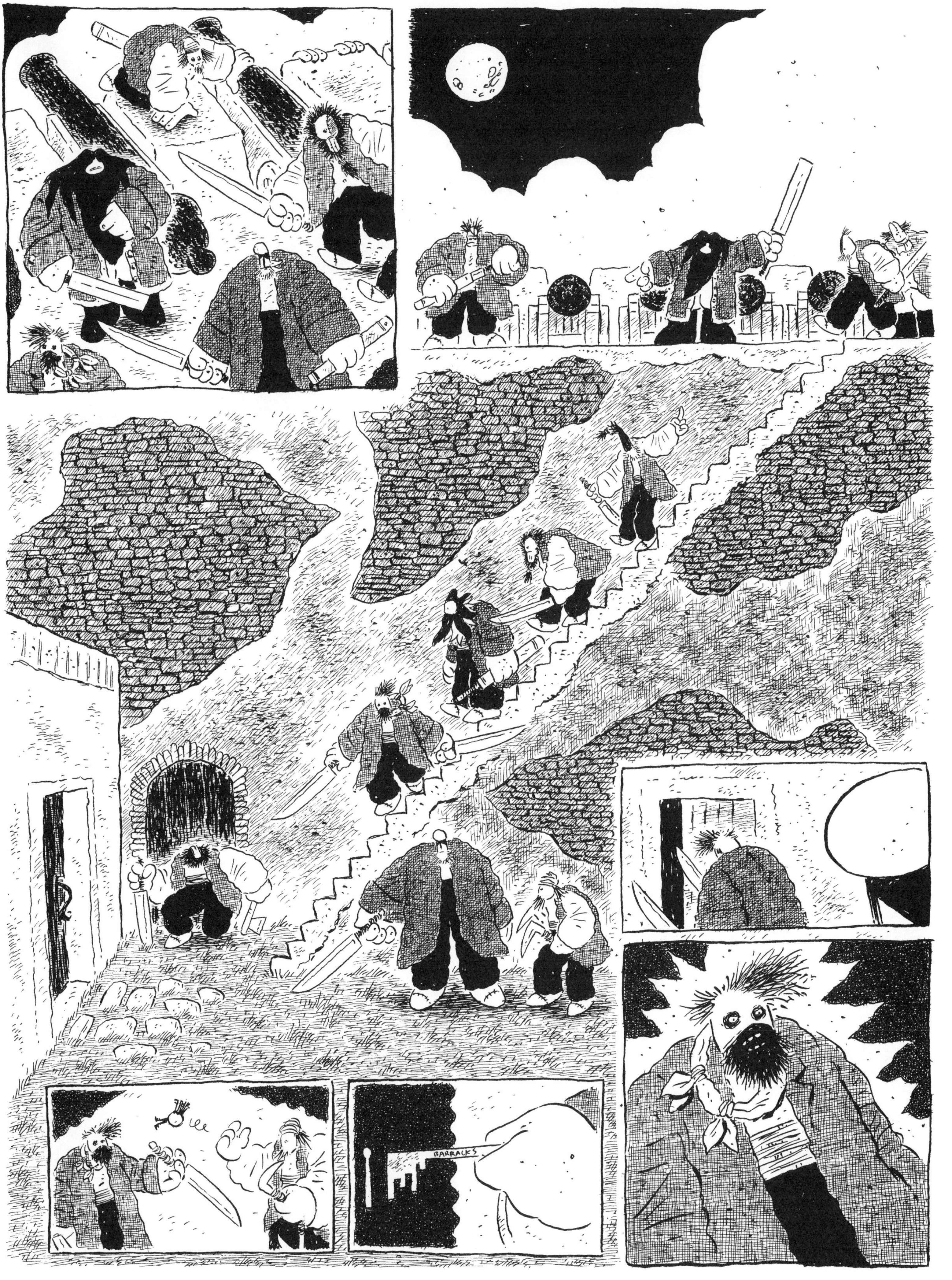
BARRACKS

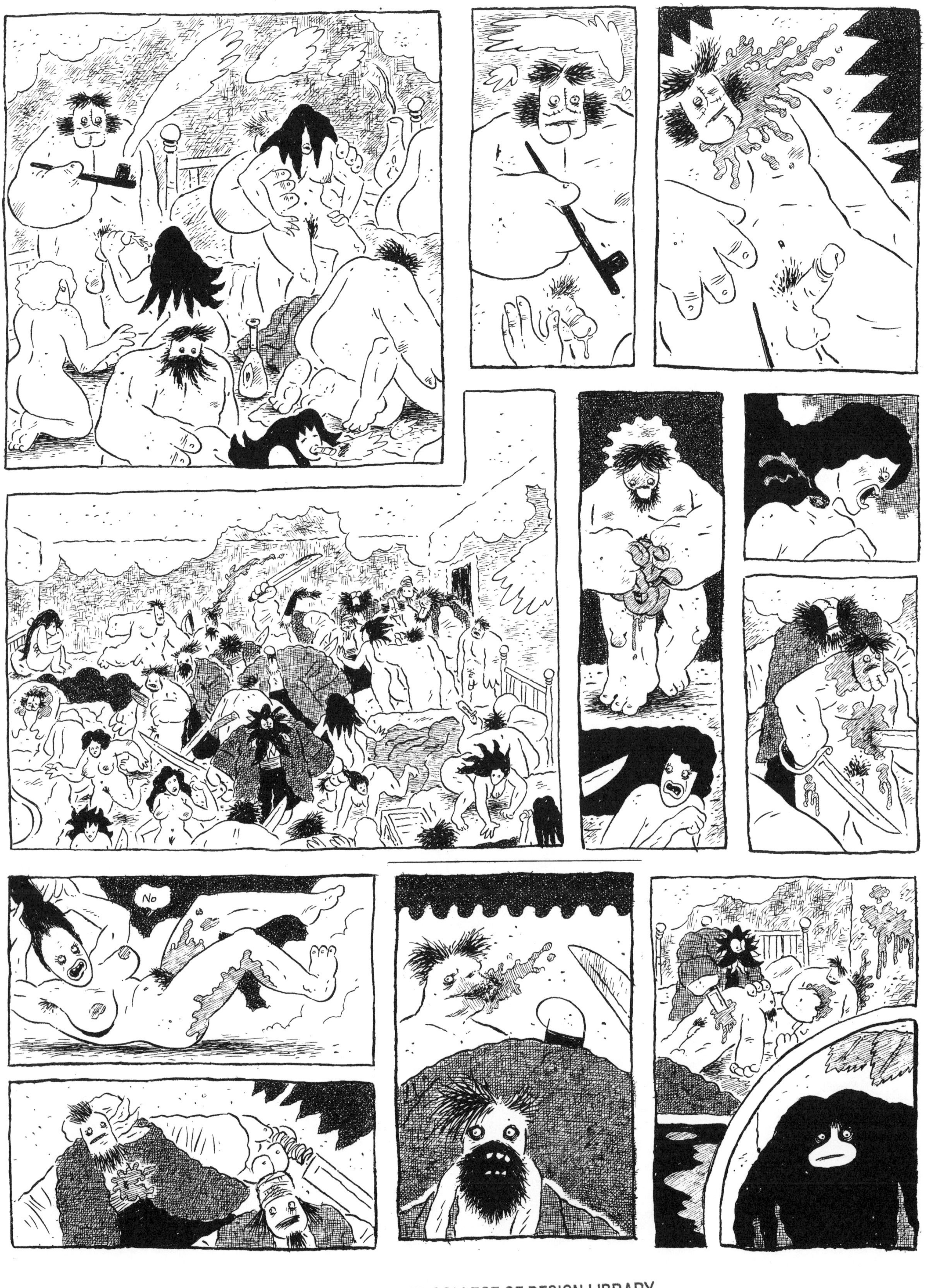
No

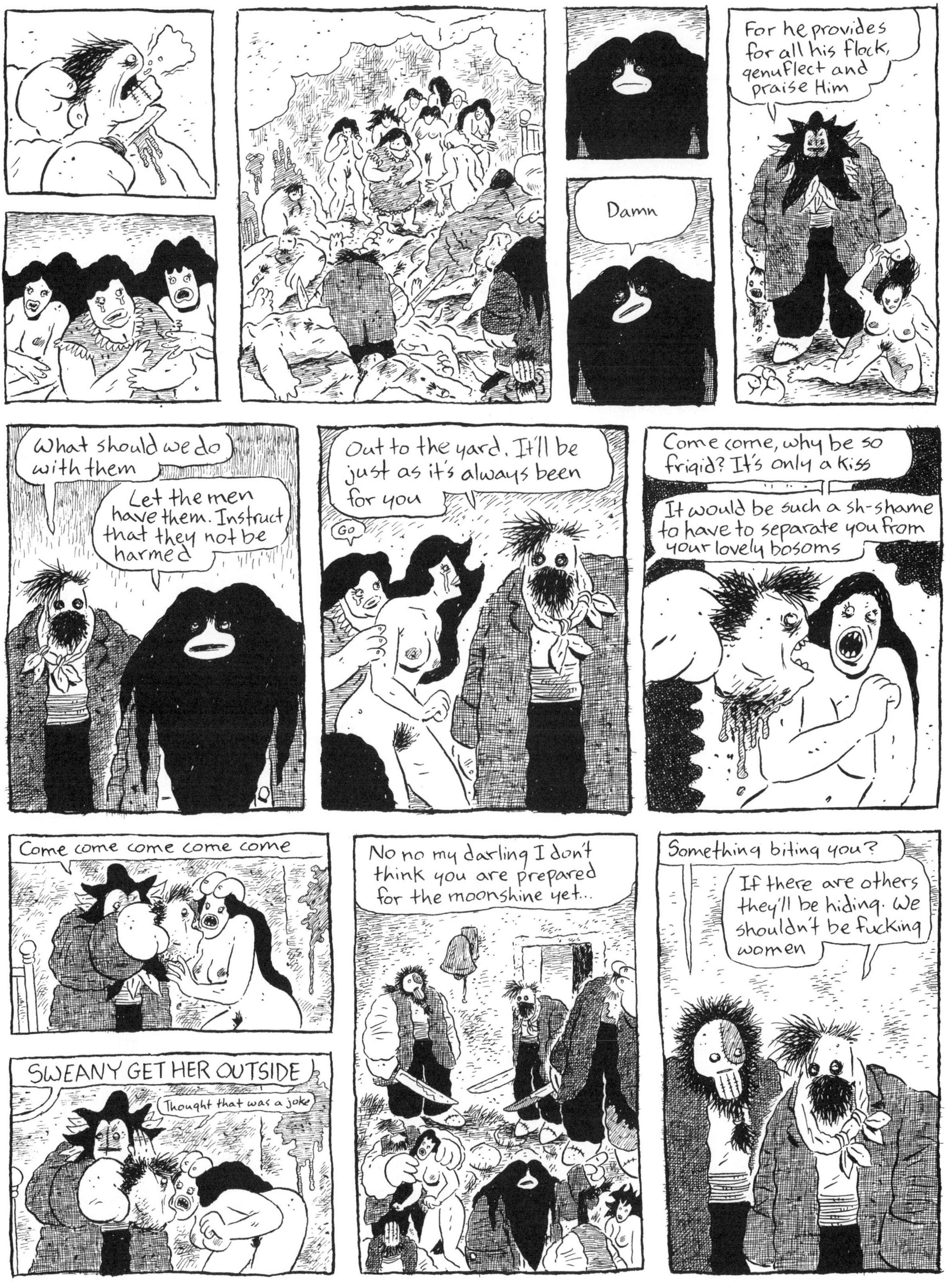

For he provides for all his flock, genuflect and praise Him
Damn
What should we do with them
Let the men have them. Instruct that they not be harmed
Out to the yard. It'll be just as it's always been for you
Go
Come come, why be so frigid? It's only a kiss
It would be such a sh-shame to have to separate you from your lovely bosoms
Come come come come come
SWEANY GET HER OUTSIDE
Thought that was a joke
No no my darling I don't think you are prepared for the moonshine yet...
Something biting you?
If there are others they'll be hiding. We shouldn't be fucking women

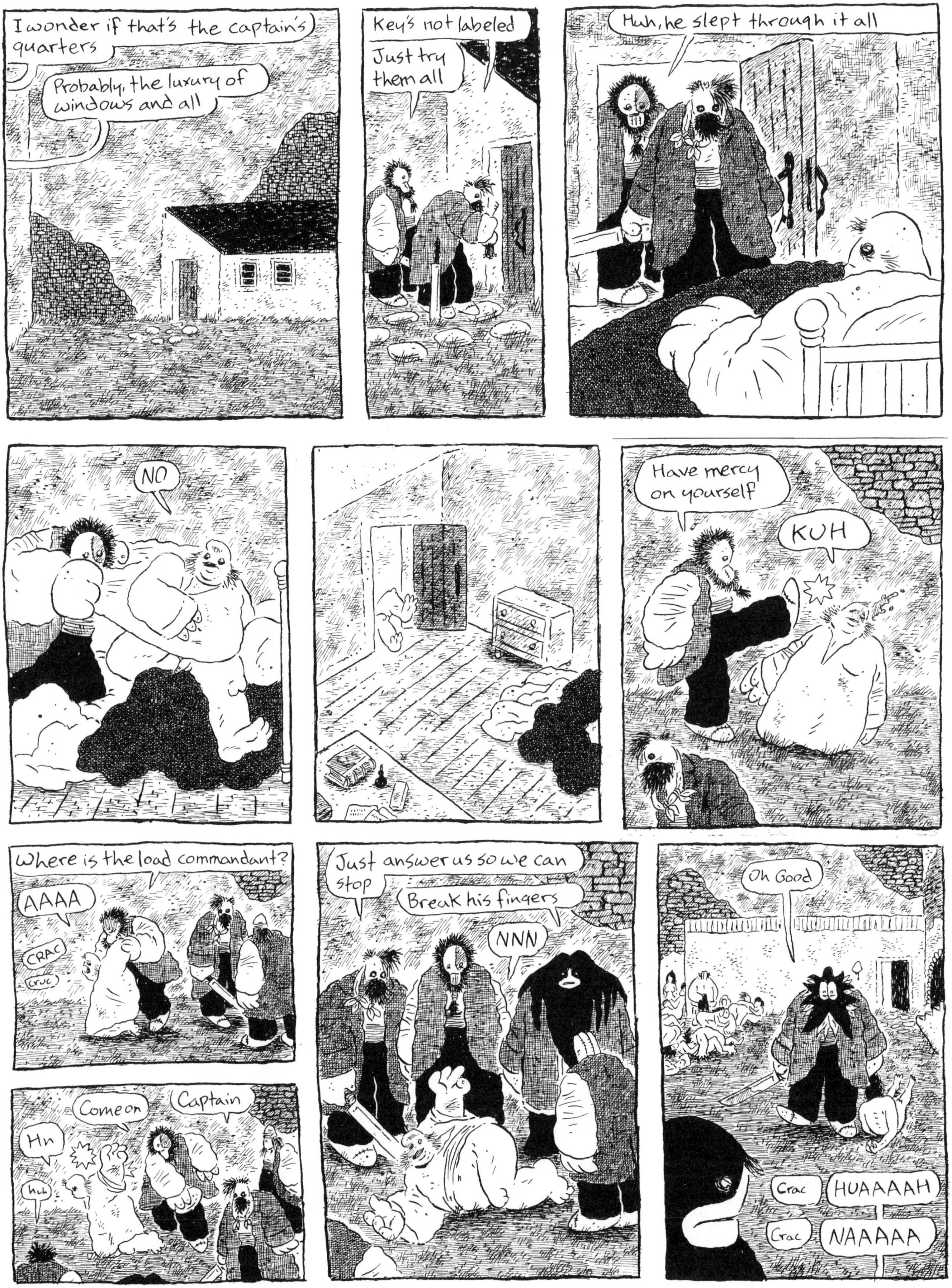
I wonder if that's the captain's quarters
Probably, the luxury of windows and all
Key's not labeled
Just try them all
Huh, he slept through it all
NO
Have mercy on yourself
KUH
Where is the load commandant?
AAAA
CRAC
crac
Hn
huh
Come on
Captain
Just answer us so we can stop
Break his fingers
NNN
Oh Good
Crac
HUAAAAH
Crac
NAAAAA

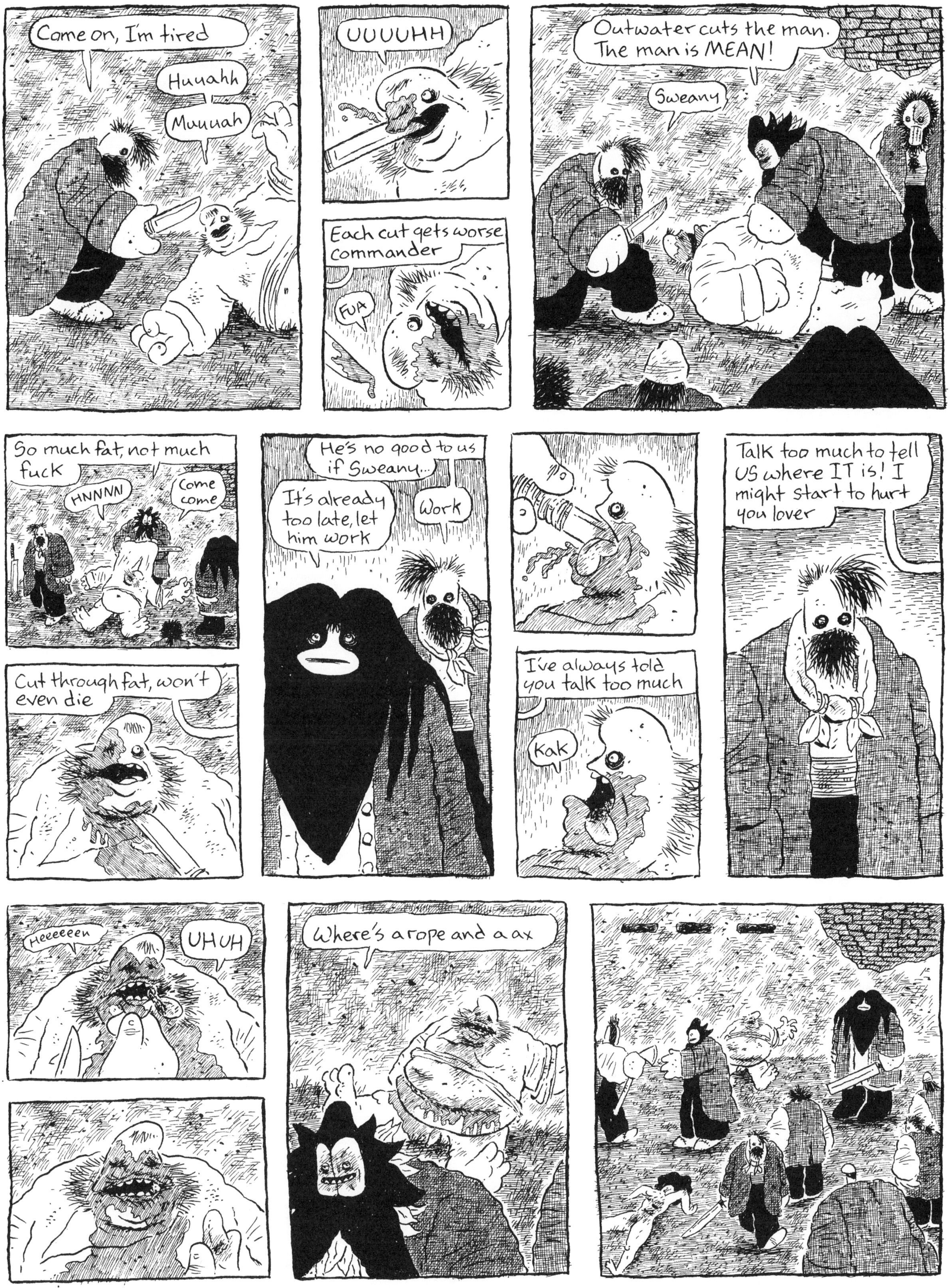
Come on, I'm tired
Huuahh
Muuuah
UUUUHH
Each cut gets worse commander
FUA
Outwater cuts the man. The man is MEAN!
Sweany
So much fat, not much fuck
HNNNN
Come come
Cut through fat, won't even die
He's no good to us if Sweany...
It's already too late, let him work
Work
I've always told you talk too much
Kak
Talk too much to tell US where IT is! I might start to hurt you lover
Heeeeeen
UHUH
Where's a rope and a ax

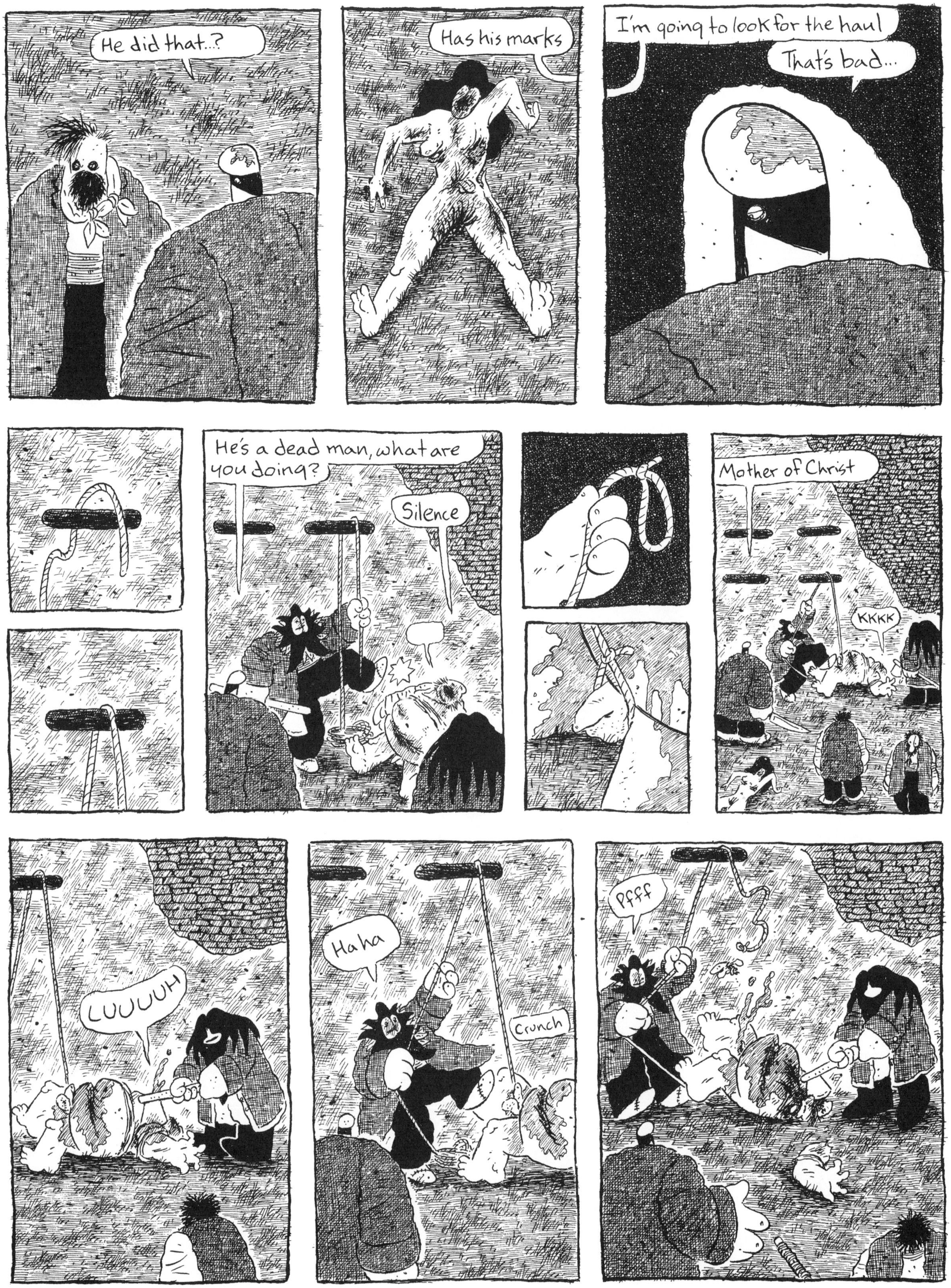

He did that..?
Has his marks
I'm going to look for the haul
That's bad...
He's a dead man, what are you doing?
Silence
Mother of Christ
KKKK
LUUUUH
Ha ha
Crunch
Pfff

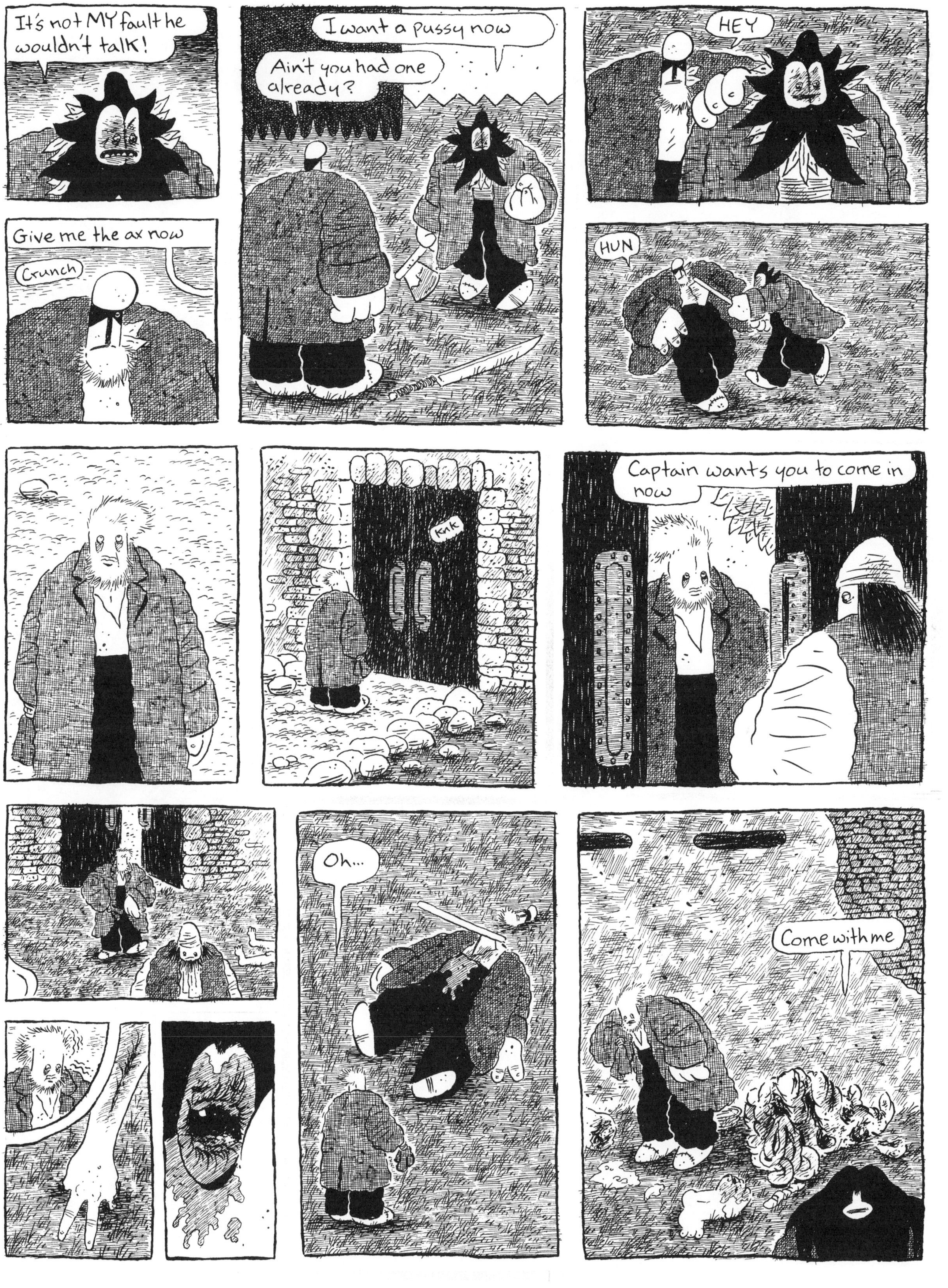
It's not MY fault he wouldn't talk!
I want a pussy now
Ain't you had one already?
HEY
Give me the ax now
Crunch
HUN
Knk
Captain wants you to come in now
Oh...
Come with me

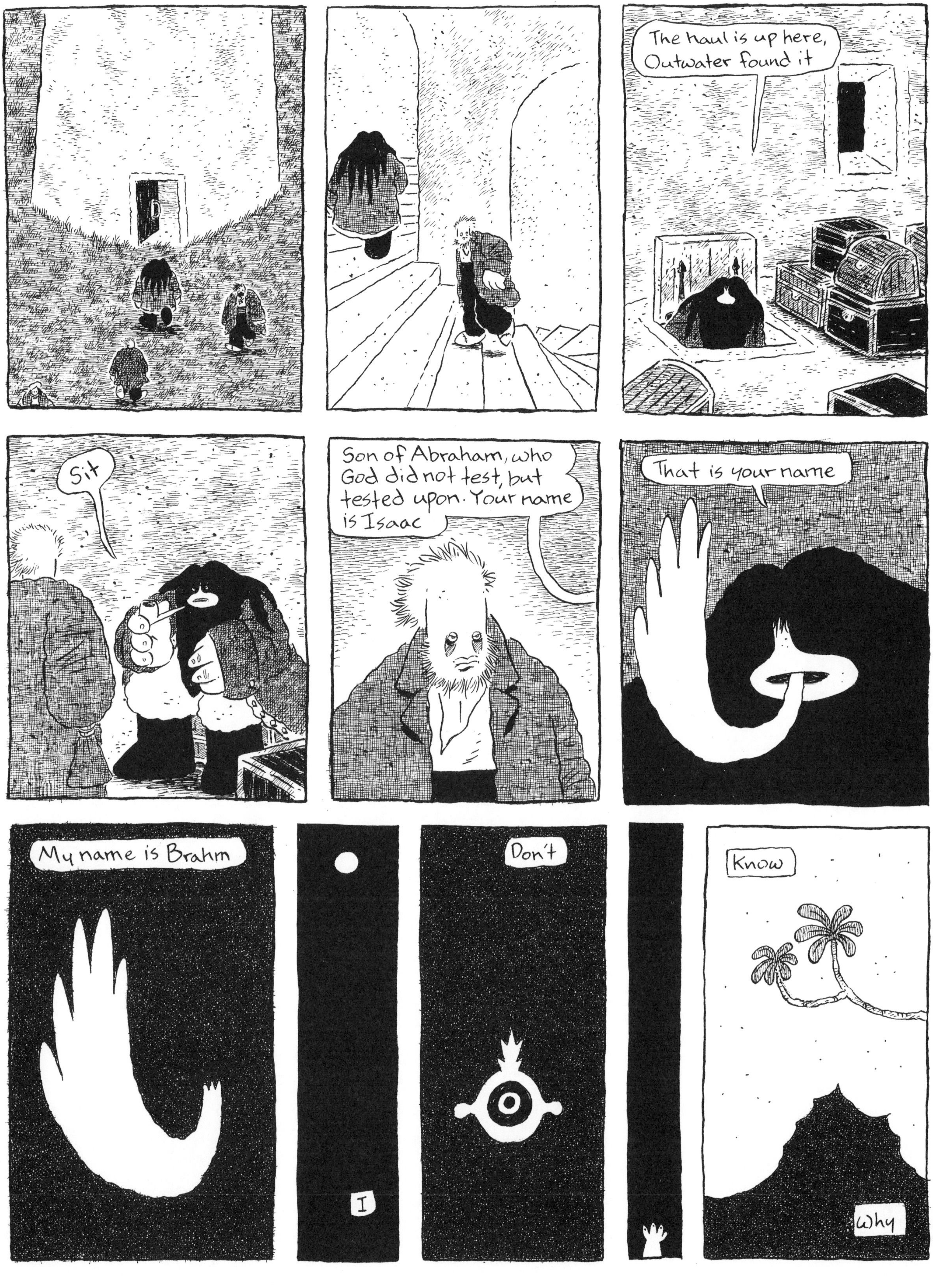

The haul is up here, Outwater found it
Sit
Son of Abraham, who God did not test, but tested upon. Your name is Isaac
That is your name
My name is Brahm
I
Don't
Know
Why

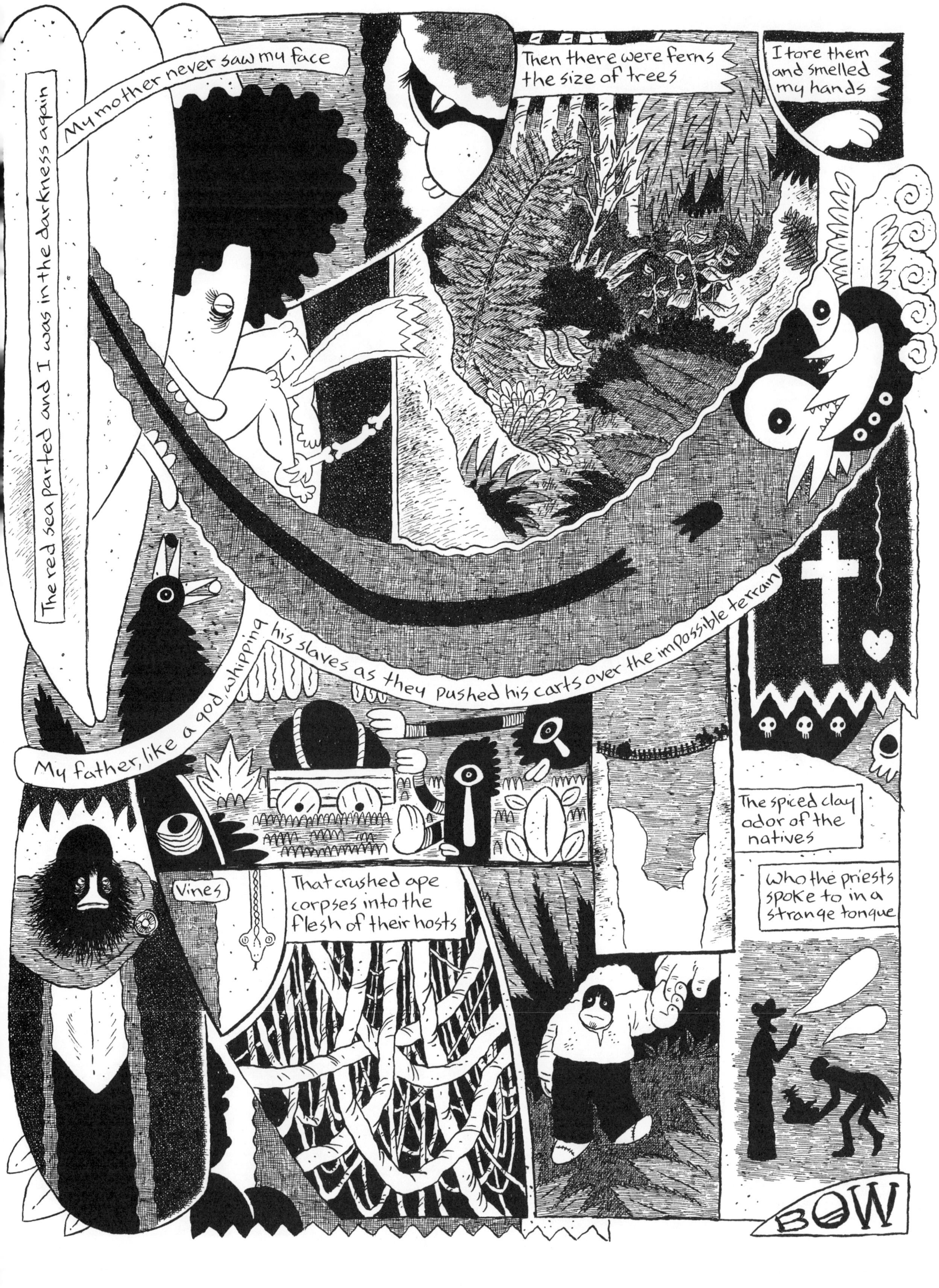

The red sea parted and I was in the darkness again
My mother never saw my face
Then there were ferns the size of trees
I tore them and smelled my hands
My father, like a god, whipping his slaves as they pushed his carts over the impossible terrain
Vines
That crushed ape corpses into the flesh of their hosts
The spiced clay odor of the natives
Who the priests spoke to in a strange tongue
BOW

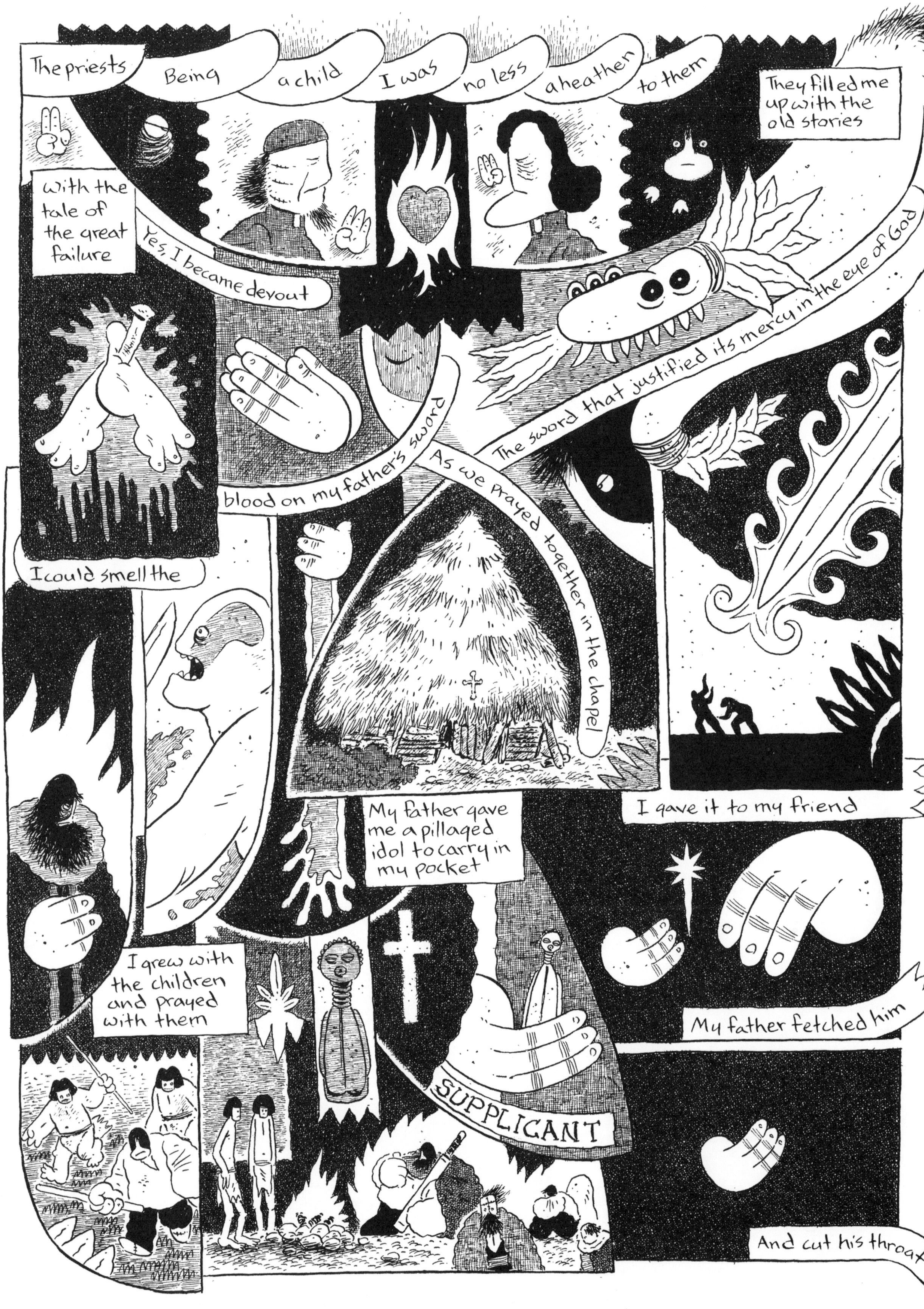

The priests
Being
a child
I was
no less
a heathen
to them
They filled me up with the old stories
with the tale of the great failure
Yes, I became devout
The sword that justified its mercy in the eye of God
I could smell the
blood on my father's sword
As we prayed together in the chapel
My father gave me a pillaged idol to carry in my pocket
I gave it to my friend
I grew with the children and prayed with them
My father fetched him
SUPPLICANT
And cut his throat

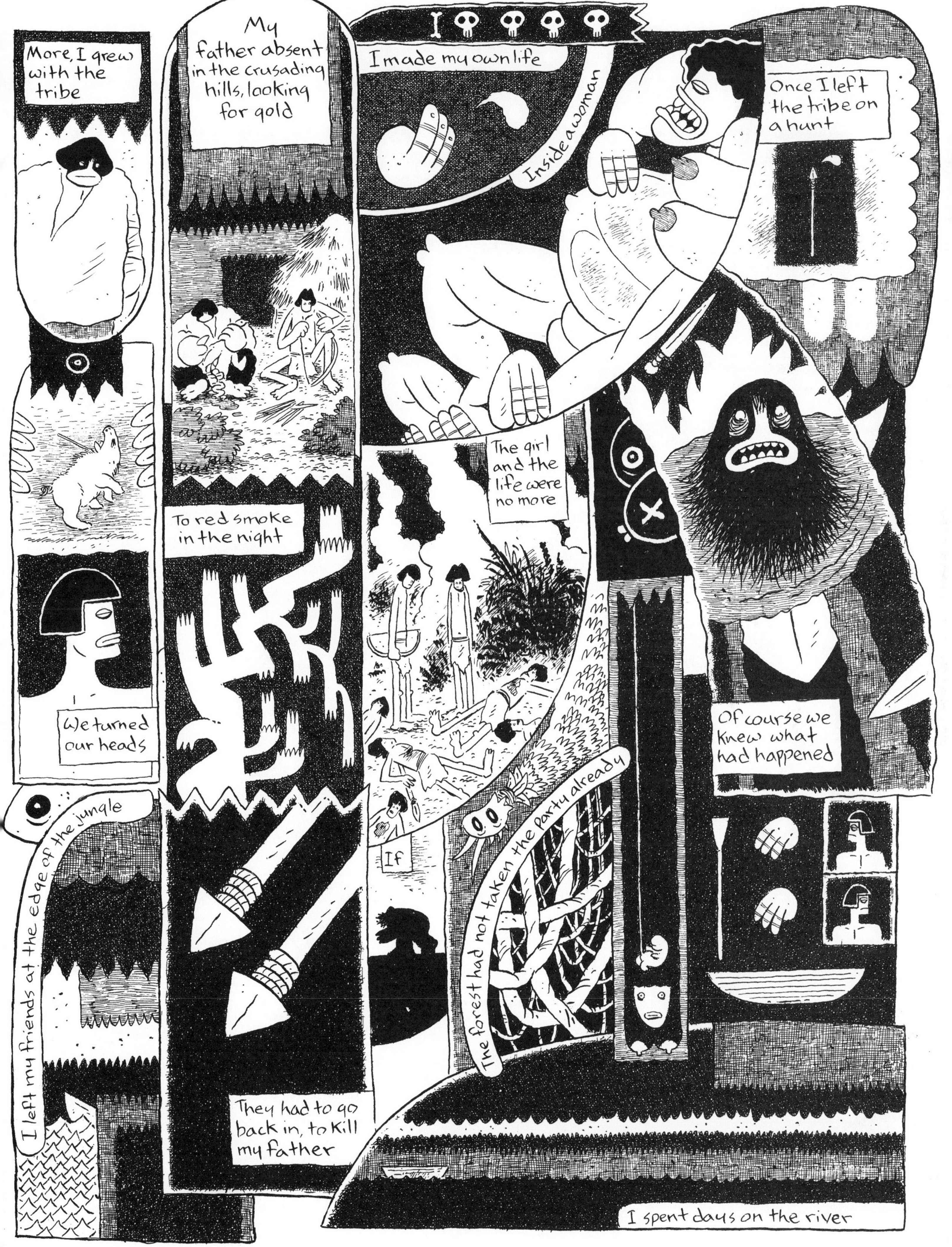
More, I grew with the tribe
We turned our heads
My father absent in the crusading hills, looking for gold
To red smoke in the night
They had to go back in, to kill my father
I made my own life
Inside a woman
The girl and the life were no more
If
The forest had not taken the party already
Once I left the tribe on a hunt
Of course we knew what had happened
I left my friends at the edge of the jungle
I spent days on the river

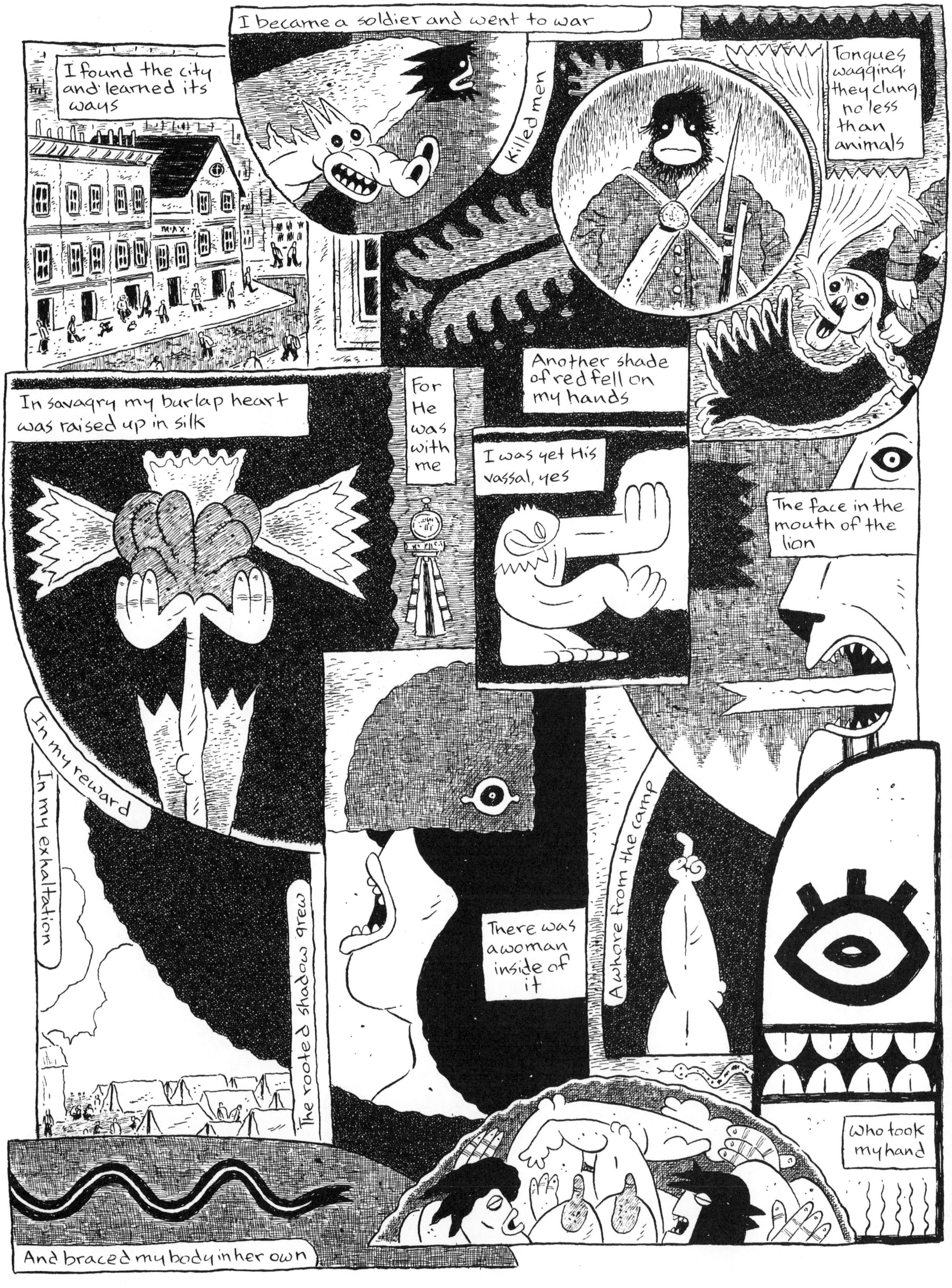
I became a soldier and went to war
I found the city and learned its ways
M·A·X
Killed men
Tongues wagging, they clung no less than animals
Another shade of red fell on my hands
In savagry my burlap heart was raised up in silk
For He was with me
I was yet His vassal, yes
The face in the mouth of the lion
In my reward
In my exhalation
The rooted shadow grew
There was a woman inside of it
A whore from the camp
Who took my hand
And braced my body in her own

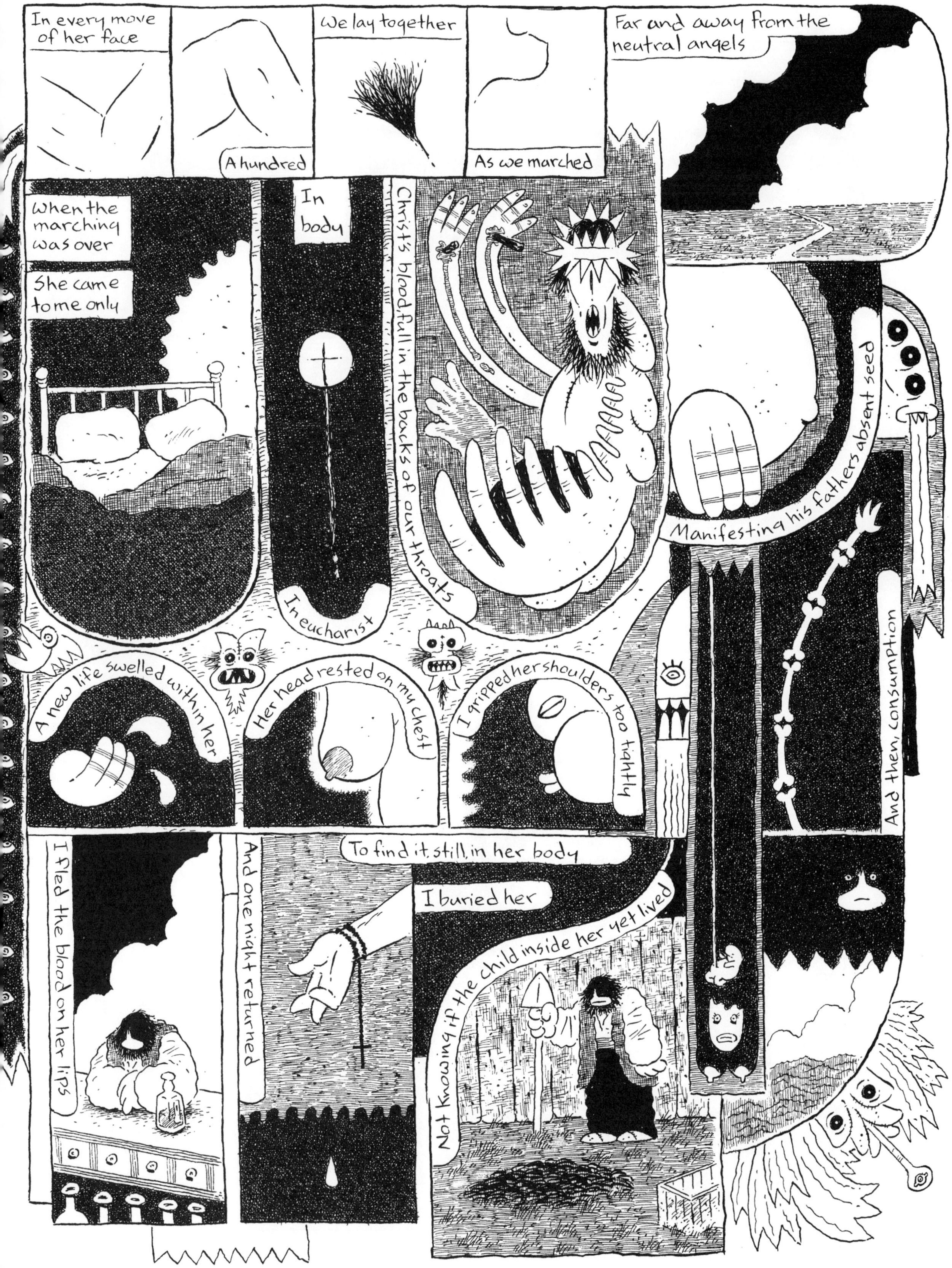
In every move of her face
A hundred
We lay together
As we marched
Far and away from the neutral angels
When the marching was over
She came to me only
In body
In eucharist
Christ's blood, full in the backs of our throats
Manifesting his fathers absent seed
And then, consumption
A new life swelled within her
Her head rested on my chest
I gripped her shoulders too tightly
I fled the blood on her lips
And one night returned
To find it, still, in her body
I buried her
Not knowing if the child inside her yet lived

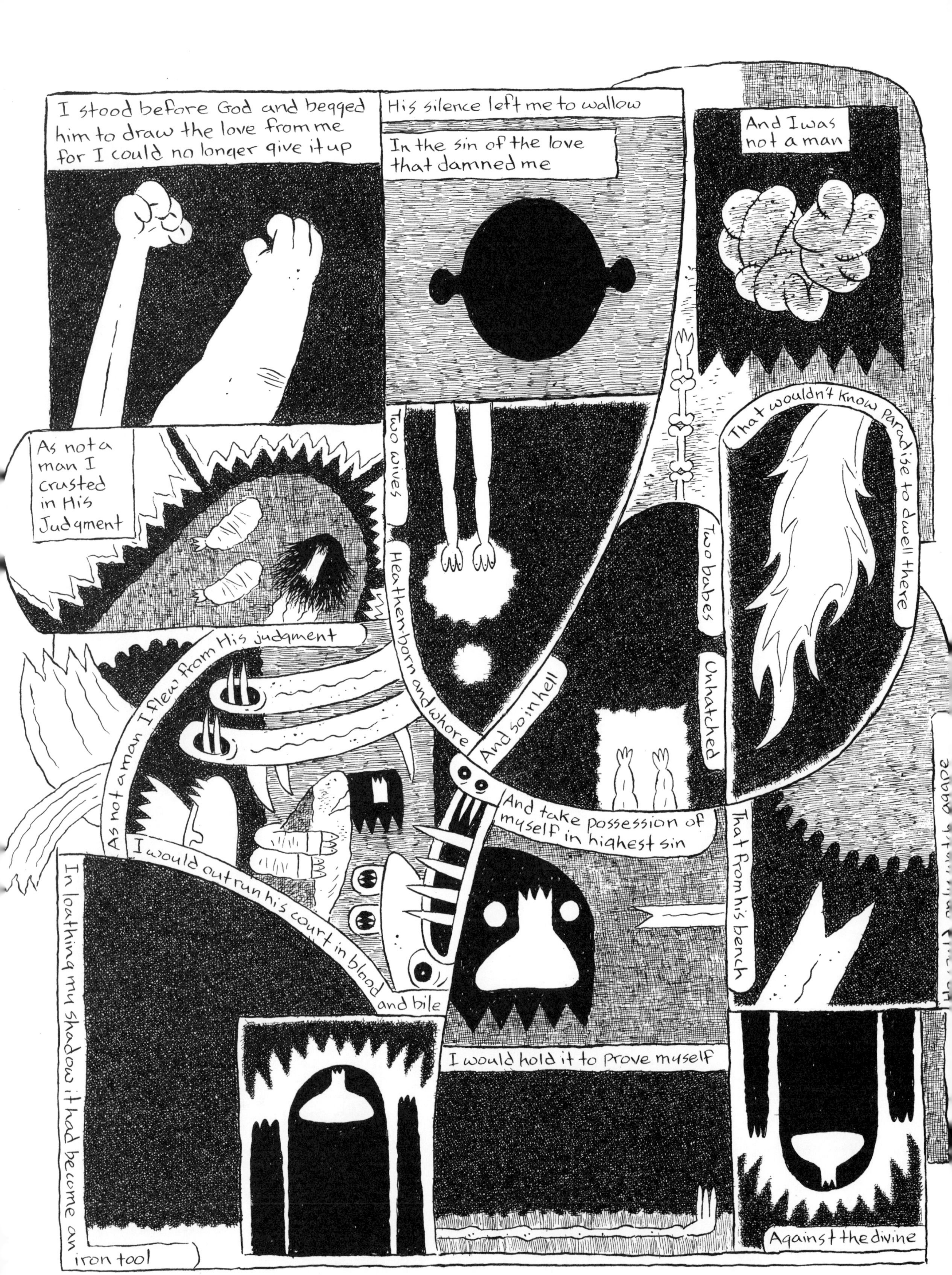
I stood before God and begged him to draw the love from me for I could no longer give it up
His silence left me to wallow
In the sin of the love that damned me
And I was not a man
As not a man I crusted in His Judgment
Two wives
Heathen-born and whore
Two babes
Unhatched
That wouldn't know Paradise to dwell there
As not a man I flew from His judgment
I would outrun his court in blood and bile
And so in hell
And take possession of myself in highest sin
That from his bench
He would only watch agape
In loathing my shadow it had become an iron tool
I would hold it to prove myself
Against the divine

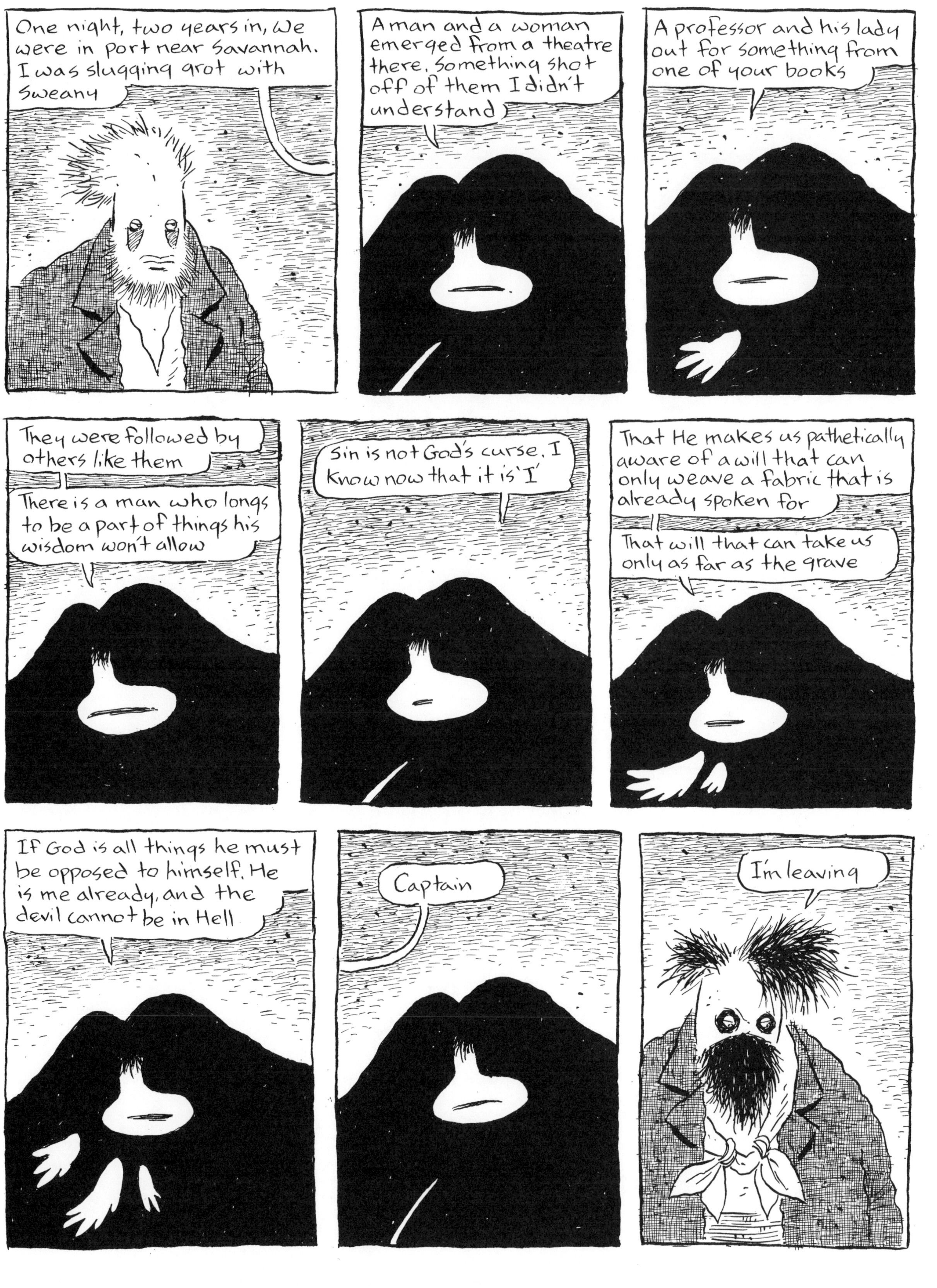
One night, two years in, we were in port near Savannah. I was slugging grot with Sweany
A man and a woman emerged from a theatre there. Something shot off of them I didn't understand
A professor and his lady out for something from one of your books
They were followed by others like them
There is a man who longs to be a part of things his wisdom won't allow
Sin is not God's curse. I know now that it is 'I'
That He makes us pathetically aware of a will that can only weave a fabric that is already spoken for
That will that can take us only as far as the grave
If God is all things he must be opposed to himself. He is me already, and the devil cannot be in Hell
Captain
I'm leaving

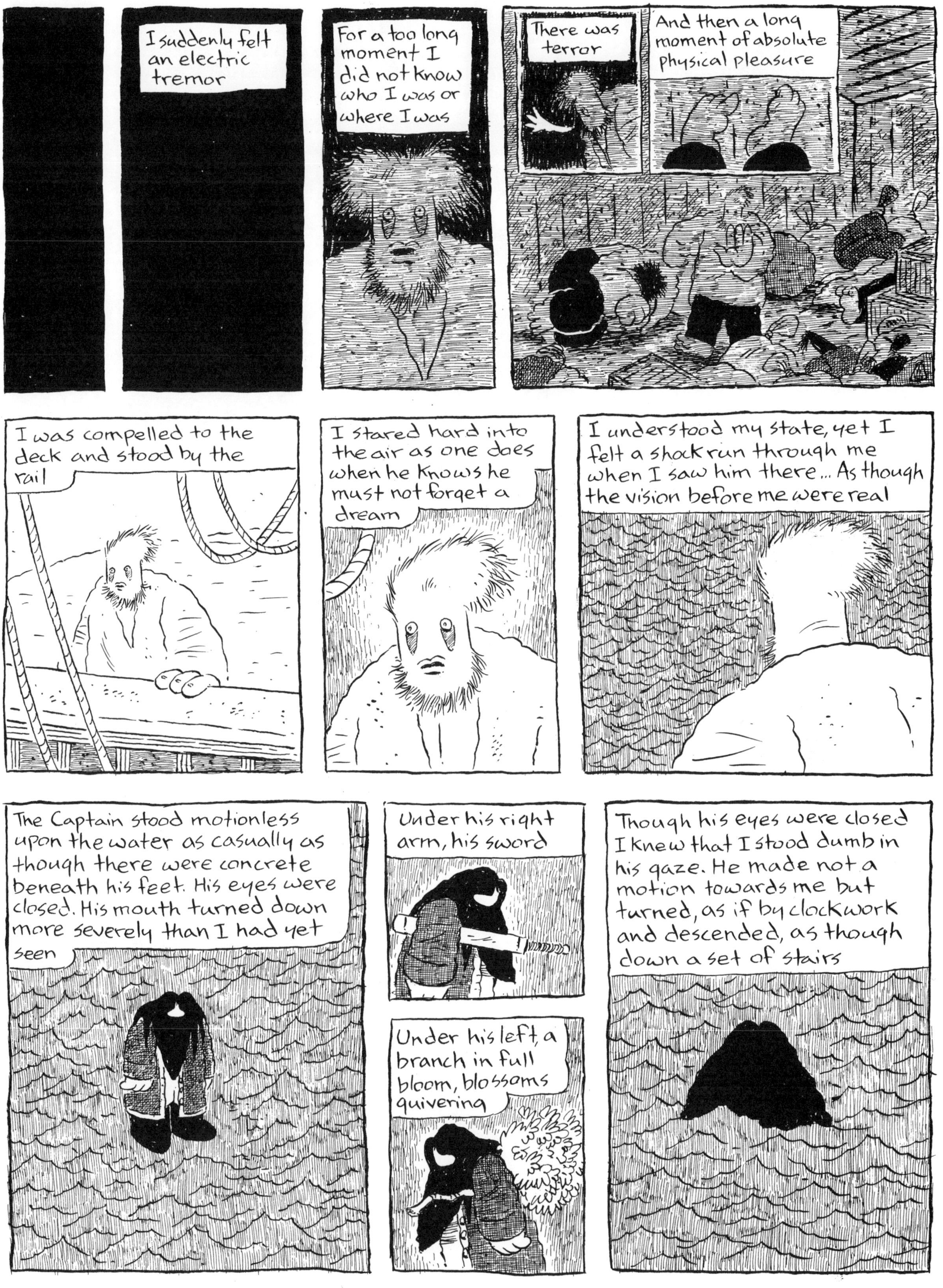
I suddenly felt an electric tremor
For a too long moment I did not know who I was or where I was
There was terror
And then a long moment of absolute physical pleasure
I was compelled to the deck and stood by the rail
I stared hard into the air as one does when he knows he must not forget a dream
I understood my state, yet I felt a shock run through me when I saw him there... As though the vision before me were real
The Captain stood motionless upon the water as casually as though there were concrete beneath his feet. His eyes were closed. His mouth turned down more severely than I had yet seen
Under his right arm, his sword
Under his left, a branch in full bloom, blossoms quivering
Though his eyes were closed I knew that I stood dumb in his gaze. He made not a motion towards me but turned, as if by clockwork and descended, as though down a set of stairs

The waves were little disturbed as they crowned about his head, He was as a child peacefully returning to the womb

I found myself back in my spot later with no memory of my return

It was like no dream of my life

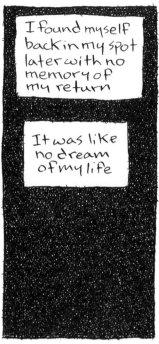

In the morning I discovered that the Captain had indeed gone missing. I could not speak

In his absence does the madman own the ship?

Outwater and a number of the crew left the company after the island massacre

I appear to have become familiar enough in the eyes of those who remain that I can walk among them unmolested. This is well, in the fact that all of my protectors are gone

I've taken to writing these pages, with the remaining supplies, to give myself cover of head and heart, to remain as stable as I might

It is remarkable to speak once again in my own voice... Or at least in its facsimile given what has transpired

I cannot date these entries, but what does it matter?

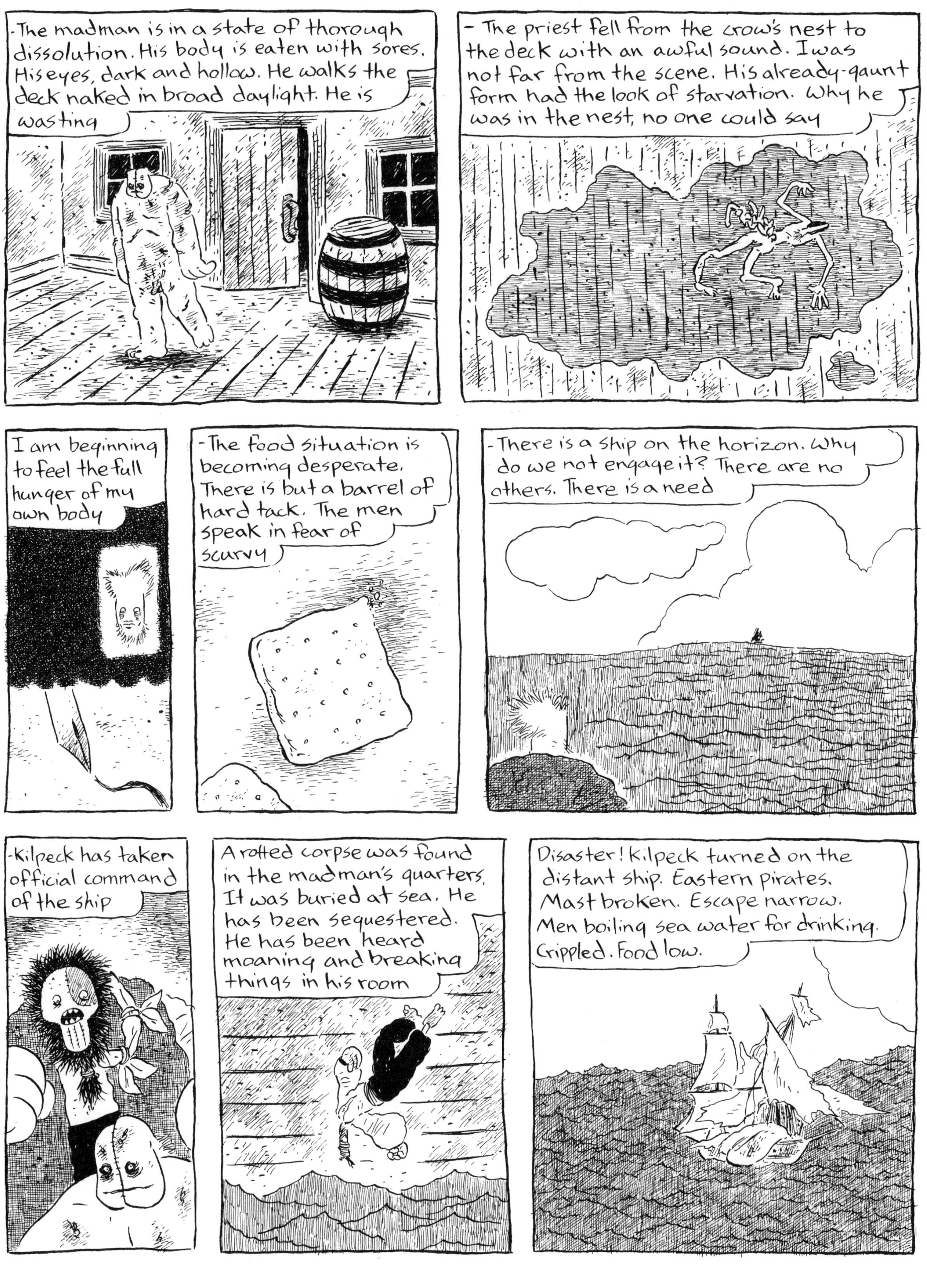
-The madman is in a state of thorough dissolution. His body is eaten with sores. His eyes, dark and hollow. He walks the deck naked in broad daylight. He is wasting
- The priest fell from the crow's nest to the deck with an awful sound. I was not far from the scene. His already-gaunt form had the look of starvation. Why he was in the nest, no one could say
I am beginning to feel the full hunger of my own body
-The food situation is becoming desperate. There is but a barrel of hard tack. The men speak in fear of scurvy
-There is a ship on the horizon. Why do we not engage it? There are no others. There is a need
-Kilpeck has taken official command of the ship
A rotted corpse was found in the madman's quarters. It was buried at sea. He has been sequestered. He has been heard moaning and breaking things in his room
Disaster! Kilpeck turned on the distant ship. Eastern pirates. Mast broken. Escape narrow. Men boiling sea water for drinking. Crippled. Food low.

- It seems that Tall Paul once sailed with a portion of the crew of the Hand under the command of a different captain. Later he underwent a conversion to non-violence, which led him here

I have no doubt that the details of his story would be fascinating, if they were remotely obtainable. Were my gifts greater I would invent them myself

Pineapple is delicious

How strange it is that they let the madman languish

They have constructed a tent for him, which is specially marked with a red x to ensure that he remain isolated

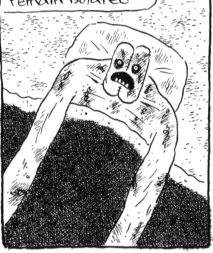

He did not seem much loved by the men. I have even been witness to cruel acts he committed against some yet in the company

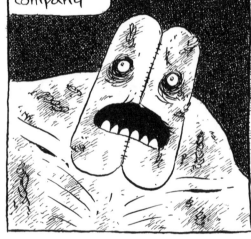

Why do they cater to him in his decay?

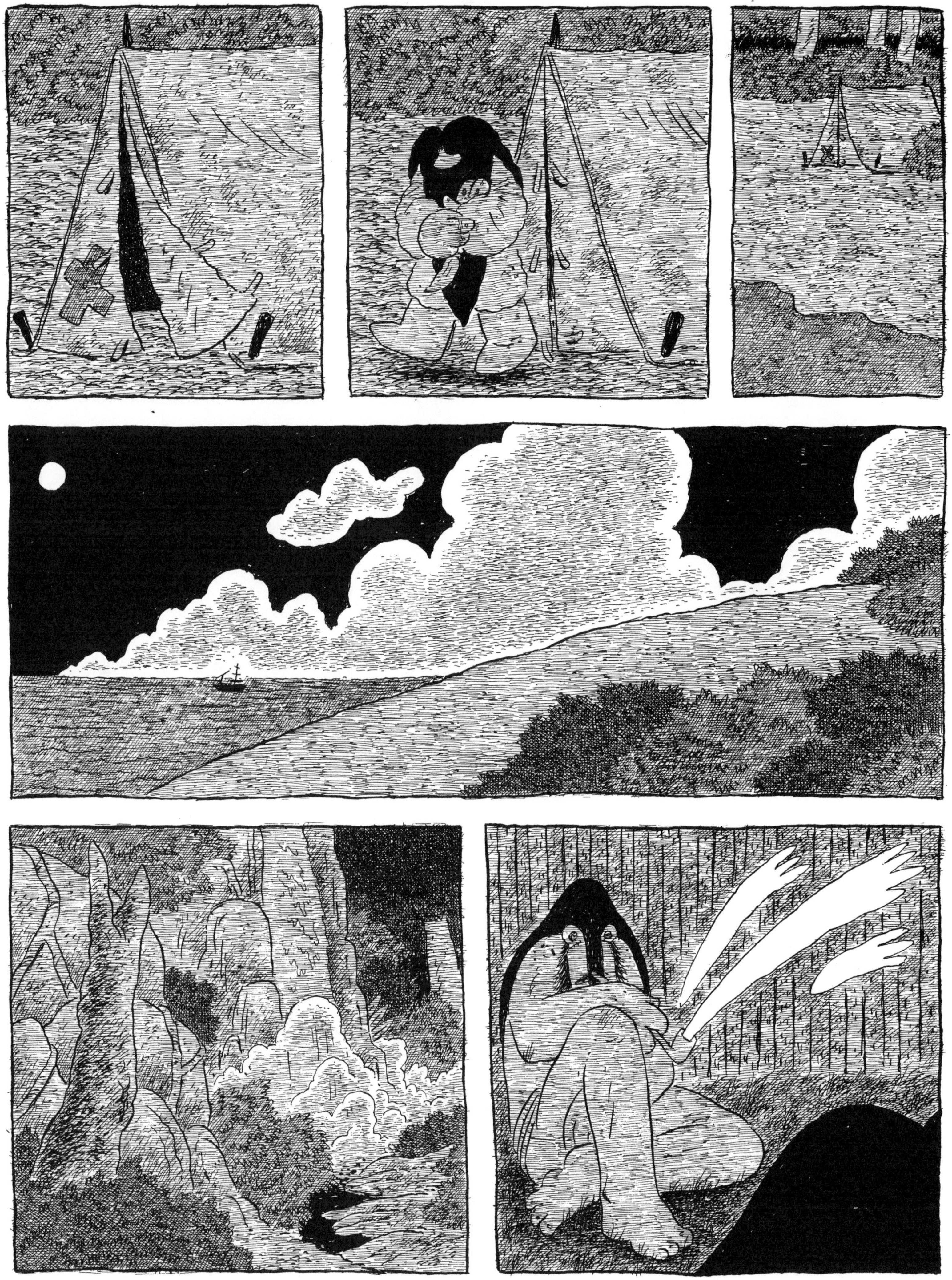

Isaac...

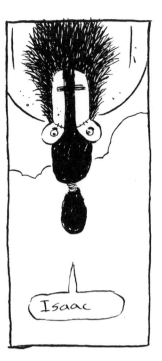

Isaac

Isaac

Your Captain came in the night. He has departed from the land of his old hand, and now departed with it. He insisted that you alone remain, and you are welcome. I have seen him in his full evil, and I have seen him changed

See

He has left you your materials and your books

I am known as Shacha

Chris Wright